IN A HUNGRY COUNTRY

IN A
HUNGRY COUNTRY
Essays by Simon Paneak

edited by

John Martin Campbell

with contributions by

Grant Spearman, Robert L. Rausch, and Stephen C. Porter

UNIVERSITY OF ALASKA PRESS
FAIRBANKS

University of Alaska Press
P.O. Box 756240
104 Eielson Building
Fairbanks, AK 99775-6240

Design by Dixon Jones
Cover design by Lisa Tremaine
Layout by Sue Mitchell, Inkworks

ISBN: 1-889963-59-3 (cloth)
         1-889963-60-7 (paper)

Library of Congress Cataloging-in-Publication Data:

Paneak, Simon, 1900–1975.
   In a hungry country : essays / by Simon Paneak ; edited by John Martin
Campbell ; with contributions by Grant Spearman, Robert L. Rausch, and
Stephen C. Porter.
      p. cm.
   ISBN 1-889963-59-3 (cloth : alk. paper) -- ISBN 1-889963-60-7 (pbk. :
alk. paper)
   1. Paneak, Simon, 1900–1975. 2. Nunamiut Eskimos--Biography. 3.
Nunamiut Eskimos--History. 4. Nunamiut Eskimos--Folklore. 5. Anaktuvuk
Pass (Alaska)--History. 6. Anaktuvuk Pass (Alaska)--Social life and
customs. I. Campbell, John Martin, 1927– II. Title.
   E99.E7 P235 2004
   979.8'7--dc22

                         2003020564

∞ This paper meets the requirements of ANSI/NISO Z39.48–1992
(Permanence of Paper).

Printed in the United States of America.

Cover photos: (top) the summit of Anaktuvuk Pass, 1961. Photo by Stephen C. Porter.
(Bottom): Simon Paneak at Tuluak Lake in Nunamiut winter clothing, 1952. Photo by Laurence Irving.

For Katy

—*John Martin Campbell*

Contents

Foreword

Grant Spearman

I never met Simon Paneak (Panniaq)[1] personally, directly. It was only through others who had that I first came to know something of this remarkable man (frontispiece). Years later, as founding curator of the museum named in his honor, I gained a fuller awareness of the significance of his contributions. While I was compiling a collection of his work, my awareness grew from an informed appreciation into a deep and firmly rooted respect. It was, I suppose, my dubious distinction to be the first anthropologist at Anaktuvuk (Anaqtuuvak) Pass not to have met, worked with, or learned from him, as he had predeceased my arrival in 1978 by nearly three years. Even so, his legacy remained strong, both within the community, through his large family and lingering influence, and without, through the writings of an impressive array of researchers for whom he had been such a vital resource and ultimately a figure who earned their highest personal regard.

It has been said that the measure of a man can best be taken by the company he keeps—and Simon kept remarkable company. Those who over the decades worked, traveled, and learned from him—and in the end called him friend—comprise a "Who's Who" of old and distinguished Brooks Range hands: Laurence Irving, Robert Rausch, Sig Wien, Helge Ingstad, George Gryc, Jack Campbell, and Ethel Ross Oliver, to name but a few. Scientists, pioneer flyers, writers, and educators, men and women of diverse pursuits—many of them individuals of considerable note in their own right—found in him a man of powerful intellect, good humor, and generosity.

Without doubt Paneak was, in many ways, an exceptional man. As Laurence Irving (1960) keenly appreciated, Simon's knowledge, understanding, and mastery of the natural world in which he moved rivaled if not exceeded, in some respects, that of professional biologists. So much so that many distinguished and first-rank scientists such as Irving quickly came to depend on the experience, insight, and judgment of this unpretentious mountain Eskimo. Yet it cannot go unremarked that within his own community and among his own people this level of knowledge and competency was, of necessity, commonplace. It was in fact but a portion of what a mature Nunamiut hunter was expected to know and master and be able to apply daily in order to survive and support his family in the arctic environment.

Nunamiut elders like Jesse Ahgook (Aguk), Iñuałuuraq Hugo, and Maptig̣aq Morry—men a generation senior to Paneak—knew all of this and more, and had they been asked, could without doubt have been as rich a source of knowledge as Simon. What they did not possess was the key attribute that helped set Paneak apart and elevated him to a position of primacy as a resource person for scientists: his facility with the English language. But this is not to say that his ability to speak and write English was the only determining factor. Had these early scientists encountered a Nunamiut speaking the King's English with the polish of an Oxford don, he certainly would have captured their attention, but without proof of his bona fides, in terms of demonstrable, practical, useful knowledge, he could never have held their interest. It was content, not form, they sought, and Simon in his own inimitable fashion offered both in one immensely bright and likable human being.

As Simon once wrote, he "was born at the Killik [Killiq] River 10 miles north of the mountain line" in the spring of 1900; born a Nunamiut, an inland Eskimo, into the arctic landscape of the north-central Brooks Range; into the cultural tradition of a highly mobile big-game hunting society based on caribou; and into the family of his father Tuṇŋana and mother Kiktuġiaq as their first child. There would be three younger sisters and a brother to come, the sisters surviving to their teens or early twenties, but only Paneak was to reach mature adulthood. Even under the best of circumstances the inland way of life into which Simon was born was a hard one. Again, in his words, "My life is not a very easy life. Sometimes it is pretty rough living."

By their own reckoning, the Nunamiut Iñupiat have always lived among Alaska's northernmost mountains, the Brooks Range. Possessors of a deep and detailed knowledge of their world, they were highly proficient hunters and fishermen who ordered their lives around the flow of the seasons. They knew no permanent home, and mobility was the hallmark of their lifestyle. Traveling by dog team and sled in winter and on foot in summer, living in tents of caribou skin and houses built of moss, they roamed the land in pursuit of game: hunting, trapping, camping, and fishing throughout their mountainous homeland. The freedom and capability to move swiftly and sometimes far in pursuit of game or other resources were critical to their success—and survival.

Although they are related to the Taġiuġmiut Iñupiat (Tareumiut) of the Arctic Coast (Map 1), the Nunamiut heritage is one of living inland rather than near the sea, their way of life built around the hunting of caribou, Dall sheep, and the grizzly bear rather than the whales, seals, walrus, and polar bears of their coastal relatives, but, above all, they were hunters of caribou (see Gubser 1965 and Campbell 1968). Skilled as they were at inland hunting and fishing, their need for marine products, especially the calorie- and nutrient-rich oils rendered from the fat and blubber of seals and whales, was acute. To secure these and other goods they established interdependent trade relationships with coastal Iñupiat. Therefore each spring groups of traders left their mountain homes to travel to Niġliq on the Colville River delta to meet with their coastal trading partners and to exchange goods,

providing one another with the supplies most needed and desired.

This way of life proceeded relatively undisturbed until the late 1880s, when a series of events was set in motion that had a profound impact on these traditional ways. Key to these changes was the New England whaling fleet, which maintained a strong presence along the Arctic coast throughout the 1890s and beyond, offering people not only jobs as hunters to keep the over-wintering crews well fed with caribou meat but also access to a wide variety of trade items like guns, ammunition, kerosene lanterns, and Western products of all types. Less congenially, they also introduced alcohol and a variety of diseases such as measles and flu for which people had no immunity, and which took a heavy toll as waves of epidemics swept inland, killing many people.

Fatefully, these epidemics came nearly hand in hand with a time when the mainstay of the Nunamiut economy, the vital Western Arctic caribou herd, was in the midst of a precipitous and disastrous decline. This circumstance led to recurrent episodes of starvation and famine among these people, further depleting their population and seriously disrupting the very fabric of their society. Driven by hunger and the need to seek relief, most surviving Nunamiut families moved to the coast around the turn of the century, where they had access to trading posts and, occasionally, jobs. Others headed eastward towards Canadian territory, where the still healthy and numerous Porcupine caribou herd remained strong. By 1920, with the exception of a few scattered families, the north-central Brooks Range, the heart of the Nunamiut homeland, had been effectively abandoned (see Gubser 1965).

As a young boy Simon found himself caught up in a cataract of social and historical currents, which eventually swept his family and his people from their traditional mountain homeland and cast them upon the shores of the Arctic coast as refugees from starvation and disease. At the age of six or seven what he was seeing and experiencing was part of the unraveling of an ancient and now vanished way of life. He also saw and experienced things no youngster should ever have had to, as he describes in Chapter 4: silent camps with caribou skin tents sheltering only the lifeless, frozen bodies of family and friends.

All of this made a strong impression on the boy, as it did on all who survived those tragic days. It was for all a central defining moment in their lives, and the impact of

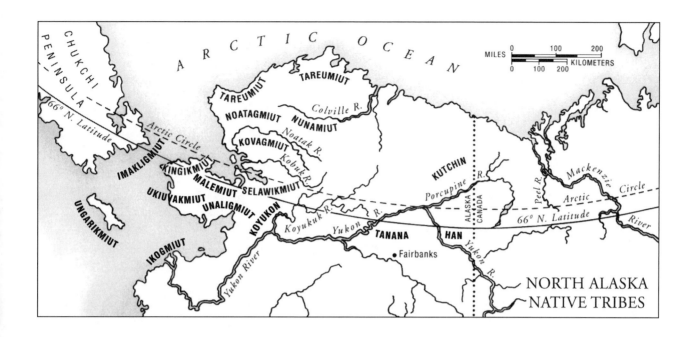

MAP 1 (Above) North Alaska Native tribes. Sources: Driver and Massey 1957; Krauss 1982; Kroeber 1939; Osgood 1936b; Oswalt 1979; Weyer 1932.

MAP 2 (Below) Alaska north of 66 degrees North latitude (after Campbell 1998a:21).

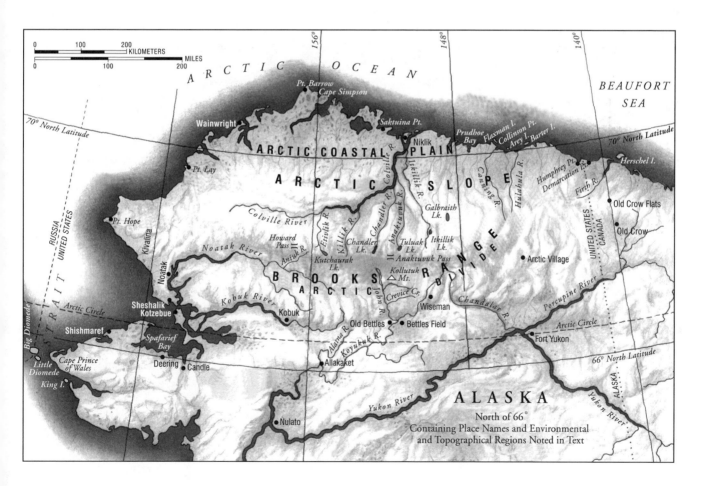

those events still echoed in the Anaktuvuk Pass community for more than eighty years until the last elder, who himself was a survivor of that great hunger, Paneak's friend and father-in-law Elijah Kakinya (facing page ix), finally passed out of the picture. Yet despite the trauma of these times, the Nunamiut faced the situation—and occasionally their fate—with a stoicism born of a strong, resilient people who lived out their lives in a demanding, unforgiving environment and who were repeatedly tested, tempered, and proved by recurrent episodes of want.

The upshot of these tribulations was, over the space of a few short decades, the total collapse of Nunamiut society, the virtual abandonment of the Brooks Range, and a period of exile in coastal areas that lasted well into the mid-1930s. During these years Simon grew from childhood into an active robust hunter, following his parents on a remarkable odyssey of travels. The coastal years were intimately linked with the rise and fall of the arctic fur trapping industry. Paneak's family traveled as far afield as the Old Crow area of Canada and made frequent forays across the crest of the eastern Brooks Range to spend periods of time in the Arctic Village and Fort Yukon areas (Map 2), as did a number of other Nunamiut families. In time Simon married and started a family of his own and for several years centered his winter trapping activities out of a sod house near Humphrey Point on the Arctic coast.

With the collapse of the fur-trapping industry in the wake of the Great Depression, Simon, now in his mid thirties, became part and parcel of the movement of highly motivated and traditionally oriented families. Led by experienced older men, including his father, they were determined to return inland and reestablish themselves and their former lifestyle in the familiar valleys of the north-central Brooks Range (see Chapter 5).

In turning from Paneak's role as an individual caught up in historical events to that of their chronicler, one cannot help but be impressed and grateful for what he has bequeathed to future generations of Nunamiut as well as to anthropologists, archaeologists, and even laymen for whom the life of nomadic caribou hunters holds unique fascination.

He was certainly not the first or the only person to tell such tales. Any number of anthropologists have, over the past fifty years of work among the Nunamiut, recorded at least partial historical accounts from men other than Paneak—accounts which, in their original telling, may

well have been every bit as detailed and moving. Yet few seem to have survived. The reasons are many. To some degree it may reflect the early unavailability of tape recorders, so useful today to capture word-for-word every detail and nuance of an account. There is also the almost inevitable filtering and sometimes condensing of a story that comes with a researcher's reliance on the services of an interpreter. More prosaically, the note-taking inclinations or abilities of a researcher, not to mention the subsequent need to condense and generalize an account in order to fit it into the context of a larger work, must also have had its impact.

This last point in particular is driven home when reading, on one hand, the 1950 field notes of the late archaeologist William (Bill) Irving and, on the other, Gubser's (1965) excellent book. The first is filled with numerous brief and occasionally cryptic tidbits of ethnographic information that today, in the absence of senior elders able to elaborate upon them, one wishes were far more detailed. The second is simply a classic ethnography—"classic" in every sense of the word, both in terms of its high quality and in its generalized presentation of data, behind which, and largely hidden from view, lie the personal detail and context in which Gubser learned what he so thoughtfully, thoroughly, and skillfully presents to us.

Perhaps another part of the explanation for this evident lack of such personal and detailed accounts in the works of earlier anthropologists was that at the time there was simply no appropriate forum in which to present these individual stories beyond those times when the researchers gathered informally among themselves, drinks inevitably in hand, and started swapping tales. Some are funny, others aren't, all are fascinating, and then there are the ones that rarely get told at all, except perhaps at times to ourselves, as we run through them in our own minds and end up wondering, "How did they do that? How did they manage?" These are the stories of famine and disease, of hardship, suffering, sacrifice, and loss, yet also of chance, fate, resilience, and fortitude in the face of what are, for most people, simply unimaginable circumstances. Perhaps the best analogy can be drawn with the men who fought in the Second World War. Only now, more than fifty years later, are our fathers and uncles finally speaking frankly of their own harrowing experiences in combat, shorn of the false glory with which too many novels and, until the film "Saving Private Ryan," Hollywood have imbued the event. As we listen to their individual accounts and hear their oral histories, we can only stand humbled and awed at what they endured and accomplished and wonder again, to ourselves, "How did they do that? How did they manage?" Another point of no less importance and which goes to the heart of the reliability and significance of these accounts is the fact that Paneak was born into an era when the Nunamiut oral tradition was in full force. It was a time when a keen mind and a steel-trap memory were the keys to survival.

In the absence of a written language there were no "how to" handbooks carried in a hip pocket to guide the inept or prompt the forgetful through new or unfamiliar circumstances. Their closest approximation to a reference book in these parts was the accumulated, encyclopedic knowledge and experience of elders. Experience they shared freely when formally instructing young men in the field, and knowledge was often imparted back at camp, in the informal atmosphere of the *qargi* or men's house, which in its own way was the nearest thing to a school that they possessed.

In those days it went without saying that when facing the challenge of a critical situation, all one had to draw upon were personal experience and whatever insights that had been gleaned from elders could be applied to the case at hand. More succinctly, you either had your stuff down cold, or you ended up that way. There was little room for a weak link in the chain of Nunamiut life. The result was a physically vigorous people with keen minds and acute senses who were perfectly suited and attuned to the vagaries, vicissitudes, and demands of the land in which they lived.

Of course there was a great deal more to the Nunamiut oral tradition than simply passing on from old to young the practical skills of physical survival. It was also a convivial avenue by which a strong and sustaining sense of cultural identity and social cohesion were regularly reinforced and strengthened. As Paneak was proud to point out, and others equally swift to reaffirm, the Nunamiut see themselves as a people distinct from all others—coastal and woodland Eskimos included—who are, at least by their own reckoning, possessed of a very long history of occupation of the Brooks Range and Arctic Slope areas. How many times across the generations, one wonders, in the relaxed and comfortable atmosphere of a caribou-skin tent or moss house, warmed and illuminated by the dim glow of a seal oil lamp, would elders lean back against their rolled up caribou-skin bedding and recount the rich and varied history of their people.

They speak first of Itchaq Imña, the dawn of oral history, a storied time of the Nunamiut creation by the giant man Ayaġumaġałqha, who taught them how to hunt and to make a living from this challenging land. It is also a time of wonder, of at once the natural and supernatural, inhabited by magnificent, if occasionally troublesome, creatures like the flying whale, giant shrews, and oversized fish, bears, eagles, and other superlative beings that find no place in Western taxonomy, yet by the Nunamiuts' own accounting, the remains of which are still to be found here and there about the landscape.

During this rather early and eventful period of the forming and reforming of their original world, the earth they knew underwent several catastrophes. First it shook mightily in an earthquake that turned everything upside down, then it was flooded as in biblical tradition, with only a few Nunamiut survivors mastheaded on a small speck of land atop the Umiat bluffs along the Colville River. After the earth had drained and dried off again, Raven brought daylight to the world. But far from being the end of their travails, this enlightening moment was merely an interlude before the giant shrews and the other Godzilla-sized creatures so prone to periodic mayhem reasserted themselves and temporarily drove the Nunamiut to the coast. Once these monsters were finally eliminated, thanks to the efforts of Qayaqtuaġuniktuuq, another important hero giant, the people returned inland—only to find that this time the climate had grown colder and great glaciers of ice were growing and advancing, choking the mountain valleys with a cryonic thrombosis that once again sent people packing coastward until the weather eventually warmed and the ice melted away. Upon the clearing of the valleys and the Nunamiut reoccupation of the Brooks Range there began an era that they term the Iŋilagaan period, a time more readily grounded in historical times and events than its preceding age. Many of the signal historical accounts Paneak tells of the Iŋilagaan period could arguably have taken place as recently as the lifetimes of his grandparents or, at most, his great grandparents. Overall, that was not a very long time ago, and given the strength of the oral tradition, the quality and quantity of detail, particularly in regard to the accounts of their conflicts with Gwich'in (Kutchin) Athapaskan Indians from whom they wrested control of the north-central Brooks Range, this nearly renders these accounts into the realm of firsthand reminiscences (see Chapter 4). Interestingly Paneak, who was in the direct line of receipt and succession of these word-of-mouth stories, represents a transitional figure in the process of rendering them from oral to written history. He actually ended up passing them along in both formats—orally on tape, which others, like Helge Ingstad (1987), then rendered into written English, but also through his own many handwritten diaries and journals.

Paneak was, among his many attributes, an intellectually gifted man who was also a true and avid student of his own culture, a point perfectly illustrated by a comment made by Ernest S. "Tiger" Burch (personal communication 1999), another of the prominent ethnographers to work with him. Burch observed that Simon was not content merely to absorb his peoples' history as it might be told among the elders of his own community; rather he deliberately and actively sought out old men with reputations for veracity and knowledge, in other far-flung communities across the North Slope, in order to learn from them. Sometimes he did this in person as opportunity permitted, but more often—by the 1960s in a practice little known outside the native community—through the exchange of reel-to-reel tape recordings that people sent to one another through the mails, to keep apprised of current events. Of course, on the other side of the ledger, Edwin S. Hall, Jr., recalls Simon once laughingly relating that when Helge Ingstad was living among the Nunamiut gathering material for his (1954) book, Helge was occasionally the object of some fun at his own expense (quite literally—at about a dollar per story.) As Simon is said to have remarked, "Yeah, we pull his leg a little bit, then we pull on his other one a little too, that way everything come out even."

Perhaps equally illuminating is another insight offered by Burch (personal communication 1999) that illustrates how the astute Paneak could tailor his presentations to fit his audience. Once, as Simon was discussing with him in broad generalities how "the Nunamiut" did this and then "the Nunamiut" did that, Burch asked, which "Nunamiut" do you mean? The Killiġmiut or the Kaŋianiġmiut or the Ulumiut? (all of which were specific bands of small, territory-based groups of the larger Nunamiut society). Somewhat surprised, Simon said, "Oh, you know about them?" and then proceeded to discuss the actions of the specific bands in great detail.

It also bears mentioning that even if we could somehow discern and discount whatever parts he may have, on occasion, ad-libbed or embellished a bit, not all of Simon's information or knowledge concerning the past came solely from Nunamiut oral tradition. From the early 1950s onward, he was in fairly regular and close association with a number of anthropologists and archaeologists—Campbell among them—who shared and discussed both their own findings and those of others, thereby providing Simon with the resources to permit him to integrate some of this new information into his narratives. I am not certain to this day if anyone has ever attempted to tackle the implications of that in regard to the content of his ethnohistorical descriptions and accounts of Nunamiut traditional life.

It is, in fact, not an inconsequential point, particularly considering, as more than one person has pointed out, that Simon Paneak was, for very good and substantial reasons, every researcher's favorite informant. As a result, our ethnographic picture of the Nunamiut, while extensive and detailed, is in large measure "the world according to Paneak." If there is any criticism on that score it is probably, at worst, one of limited perspective (see Burch 1998). In fact, the process of drawing a fuller, more rounded picture of Nunamiata is gradually yielding fascinating and valuable dividends as the first-person accounts of a number of other senior elders gradually come to light.

Nevertheless, the fact remains that despite whatever minor qualitative quibbles linger about the information he has left us, Paneak has made the major contribution to our knowledge of his people, both in presenting researchers with detailed accounts of earlier days, as they were handed down from generation to generation, as well as through his writings, recordings, and drawings on the life he personally led during some of the most tempestuous, provocative, and interesting times in all of Nunamiut history. What follows is an account to be read and savored and appreciated as a nearly one-of-a-kind, straightforward and unvarnished presentation of a way of life that has only recently passed out of existence and is now drifting into history. We owe him a great deal. More, I think, than we know.

Acknowledgments

The following chapters are the product of Simon Paneak's creativity and intellectual enthusiasm. As contributing authors, Grant Spearman, Robert L. Rausch, and Stephen C. Porter have enhanced and explicated Simon's narratives. As beloved critics and advisers, Katherine "Katy" Kallestad and Marjorie Kilberg Shea have been indispensable in arranging and composing the manuscript. Indispensable, too, have been William B. Workman for his bibliographical expertise and James Nageak for his Iñupiaq equivalents of anglicized native words.

Among the students this editor introduced to the Arctic or Subarctic, and who went on to distinguish themselves in northern studies, are several whose work, as expressed both in conversation and in writing, has been of special value. These scholars include Herbert L. Alexander, Jr., Charles W. Amsden, Annette McFadyen Clark, Nicholas J. Gubser, Edwin S. Hall, Jr., Robert L. Humphrey, Richard E. Morlan, and Dennis J. Stanford (see References).

Other sources of information and assistance include Keith H. Basso, Philip K. Bock, Nancy M. Brown, Richard Carl Chapman, Roger Colten, Veree Crouder, George Gryc, Frederick Hadleigh-West, Muriel Hopson, Larry R. Jordon, Mary Mekiana, Sverre Pedersen, Richard E. Reanier, Howard Rodee, the Reverend Hunter Silides, Joseph Winter, and Karen Wood Workman. Mary June-el Piper, with remarkable editorial skill, put the finishing touches on the manuscript; and our efforts were encouraged most abidingly by Jennifer Collier and Erica Hill of the University of Alaska Press.

We are grateful for the generous help of each of them.

Financial backing for this and related north Alaska endeavors was provided by the American Museum of Natural History, the Arctic Institute of North America, the Doris Duke Foundation, the Explorers Club, The George Washington University, the National Science Foundation, the United States Navy, the University of New Mexico, and Yale University.

John Martin Campbell

FIGURE I   (Top) A November 1947 camp near Chandler Lake. Except for the lone white man's canvas-wall tent and a tin stovepipe, this encampment of caribou-hide, hemispherical houses is identical to camps typical of the early Nunamiut. Rasmuson Library, University of Alaska, Fairbanks. Photograph by Laurence Irving.

FIGURE 2   (Above) Suzie Paneak, left, and Ellen Hugo beside the stone tent rings that mark the same 1947 Nunamiut encampment shown in Figure 1. Chandler Lake is in the background. This lake, on the Brooks Range Divide, appears prominently in Chapter 4 (and see Figure 5). Photograph by Grant Spearman, 1985.

Introduction

John Martin Campbell

In his Foreword, Grant Spearman, with typical eloquence, treats the history of Nunamiut society and salient attributes of Simon's life. Here I will comment on Nunamiut origins and will describe certain characteristics of Simon's own history and personality that bear on this book's conception.

Until its dissolution the Nunamiut was one of numerous Eskimo tribes scattered from northeast Siberia and northwest Alaska eastward across the top of North America to East Greenland. As attested by archaeological evidence, Eskimo history reaches back at least 5,000 years, and as expressed in distinctive artifact types and assemblages, Eskimo material culture, as distinct from that of northern North American Indians, developed first in the region of the Bering Strait.[1]

As concerns possible early genetic and social relationships between Eskimos and American Indians,[2] the jury is out. Indians have occupied the Americas for more than twelve millennia, and probably over the past several thousand years—certainly during the past several centuries—America's northernmost Indians have lived within hailing distance of the Eskimos. Accordingly, one would think that given this long time-span a conspicuous mixing of both genes and culture traits would have occurred. Nevertheless, there are noticeable genetic differences between the two populations, and historically the Eskimos differ from their Indian (and Siberian) neighbors in language, social structure, political organization, and religion. Further, on both ethnographic and archaeological evidence, the latter of which embraces several thousand years, Eskimo material culture is similarly distinctive.[3]

With few exceptions the far northern Indians have been interior forest dwellers. And with equally few exceptions their Eskimo neighbors have occupied treeless arctic coasts from whose shores they have made their living by hunting whales and seals. At various times in the past, however, a few Eskimo tribes, the Nunamiut among them, abandoned the typical Eskimo sea-hunting way of life in favor of land-mammal hunting based overwhelmingly on the inland-dwelling caribou (see Foreword). The question of when the Nunamiut reached their interior tundra territory has not been resolved, nor has the question of where in the Western Arctic they lived before moving inland.

According to Nunamiut oral history, as Spearman describes, they have occupied the Arctic Slope and northern Brooks Range for countless generations. On the other hand, not all, but most, of the archaeological evidence implies a tenure of a few centuries (Campbell 1976). And the same evidence suggests derivation from the Eskimo tribes of the Arctic Alaska coast. In any event, the Nunamiut have lived inland for generations, and today their descendants in Anaktuvuk Pass continue to base their subsistence economy on caribou hunting (see Epilogue).

In the half century preceding Simon's birth the Nunamiut had acquired, via their coastal Eskimo neighbors, white man's goods and white man's diseases, which together initiated the disintegration of the Nunamiut tribe. Prompted by the fur trade, the introduced goods included, among other desirables, glass beads, metal pots, steel blades, and, most notably, firearms; the latter of which had made obsolete the compound, sinew-backed bow, a universal hallmark of Eskimo culture. But in 1900, and

FIGURE 3   Simon Paneak in 1949. Among the more useful of white man's introduced artifacts were various "bug dopes" (insect repellents) and mosquito head nets of the kind Simon is wearing here. Photograph by Robert L. Rausch.

during much of the first decade of the twentieth century, most of the old artifacts, including skin tents, were in use still (Figures 1 and 2), and Simon's elders knew perfectly well the techniques of manufacture of those that had gone out of style. Simon and his age-mates learned as teenagers how to make the numerous surviving native implements (dozens were in use until Simon was a grown man), but I feel Simon took a more than ordinary interest in learning the details of making the old, out-of-fashion artifacts. I would guess, for example, that few of his fellow teenage boys were interested enough to sit down and learn the complicated and tedious procedure required to make a compound bow. He was a boy antiquarian of sorts; he wanted to know about the old things in the same way that the uncommon American farm boy is fascinated as much by antique horse-drawn wagons as by pickup trucks. And until he died Simon could make lances and arrows and compound bows that were elegant and accurate in every detail. (In these regards, in the 1950s he showed me, on my field maps, places where his great grandfather had quarried flint for flaked-stone arrow points.)

Further, I think that Simon in his youth took more than ordinary interest in the natural history of the Nunamiut world. From necessity, Simon and his contemporaries learned the habits and physical characteristics of the wild animals (fishes, birds, and mammals) upon which they depended for survival, or in the case of furbearers, for trade. But beyond this essential knowledge, and knowledge of the few plants valuable as food or as the raw materials of manufacture, neither the majority of Simon's contemporaries nor most of their elders knew or wanted to know the habits and Eskimo names of, for example, the

150 or more species of birds in Nunamiut territory. But Simon wanted to know.

I did not meet Paneak until he was 56 years old, but both he and Kakinya (his best friend and father-in-law, who was five years his senior) were more than ordinarily friendly and outgoing. They liked people, and they liked to talk and tell stories and explain things—Kakinya's lack of English did not stop him from talking and explaining things to white men such as I who had not the foggiest notion of what he was saying. The personalities of both were strikingly different from those of the other old Nunamiut men I met in 1956. Thus, when the likes of Irving and Rausch, to name two of several scholarly white men, appeared on Simon's native heath in the 1940s, they were lucky indeed to have been met by the indomitable Paneak (Figure 3).

As the years passed and Paneak became known among what may be termed the academic crowd, he was often paid as a consultant, or as a native artisan; but just as often he offered his mental hospitality free of charge. When in the late 1960s a small landing strip was bulldozed on the edge of the Nunamiut camp, Simon built, as his family summerhouse, a plywood shack at the end of the runway from which he served as an unofficial greeter of arriving tourists. A tall, robust man, his greetings were impressive, the more so when the tourists found that he had nothing to sell.

For this and for the other reasons noted here, numerous outsiders from varied lands and climes came to know Simon to the degree, at least, of having met and talked with him. However, and by his own choosing, he had few close non-Nunamiut friends. His closest was Larry Irving, who was about his own age, and the two of them became bosom pals. Next were Bob Rausch, a loyal friend, and then the youthful Nick Gubser, in his early twenties when Paneak was in his sixties, but who in his fabulous year of hunting and traveling afoot and by dogsled with Simon and his family became more of a much-esteemed, hardworking adopted son than a friend of the status of Irving and Rausch.

Ironically, the two most promising of Simon's prospective biographers, Ed Hall and Grant Spearman, knew him only in passing, or not at all. Grant missed him by three years. I introduced Ed to Simon in the summer of 1959, and for several years thereafter the two met infrequently until, shortly before Simon's death, Ed embarked on an in-depth biography. In the 1980s this commitment of Ed's involved his making annual summer visits to Anaktuvuk for purposes of acquiring pertinent data from Simon's relatives and friends, but the project was abandoned when Hall contracted a debilitating illness. Grant, meanwhile, with his long residence among the Nunamiut, his command of the appropriate literature, and his file of the field notes of scholars like W. N. (Bill) Irving, knows more about Simon Paneak than anyone else. So hopefully, he will one day write the much desired biography.

Always, travels with Simon were delightful courses of study in Nunamiut lore, transmitted more often than not by sheer chance. One morning at one of our John River camps (see below) a small company of ravens passed by, talking, as ravens do, in their bell-like language, and Simon, picking up his rifle, said, "Wolves."

"What wolves?" I asked.

"When they fly like that," Paneak said, "they are following wolves to eat what's left" [of the moose or caribou], and putting his rifle on his back, he slinked off through the spruce woods. (In those years the Nunamiut were always on the lookout for wolves. Even in summer, when their pelts were poor, wolves fetched a bounty of $50 apiece.)

On that same John River journey Simon spent parts of several days searching the woods for a canoe birch from which to carve a pair of snowshoe frames. He spent hours looking at hundreds of birches until finally he found just the right tree. But for once his exceptional powers of explanation failed him. Try as he might, he could not tell us just why it was the only right tree among the several hundred. But it *was* the only right one, I am certain.

In a rocky gorge through which we took the kayaks he showed us a gyrfalcon aerie from which long ago the Nunamiut got feathers for arrow fletching. At the mouth

of a certain little creek, which he had not seen for years, Paneak insisted we stop to collect a few waterworn pebbles of a special kind that made the best whetstones in the country. As we floated down a long pool on the lower river, he demonstrated both his abiding, esoteric interest in natural history and his impressive memory when he said that at this very pool he had once seen an osprey—a scarce bird in those parts. And when I asked him when, he said that it had been in the summer of 1917.

Often, his well-developed sense of humor was instructive. One day when the two of us were walking a trail on the outskirts of the Nunamiut camp in Anaktuvuk Pass we found a small boy who had strayed from home, and who, when he saw us, had the look of a child who had been caught with his hand in the cookie jar.

"Well, it's Tulakana!" boomed Paneak in English, and then in his native tongue he went on and on about Tulakana (Tulukkana) until finally the wide-eyed five- or six-year-old turned and started back the way he had come.

"What was that about?" I asked, and Simon explained that, pretending the boy was Tulakana, a legendary Nunamiut man of the eighteenth century, Paneak had asked him how the hunting had been, and if he had tried hunting at the head of the Killik, and that given the weather and all, it was time for Tulakana to head back to camp.

Between 1956 (the year I met Simon) and 1968, I worked in the central Brooks Range a total of nine summers, during which our friendship included hunting and traveling adventures and brief get-togethers both in Simon's native mountains and in Fairbanks. Additionally, we corresponded by mail. My Brooks Range research interests during those years were twofold: the first being archaeological discovery and interpretation, the second an assessment of the central region's human subsistence resources (Figure 4).

The two objectives were of course closely related, but the latter was generated most particularly by the fact that, because of its remoteness and the grievous reductions of its former Nunamiut populations (see Gubser 1965), nearly all of traditional Nunamiut territory lay fallow. Except for the above-noted Nunamiut, whose mid-twentieth-century subsistence base was founded overwhelmingly on hunting in the country lying in and near Anaktuvuk Pass, human exploitation of plants and animals had become practically nonexistent. Here, then, was an immense landscape whose flora and fauna, with the exception just noted, were quite probably more abundant than they had been for centuries,

FIGURE 4   Our 1969 endeavors were aimed at assessing native fish resources in central Brooks Range streams that had lain fallow for many decades. Here, on the John River, Donald M. Campbell and Mary E. Nutt are preparing to set two 120-foot experimental gill nets. Photograph by JMC.

a condition that invited questions relative to the nature and carrying capacity of its native human food sources.

By 1968 my regional archaeological work had resulted in several published essays, but I had become increasingly interested in Nunamiut ethnography—primarily, and not surprisingly (see above), as it related to the traditional Nunamiut food quest. This interest developed both because of my associations with Simon and because of the growing body of literature having to do with tundra and coastal north Alaska, a literature that permitted and encouraged cultural-environmental studies.[4]

Simon's influence in directing my interests toward Nunamiut ethnography derived mainly from three weeks in 1959 when the two of us, together with Thomas H. Follingstad and Nicholas J. Gubser, boated the length of the John River (Map 2, and see Campbell 1998a:7–8), and a week in 1967 when Simon, Loren D. Potter, Donald M. Campbell, and I camped on the shore of Akvalutak (Aqvalutaq) Lake near the head of the Chandler River (Map 3 and Figure 5). Removed from the hustle and bustle of the Nunamiut camp in Anaktuvuk Pass, and finding himself in the wilderness with, in each instance, three sympathetic and attentive white men, Paneak came into his own. His knowledge of the Brooks Range and how to survive there was extraordinary, and his accounts of traditional Nunamiut life were so inspiring that Nick took a year off from his undergraduate career at Yale to travel on foot and by dogsled with Paneak and Kakinya and their families, after which he wrote his exemplary book on the Nunamiut (Gubser 1965).

Following our days together at Akvalutak Lake in 1967, and realizing that Simon had more to say about Nunamiut history than had appeared in the publications by Gubser, Rausch, or Ingstad (see note 1), I gave him an artists' sketchbook in which, by the summer of 1969, he had completed a series of drawings having to do with the lives of the aboriginal Nunamiut. Most of those pictures, together with my own summaries of his career and of the natural and cultural environments of north Alaska, appear in Campbell 1998a. In the same sketchbook he included several handwritten stories relative to north Alaska history, which together total 16,000 words but which, except for short passages, are not contained in the above-noted 1998 book.

Paneak's drawings and their accompanying texts turned out to be so instructive, and at the same time so engaging, that it seemed obvious that I should ask him to record further Nunamiut lore, a request with which he agreed. Fortunately and coincidentally, with the completion of Simon's sketchbook, funds from the recently inaugurated American Indian Oral History Project became available to University of New Mexico anthropologists and historians, and with this resource I provided him with a small tape recorder, tapes, and an honorarium.

Accordingly, in 1970 and 1971, Simon recorded additional Nunamiut history, including lengthy accounts of his own experiences in hunting, trading, traveling, and having been a participating witness to a prolonged period of famine. Further, his taped stories, totaling 29,000 words, tell of aboriginal north Alaska warfare and of Nunamiut remembrances of mythic episodes in the ancient past. Most

MAP 3   Central regions of the Arctic Coast, Arctic Slope, and Brooks Range (after Amsden 1977).

FIGURE 5 "Big" Chandler and "Little" Chandler Lakes, looking south. These two bodies, connected by a short narrows, have a combined length of eight miles, and because of their food fishes, and their position on a major caribou migration route, their shores were occupied frequently by the old-time Nunamiut, and sometimes even by Indians (see Chapters 3 and 4). Photograph by Edwin S. Hall, Jr., 1961.

of these written and oral histories, both verbatim and as annotated by this writer, appear in the following pages.

As presented here, their contributions to north Alaska history and ethnography embrace three main spheres of interest. First, as Keith H. Basso, my colleague at the University of New Mexico, has suggested in conversation, the book's layout—in which Paneak's verbatim, unedited accounts are accompanied by my renditions into standard English—is an unusual approach; he feels that our presenting Paneak's fascinating English "as is" is of value to anthropologists and linguists whose interests include that of how traditional Native Americans learn to use this language. Beyond this attribute, the book contains two closely related kinds of evidence. About half of its content is autobiographical, beginning with Paneak's earliest

memories (as a five-year-old in 1905), and accordingly it belongs squarely with those published accounts of arctic and subarctic native life histories that, while popular, are decreasing in number because of the passing of the old Eskimos and Indians.

And entwined commonly with this autobiographical characteristic is its contribution to north Alaska history. For example, most of Paneak's accounts of protohistoric and more recent north Alaska trading (including that with Siberia), as well as most of his tales of war and hunger, add new dimensions to related works.[5]

Not surprisingly, given Paneak's popularity among scholarly writers, three of whom (Irving, Rausch, and Ingstad) were relying on his expertise as early as the 1940s, some small parts of this book's contents have

FIGURE 6   The traditional Nunamiut hemispherical tent of caribou hides was adapted to both summer and winter use. This house belonged to the Homer Mekiana family. Homer was a Pt. Barrow Tareumiut man who had married a Nunamiut woman, and when this picture was taken their hide dwelling had just begun to serve, in addition, as the first U.S. Post Office in Anaktuvuk Pass, with Homer as postmaster. Rasmuson Library, University of Alaska, Fairbanks. Photograph by Laurence Irving, 1951.

been published elsewhere, either as fragments of the narratives contained here or as described in English by writers for whom Paneak served as a principal advisor. Where such overlapping correspondences occur in the following chapters, they are acknowledged, but this book is new and unique because its stories are set down quite precisely as Paneak wrote them or told them. Page by page, as the reader will note, I have smoothed his testimony into standard English, hoping fervently that while I revise, sometimes radically, his sentence structure and grammar, I transcribe faithfully what he means to say. For the most part I am satisfied with my attempts, mainly because of my years of personal association with

Paneak. However, in a few cases, after reading over and over again one or another of his remarks, I was left with an understanding that can best be described as opaque. So the imaginative reader is invited to try his or her own renditions of Simon's English.

Additionally, each of the five chapters contains my own prefaces and notes, meant to place in broader context the people, places, and events in Simon's narratives. Then, Grant Spearman's Foreword and Bob Rausch's and Steve Porter's appendices round out and enhance this final of Simon's personal contributions to Native American literature.

Simon Paneak in a summer parka made of cloth shipped in from "outside" and fitted with a wolverine hood ruff that can serve as a mosquito bar. Photograph by Stephen C. Porter, 1960.

Elijah Kakinya—hunter, trader, mystic—at Anaktuvuk
Pass in 1967 (see Campbell 1998a:22). Photograph by
JMC.

THE SUPERNATURAL

Aboriginal and early historic Nunamiut tribal territory encompassed most of the tundra land lying between the Arctic Divide and the coast of northernmost Alaska (Map 1, and see Grant Spearman's Foreword, and Campbell 1968).[1] Most of their scattered bands were so isolated that with the exception of trading expeditions in which from time to time they met white people—most often at Arctic Coast trading posts in Tareumiut territory—they remained unknown to the outside world until the end of the nineteenth century. Indeed, the locations, or former locations, of their several tundra interior bands were not recorded until the middle years of the twentieth century, and Paneak, born in 1900,[2] was five years old before he saw a white man (Simon Paneak, personal communication).

Still, by about 1900 many of the Nunamiut had become Christians, mainly because of the efforts of Moravian and Presbyterian missionaries domiciled at Kotzebue Sound and Pt. Barrow, respectively (Map 2, and see Stefansson 1913:81–83; Spencer 1959:378, 382; and Gubser 1965: 15–20).[3] When I reached the Brooks Range in 1956 all of the adult Anaktuvuk Pass Nunamiut had knowledge of Christianity, and many or most of them were church-going Presbyterians. Their lay preacher was Homer Mekiana (Mikiana) (a Tareumiut man married to a Nunamiut woman), whose church was his caribou hide tent or his sod winter house, and who on Sunday mornings preached in Iñupiaq (Eskimo) and English from lessons mailed in by bush plane from Reverend William C.

Wartes, the white Presbyterian missionary at Pt. Barrow (see Campbell 1998a:35, and Figure 6).

Some of the older men and women did not attend, possibly because they remained unpersuaded that Christianity was better than the native religion they had learned as children. But for others, Christianity was attractive and convincing, one reason, I feel, being that of the close parallels between supernatural phenomena chronicled in the Old and New Testaments and those contained in traditional Nunamiut lore. Traditionally, the Nunamiut believed in the truths and practical applications of prophesies, spirits, dreams, and taboos, as well as in the unique abilities of their own religious practitioners, whose miraculous powers ranged from that of causing a gun not to fire (see Chapter 3) to curing the sick. Since ancient times these and other religious elements and themes had loomed large in Nunamiut society, and in native Arctic and Subarctic life in general,[4] and during the 1950s and 1960s, if not more recently, some of these old beliefs survived among the Nunamiut as adjuncts to, or despite, Christianity.

Among the examples collected by this writer, Elijah Kakinya was able, supposedly, to make boots walk without feet in them, and one of Paneak's distant uncles, Tulukana, had possessed the power to kill caribou magically (Campbell 1998a:22, 24). Further, on one long overland trip between Anaktuvuk Pass and Chandler Lake, I was warned beforehand to avoid the highest peaks and ridges because they were occupied by malevolent spirits in human form. Similar sorts of supernatural happenings or observations are reflected in the following stories.

Gubser (1965:28) writes that "The Nunamiut distinguish between what they consider to be true history (*koliaqtuaq*) and imaginary folklore (*unipqaq*)." These two categories are separate and distinct from the pragmatic oral history accounts described in the following chapters, but as Gubser says, the first of them, *koliaqtuaq* (*quliaqtuaq*), contains supposedly true events. One such account related to me by Paneak in conversation has to do with the tall hill near Umiat (Map 3) upon whose top the Nunamiut escaped the terrors of the flood. Another is the story of the first mammoth hunt (Campbell 1998a:19, pls. 1–6), and in his Foreword, Grant Spearman notes the story of the hill near Umiat and other such tales. The first four and the sixth of the following are of this kind. The fifth treats religious avoidances and cautions, the seventh is a personal account of Paneak's boyhood experiences with magic, and the last two belong squarely in the *unipqaq* (*unipkaaq*) group: stories designed for the entertainment and betterment of Nunamiut children.

Paneak begins with the brief and matter-of-fact Flying Whale story, among whose purposes is that of reminding us of the truly incredible food source provided by whales, a sea bounty that permitted the Tareumiut a more elaborate way of life than that of the Nunamiut. From Paneak's drawings this particular animal is most likely a blue whale (*Sibbaldus musculus*), which may reach lengths of one hundred feet and whose weights are reckoned at one ton per linear foot. The Three Brothers story provides insight to early relationships between the Nunamiut and other Eskimo tribes. It is one of several Nunamiut "giant" tales, and it mentions an interesting penalty for committing incest.

The Raven story, because it tells of how the Nunamiut were given daylight, would belong at the head of these *koliaqtuaq* if it were not that parts of it, as Paneak implies, smack of *unipqaq*. Further, it introduces the Muskoxen tale which, in addition to its reflections on the age-old human fear of menstruation, is of practical interest to anthropologists and biologists. Arlvalioruak (Alvaluiḷiruaq) is a hair-raising tale of the dangers of the dead—another ancient and worldwide fear—and Scary Story abides in Paneak's mind as the time when as a small boy he was frightened half out of his wits by a failed attempt at contagious magic. Parent of All Mosquitoes imparts a certain humanity to the single arctic and subarctic animal that qualifies as an unredeemable scourge, and while The Story of Mouse carries with it no such child-rearing benefit, it has a Mother Goose sort of charm.

Koptogak

Flying whale can be heard from long away off – Sharp whistle from wing hole. Early peoples know how to bring the whale down to ground. When the flying whale flown by close by all the peoples make a noise in loud voise even childrens can Screamed. And soon flying whale hear the noise of peoples he get nervice lost his power and landed on the ground. Can never took off the ground again. And then peoples killed by spear (harpoon) and said flying whale is thin blubber except plenty meat & Muktuk.

An among Eskimos saying in early days was waiting for flying Whale and watch in every day & night because big mammals is large of food for many peoples. This is Short Story. – end

Koptogak (Quptuġaq)

The flying whale (Figures 7 and 8) can be heard from a long way [as he makes a] sharp whistle from his wing hole. The early people knew how to bring the whale down to the ground. When the flying whale flew close by, all the people shouted in loud voices and even the children screamed.

As soon as the flying whale heard the noise of the people, he got nervous, lost his power and landed on the ground. Once on the ground he could never take off again. Then the people killed him by spear (harpoon). They said that the flying whale has thin blubber, but plenty of meat and muktuk [*maktak*; whale skin]. And in the early days the Eskimos say they watched day and night, waiting for the flying whale because the big mammals provided food for many people.[5]

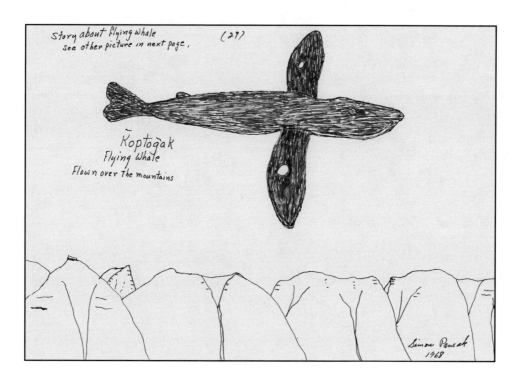

FIGURE 7   Paneak's illustration of the flying whale story.

Koptogak — flying whale can be heard from long away off — Sharp whistle from weng hole (28)
Early peoples know how to bring the whale down to ground. when the flying whale flowry
close by all the peoples make a noise in loud voise even Childrens can Screamed
flying whale hear the noise of peoples he get nervice lost his power landed on the ground
Can never took off the ground again then peoples killed by spear (harpoon) and said
flying whale is third blubber except plenty meat & Muktuk
    An among Eskimos saying in early days was waiting for flying Whale Watch in every day & nig
because big mammals is large of food for many peoples, This is short story. — end.

Simon Pan
1968

FIGURE 8   Paneak's illustration of the flying whale story.

A Story About Three Brothers

A story about three brothers their mother name is Aknaniak. She are ordinary woman. Father of three brother … could not remember name but said he is ordinary man. Ilagannik older & Kovravak is second which is standing in between of his 2 brother and Aksik youngest and all of them are mighty strongmans.

In the day of 3 brothers there was giant animals peoples Killer. And Ilaganik & Kovravak kill all giant animals. Kovravak hand had webbed as goose foot and he can dive in the Water for while like Oogrook – (Bearded Seal). And 2 big shrews one in Colville in above about 20 miles from Killik river mouth and one was in Ikpikpak river. And said the 2 animals are hair on like sea animals. When a look for animal Ilagannik riding his kayak and Kovravak are diving. And found and animal chasing who ride in kayak & paddling into shore of the lake & jumb out of his kayak. Two man attacking the big animal with flint sword made of flint and killed. And said after the big animal killed and butchered & found many flint arrow head just under the skin of giant animals. And one big fish located near Noatak river. Cannot kill the big fish and said Kovravak almost swallowed by fish. Kovravak trying to kill with his flint made sword but said the big fish very difficult to kill or tough to kill leave the big fish alone and told peoples would not come near of lake shore and in winter do not walk or driven dogsled on the lake ice.

Ilagannik wife name are Ottoktak and all three are moved over to Kotzebue Sound after race in Colville river. In over Kotzebue an among old peoples must have a story what they doing in over there. Said in story and telling Ilagannik was killed by his wife Ottoktak, wife jade adze after Ilagannik sleep with own daughter – Ottoktak got jealous. And Kovravak died by himself. He is great swimmer and swimming across from Kotzebue to Shismaref in near Deering. And Aksik was killed by Shismaref peoples.

Ilagannik house could be found in west of Kotzebue in island built by flat stone on roof & side no man can moved. One times his enemies came with two skin boat full load with mens. When two boat came near he told them. No more Ilagannik, no more power to fight. He put his face with Salmon Eggs. He told them the sickness make him weak, (Pu pik) meaning Chicken pox or Small pox or Measle any one of these. He walk over to his big

A Story About Three Brothers

There were once three brothers (Figure 9). Their mother was an ordinary woman named Aknaniak (Aġnaniaq) and the father whose name I can't recall was also ordinary. The older brother was called Ilagannik (Iḷaŋanniq), then there was Kovravak (Kuvravak) and Aksik (Aqsik) was the youngest. All of them were mighty strongmen.

At this time there lived giant animals—people killers. Ilagannik and Kovravak killed all of the giant animals. Kovravak had webbed hands like goosefeet and he could dive under water like Oogrook (ugruk), the bearded seal.[6]

There were two big shrews. One was in the Colville River about twenty miles above the Killik River mouth and another in the Ipikpak River (Map 3). It is said that the two animals had hair like that of sea animals. When looking for the animal, Ilagannik was in his kayak (qayaq) and Kovravak was diving. They found the animal and it chased Ilagannik in his kayak. He paddled into the shore of the lake and jumped out of his boat, then he and Kovravak attacked the big animal with a flint sword and killed it. They said that after the big animal was killed and butchered they found many flint arrowheads just under the skin.

There was also a big fish located in a lake near the Noatak (Nuataaq) River (Map 2). The big fish was hard to kill and Kovravak was almost swallowed by it. He was trying to kill it with his flint sword but couldn't and decided to leave the big fish alone. He told the people not to come near the lakeshore and in winter not to walk or drive dogsleds on the lake ice.

Ottoktak (Uttuktaq) was the wife of Ilagannik and she and the two brothers moved over to Kotzebue Sound after a race in the Colville River. Over in Kotzebue, the old people have a story [about what happened]. They tell how Ilagannik was killed by his wife, Ottoktak, with a jade adze after Ilagannik slept with his own daughter and Ottoktak got jealous.

The second brother Kovravak died by himself. He was a great swimmer and could swim across from Kotzebue to Shishmaref near Deering (Map 2). The third brother, Aksik, was killed by the Shishmaref people.

Ilagannik's house could be found west of Kotzebue on an island. The roof and sides were built of flat stones, which no ordinary man could move. One time his enemies came with two skin boats full of men. When the two boats came near, he told them, "No more Ilagannik; no more

A Story about three brothers their mother name is Aknaniak she are ordinary woman. Father of three brother could not remember name but said he is ordinary man. Ilagannik older & Kovravak is second which is standin in between of his brother Aksik youngest all of them are mighty strong mans
In the day of 3 brothers there was giant animals-peoples Killer Ilagannik & Kovravak kill all giant animals. Kovravak hand had webbed as goose foot he can dive in the water for while like Oogrook (Bearded Seal) 2 big Skews one in Colville in above about 20 miles from Killik river mouth one was in Ikpikpak river said the 2 animals are hair on like a sea animals when a look for animal Ilagannik riding his Kayak Kovravak are diving found animal chasing who ride in Kayak &

conts'd in next page   Simon Paneak
                                              1968

FIGURE 9   Paneak's illustration of the three brothers story.

pile of flat stones and he took one and throw to boats and the boat was boat wrecked and other boat wrecken too. Both boats Completely perish with two flat stones. All men of two boat are drowned to death. More story about Ilagannik in next page.

Ilagannik was in above camp with a man. They had some caribou in the lake. By that time Ilagannik is head of mans towing bull caribou and he reach the camp. He was floating along in front of camp and all the woman see him with caribou. And all the childrens was so happy to see nice looken caribou they can tell by the horn used to be fat caribou or see big horn on caribou.

Ilagannik carried by Swift Current water. Finally he was beyond the camp. He know will bring the caribou

power to fight." He put salmon eggs on his face. He told them that he was sick with Pupik, meaning chicken pox, smallpox, or measles, and it made him weak. He walked over to his big pile of flat stones and he took one and threw it at the first boat and wrecked it. He wrecked the other boat too. Both boats completely perished from the two flat stones and all of the men in the boats drowned.

Ilagannik was above the camp with a man. They had some caribou in the lake. Ilagannik was ahead of the man, towing a bull caribou, and he reached the camp first. He was floating along in front of the camp and all the women could see him with the caribou. All the children were so happy to see such nice looking caribou. They could tell by the big horns [antlers] that it was a fat caribou. Ilagannik up Against the Swift Current water. And Finally one of woman was told him. Ilagannik! Kamatkotsillasigatin! Meaning you would be off too much. And Ilagannik sounded Ays. Meaning Oh! Oh! And He is started paddling & Against the Current his tow bull caribou coming up & down in the water Nothing do it like willow leave he tow. And he must be fast and make water rough because his paddle blade is big enough to cover Kayak opening when a rain.

His youngest brother Aksik is powerful also. Story was telling when Shismaref peoples are loading up his Kayak and when he got in his Kayak tie by raw Qogrook line to his Kayak rim so won't be leaken when he riding in rough sea. And Severals man are ready with Bow & Arrows behind the Crowd. Soon After ready off the shore the crowd run but the Severals Man Shoot Aksik from behind with Severals Arrows him and then Aksik feel ache on his between Shoulders. And he hit Severals persons by his big paddles and killed Severals persons and he died in his Kayak.

And Kovravak are died by his own illness.

Ilagannik was camping one summer at Kootchiakruak Lake located about ten miles west of Killik in mountain lines in near outlet of big lake. And he piling many horn of caribou he kill even now could be found there.

According to story talk about three brothers and are not very much tall than ordinary man but they are dynamics powerful & strong. And Ilagannik always bring to his camp at Kootchiakruak by foot ball playing and his wife Ottoktak waiting with large food for the big group of Killik Eskimos – he is nicely playing on foot ball. He could run better than ordinary men. And Same things with his two brother.

and the caribou were carried by the swift current beyond the camp. Finally, one of the women cried "Ilagannik! Kamakotsillasigatin! (Qamatqullasigaatin)" meaning, "you are too far off." And Ilagannik replied "Ays (Aiy)," meaning "Oh! Oh!"

And he started paddling against the current and the bull caribou he was towing was bobbing up and down in the water. There was nothing to it. It was as if he were towing a willow leaf. He was fast and made it through the rough water because his paddle blade was big enough to cover a kayak opening when it rained.

His youngest brother Aksik was powerful too. The story is told that the Shishmaref people were loading up his kayak and when he got in, he tied a raw Oogrook line to his kayak rim so it wouldn't leak when he was riding in rough sea. Several men were ready with bows and arrows behind the crowd. Soon after he was off the shore, the crowd ran and several men shot Aksik with arrows from behind. Then Aksik felt an ache between his shoulders. He hit several persons with his big paddles and killed them; then he died in his kayak. And Kovravak died of an illness.

Ilagannik was camping one summer at Kutchaurak (Kuutchiaġruaq) Lake, located about ten miles west of the Killik River in the mountain line near the outlet of the big lake. He piled up many horns [antlers] of the caribou that he killed and even now they can be found there. According to the stories, the three brothers were not very much taller than ordinary men but they were dynamic, powerful, and strong. Ilagannik always played football at his camp at Kutchaurak and his wife Ottoktak always waited with a lot of food for the big group of Killik [Nunamiut] Eskimos who played football. [Ilagannik] was very good at playing football and could run better than ordinary men, as could his two brothers.

Raven

This story ... They want a very old story, before the days of the Flood. People where talking about it, somehow that ... more and more and ... one was living together. They probably these rich men having labrets on their lower lips, cause he is richest men in this group. The family, they was traveling during winter time. So very hard to find dry wood for fire in the home, and they were collecting, testing by lick, to pass tongue over the surface in cold weather. Green oil can stick to the tongue, and if dry wood stick to the ... stick to the tongue, because the ... no wet in it. In those days, in these groups rich men live and stayed with the people a very rich man. Had a daughter. She is Princess who would not like to have husband. Many young men were going after her, but she did not mate. They did not make it.

And this rich man have two lights, which is a carry one, bright one shaped like a football ... this is in the story, and the light too, real bright during the darkness, shinning far away good enough to see the animal from distance when they carry out during the hunting. And he also have, he also have one dark one that he use at home for ... to get some wood and water and probably some ice too for drinking water. Rich man went out to hunt and everybody was follow along and catch animal, other wise that they don't see no animals during the winter time. Like up around North Pole, near North Pole.

I would say that also the raven and the crow who can speak in their language ... And the man was talking about bright lights could be busted. They know that if someone busted the bright light and the country would be in day light all the time. Then everybody would have a light in the country, whenever they go hunt, there is no way to fall ... no way to follow the rich man. And that the rich man was so great so smart, than other people, and finally Mr. Raven was told that ... told the man could bust it ... rich man light, bright light. Everybody told Mr. Raven, if you could bust the rich man's light, and we would give you, we would give you all you need, the rest of ... your life.

That was agreed. Mr. Raven was so happy he think it might be. It might somehow fall the rich man and bust the rich man's light. But they never know yet. And Mr. Raven says, I could try tonight. He told the people like

This is a very old story. Before the days of the Flood, the people told about these rich men who had labrets in their lower lips.[7] There was a family traveling during wintertime. It was so very hard to find dry wood for fire in the home. As they collected wood, they tested by licking the wood, passing their tongues over the surface. In cold weather, the oil from green wood can stick to the tongue but dry wood will not because there is no wet in it. In those days, a very rich man lived with this family. He had a daughter, a princess who did not wish to marry. Many young men were going after her, but she did not mate.

This rich man had two lights, one bright one, shaped like a football, which he carried during hunting. This light was real bright in the darkness, shining far away, good enough to see an animal at a distance. He also had a dark one that he used at home to get wood and water and probably some ice too, for drinking water.

The rich man would go out to hunt and everybody would follow along to catch the animal; otherwise, they could not see animals during the wintertime. It was like up around the North Pole.

I would also say that Raven and Crow can speak in the Eskimo language. One of the men was talking about bright lights that could be busted. They knew that if someone broke the bright light the country would be in daylight all the time. Then everybody would have a light in the country; whenever they went hunting, they wouldn't have to follow the rich man who was so great, so much smarter than the other people. Finally, everybody told Mr. Raven, "If you could bust the rich man's light, we will give you all you need for the rest of your life." This was agreed to. Mr. Raven was so happy. And Mr. Raven said he might try that night to somehow follow the rich man and break the bright light hanging from the roof of the rich man's house.

The two lights were hanging all the time, and no man could reach the bright light. Mr. Raven was figuring out how he could get in. He went over to the side of a little pond where the princess usually got water towards evening. Mr. Raven was sitting there at the shore of the little pond and finally the young princess showed up with the dark light. Mr. Raven was so scared that the princess would see him and be frightened and not come to that. He said he could try and bust the rich man's bright light which is hanging on the roof of the rich man house. And two of his light is hanging on the roof of the rich man, hanging all the time. And no man could reach, reach the bright light. And Mr. Raven was figuring out how he could get in. He went over to the side of a little pond to where the princess usually get water towards evening. And Mr. Raven was sitting there at the shore of the little pond, finally young princess showed up with the dark light and Mr. Raven so scared that princess saw him or the princess would be scared she would not come to the pond to get water. But Mr. Raven was turned to raven fathers and raven was hoping the princess would get thirsty. Soon as she get to the little pond and drink water before filling her bucket. Soon after the princess reached the pond, she dipping her dipper for water and drank and swallowed feather of Mr. Raven. She could feel in her throat, but she swallow it already. And fill it up for her water bucket. She went home, told her mother that she had swallowed something but she could not figure out what she had swallowed in the pond. Mr. Raven are not home in these evenings to the people, some men and women wondering how Mr. Raven is sneaking over to rich man's side. Young princess was filling belly and growing fast and something in there. And little later she could feel she was going to have a baby, without man approach her. She don't even have a friend, no boyfriend does she have … This is kind of funny situation, I guess, to the rich young princess. Princess told her parent that she was to conceive, pregnant. The rich man was so glad but he hoped that the child should be boy because he is getting old already. And he decided I am getting old, I might need hunter when I am old to do all my hunting gear. And my richness too, richness. Rich men happy to have a first grandchild on the princess, daughter. Before too long, after princess had big belly, almost ready to be born, that child. Some night child was born, and child was little boy. How glad the rich man he was.

And grandmother … that little boy had little lumps on forehead. The little boy was healthy and happy. And shortly after he was born he was laughing and happy all the time. He was growing very fast as an ordinary child, and grow and grow every day. And then finally light boy was crying and looking up there, bright lights on roof of the house. And he pointed his hand up and bringing down … old man to bring down this … bright light to him, like to play with bright light. But grandfather give

the pond to get water that he turned himself into a raven feather, hoping that she would be thirsty.

As soon as the princess got to the pond, she dipped her dipper into the water and drank, swallowing the feather that was Mr. Raven.

She could feel it in her throat but swallowed it anyway. Then she filled up her water bucket. She went home and told her mother that she swallowed something from the pond but she could not figure out what she had swallowed. Mr. Raven did not come home to the people in the evening and some men and women were wondering if Mr. Raven was sneaking over to the rich man's side. The young princess's belly was filling and growing fast. Something was in there.

A little later on, she could feel that she was going to have a baby without any man ever having approached her. Because she had no boyfriend, this was a kind of funny situation to the rich young princess. So the princess told her parents that she was pregnant. The rich man was so glad and hoped that the child would be a boy because he was getting old. And he thought, "I am getting old, I will need a hunter when I am old and what about all my hunting gear and my riches, my riches?" The rich man was happy to have a grandchild from his daughter the princess. Before too long, after the princess had a big belly, the child was ready to be born and when it came it was a little boy. How glad the rich man was!

And the grandmother saw that the little boy had little lumps on his forehead, but he was healthy and happy. Shortly after he was born, he was laughing and happy all the time. He was growing very fast like an ordinary child and grew and grew every day. One day the boy was crying and looking up at the bright light on the roof of the house. He pointed his hand up—he wanted the old man to bring down this bright light to him so he could play with it. But his grandfather gave him the dark one, he didn't let him near the bright one.

He was a healthy little boy even if he had lumps on his forehead and his grandfather and grandmother loved him very much. They held him on their laps and gave him very good food. And the little boy was so happy to have the dark light to play with because grandfather told him that it was easier to handle than the bright light and the little boy looked like he understood what the grandfather was telling him. But then the little boy got tired of the dark light and again wanted the bright one, but grandfather would him dark one, he don't let him near the bright one. He was a healthy little boy, but with that ... he had lumps on the forehead and anyway grandfather loved him very much and grandmother too. They had him on the laps and in the hands and gave him very good food. And little boy was so happy to have dark light cause grandfather was told him it is easier to handling than bright light and then look like a little boy understood what the grandfather was telling him. And in those days little boy was getting tired of the dark one, he want a bright one. But grandfather would not let him have. But Mr. Raven, little child, was crying and crying day and night. Finally grandfather can hardly sleep cause the little boy was crying all the time, real loud too.

And sometime princess took little child on the back and tried to make the little boy go to sleep, but never did ... never did go to sleep. Even on mother's back. And then he cry and in several days, didn't want to eat ... they give him some food, but he don't want to eat, the little boy. Finally, the grandfather took the bright one from the roof and hand it over to the little child, the little boy. The little boy get up walking along on the floor already, in a few days ... maybe a few weeks, he is really fast growing in the story telling. When he comes ... the little boy was nicely handling the bright light and very easy then he go to sleep. Then he go to sleep. Then when he wake up he eat some food, good food. Because rich man has got all kinds of food. Another time he want to play with the bright light all the time, they give him the dark one but he don't want it. Don't want the dark one. I mean don't want the dark one. He want the bright one. And then grandfather gave ..., the bright one ... that was nice ..., boy was very nice to be singing, him singing ..., happy, and dance little maybe. And then when they get tired to play with bright light, then he give it back to grandfather carefully.

Finally the little boy could talk in their language and could understand very well, his voice is very beautiful noise. In the evening after the grandfather come home from hunting, he wanted to play with the bright light one again. And then the grandfather handed it over to him and tell him to be careful ... be careful my kid. And then the little boy was handling it nicely and they ... nobody in this house is scared to bust the light cause the little boy was very careful in handling that light. And mother was cooking while the little boy had the bright light. And then immediately the little boy was jumping and go out from house. And mother sees the little boy was going out

not let him have it. But Mr. Raven, the little child, was crying and crying day and night. The grandfather could hardly sleep because the little boy was crying all of the time and real loud too.

Sometimes the princess took the little child on her back and tried to make the little boy go to sleep but he never did, even on his mother's back. He cried for several days and didn't want to eat, even though they gave him food.

Finally, the grandfather took the bright light down from the roof and handed it over to the little boy. The little boy had been walking on the floor already—really fast growing. So when the grandfather gave him the bright light the little boy handled it nicely and easily and then he went to sleep. When he awoke, he ate some food, good food, because his grandfather, the rich man, had all kinds of food. Another time, he wanted to play with the bright light and they gave him the dark one but he didn't want it, he wanted the bright one. So his grandfather gave him the bright one and the boy was happy and was singing and dancing a little. Then when he got tired of playing with the bright light, he gave it back to his grandfather very carefully.

Finally the little boy could talk in their language and could understand very well. He had a beautiful voice.

In the evening after the grandfather came home from hunting, the boy wanted to play with the bright light once again. And then the grandfather handed it over to him and told him to be careful. The little boy was handling it nicely and nobody in the house worried that he would break the light. The mother was cooking while the little boy had the bright light. Then suddenly, the little boy jumped up and ran from the house with the bright light. The mother went after him but she was too late, because the little boy was breaking up the bright light with his beak.

The little boy had turned into a raven and flew away and there was no way the princess could catch him. Mr. Raven flew all over the country, which was bright all over, after he had broken up the light. Then, according to the story, the princess was talking about dark and light and said darkness could be called night—*unyak* (*unnuaq*)—and bright could be called day—*uvuluk* (*uvluq*)—and, my God, they had day and night. Then everybody was so happy and they had a big celebration. And they promised Mr. Raven that they would give him all they had for the rest of his life. The rich man was very sad at losing the bright light. He was crying and the old lady was crying too.

with bright light and she went out shortly after the little boy went out. But she was too late, little boy busting up the bright light with his beak. Little boy was turning to raven, fly ... and princess could not catch ... , no way. Flying all over country, very bright all over ... , after Mr. Raven busting up the light. Finally princess says it could be divided into two item; one is, princess says ... one could be ... darkness, call it night, unyak and bright could be called day ... uvuluk. Then according to story princess was talking about dark and light and my God, they had day and night. Then everybody was so happy, and they have a big celebration and happy. And they promised Mr. Raven that if they could give all they had there for the rest of his life.

Then the rich man, he was very sad loosing the bright light. He was crying and the old lady cry too ... all of them crying. But they could not help. Then while the rich man was crying at the same time he took the dark one and he busted it. He says, I don't want the dark one. It was nothing to me. And we had the light anyway in the outdoor over the country, no way to see the dark one. I don't know how they kept the bright lights, said the rich man. In the story nobody talking about where he get the light.

And then after that, they live in same place down there ... near mouth of Killik River in Colville. Everybody so happy. And then they was hunting and they round up the muskox.

All of them were crying but they could not help. Then while the old man was crying, he took the dark lamp and broke it.

He said, "I don't want the dark one, it is nothing to me. We had light anyway in the out-of-doors, no way to see the dark one. I don't know how they kept the bright lights," said the rich man. In the story, nobody is talking about where the light came from.

Then, after that, the people were living in the same place near the mouth of the Killik River on the Colville River. Everybody was happy and they were hunting and rounding up the musk ox.

Why the Muskoxen were Turned to Stone

———

They round up the muskox and bring in the muskox to their home and then kill it, spear it. Spear or bow and arrow ... and they say that they say that they spear the muskox in the very old days before they know about the bow and arrow, that is true I think. And some other time a bunch of boys went out and running up the muskox. Then one young boy was a good runner and he was lead all the young boy cause he is quick running than everybody else. They also carry dogs to help them drive the herd. And in those days in the village, all the women and kids and old men went out and holler and happy.

And there was a young lady who was beginning the monthly bleeding, who should not look out into the outdoor from this tiny tent. It must be moss house in the winter time. And then everybody was happy and screaming and the kids jumping up and down and making a lot of noise while a young bunch of boys and bringing the herd, muskox herd. And come near and people were so happy that they would have a lot of meat. And then young lady going out from this little moss house and look at the boys who was driving the muskox herd. The muskox just stop up there about a couple miles from the river. No move at all. Young men who can run better than all, he was near the front of the muskox herd. And then finally someone was going up to see after they all stop the herd and the boys, went up to see. Muskox and men and dogs turn to rocks.

When they are going up there, nothing else but rocks. Turn to rocks. And then pretty soon in the village find out about young lady. She is driving the herd and boys ... they know that young lady make them turn to rocks. And when they saw her and then old man took some sticks and killed the young lady with the stick cause he was very sure to lose his son.

Now even today we could see from distance like a caribou herd lining together towards the river ..., some men nearby, they heard it looked like a man nearby the rocks lying.

I don't know if it was true or not, but they, the old people, were talking like this. Some thinks that it was down at the Anaktuvuk River. And another herd of muskox turns into rock too ..., same, about same look like down at the Colville. Same thing as that young lady, she turned ..., make them turn into rocks. I don't know after that ... that is enough, this story.

How the Musk Ox were Turned to Stone

———

In the old days, the people rounded up the musk ox and brought them to their homes where they killed them with spear or bow and arrow.[8] They say that in the very old days, before they knew about the bow and arrow, they always speared them. One day a young boy who was a good runner led all the other young boys because he was the fastest. They also had dogs to help them drive the herd. And in those days in the village, all the women and kids and old men went out and hollered and were happy.

There was a young lady who was beginning the monthly bleeding, and who was in a tiny tent where she was forbidden to look outdoors. In the wintertime, it must have been a moss house (Campbell 1998a: pls. 17, 18). Everybody was happy and screaming and the kids were jumping up and down and making a lot of noise when the bunch of young boys brought in the musk ox herd. As they came nearer the people were so happy that they would have lots of meat. And the young lady came out of the little moss house and looked at the boys who were driving the musk ox herd.

The musk ox just stopped there about a couple of miles from the Colville River not moving at all. The young man who could run the best was near the front of the herd. Finally, someone went up to see what had stopped the herd, and when they got to the front of it, they saw nothing but rocks; musk ox and men and dogs had turned to rocks. Then, in the village, they found out about the young lady. She had changed the herd and the boys, and the people knew that the young lady made them turn into rocks. Then an old man took some sticks and killed the young lady because he was very sure that if he didn't he would lose his son.

Now, even today, we can see from a distance, like a caribou herd lined up together toward the river, the musk ox herd and the boys and the dogs that had turned into rocks. I don't know if it was true or not, but this is what the old people said. Some think that down on the Anaktuvuk River another herd of musk ox was turned into rock also. It looks about the same as down at the Colville River. It was the same thing, a young lady—she made them turn into rocks. I don't know what happened after that. That is enough of this story.

Taboos

I could talk a little about what I hear on the Eskimo in the early days before they know about the religion. They have all kinds ... just like the law, and people should not. In the first place they should not make a ... never use skins that has been, but never used new skin ... , what they call that, like that where they don't have to make socks or mittens or pants and parkas during the fishing in the fishing hole. I believe some time they died after ... after ... , they would make very clean skin ... , all the skin ... somebody make it and this group always get sick. That is why they don't want to make any more mittens and socks or pants and parkas in the fishing holes during fishing time. And another thing, when the man gets a wolf or wolverine should not drink from family water bucket for four days for male and five days for female. This is another law of the old Eskimo. And third, and when the people get grizzly bear or a brown bear, should not bring the fresh meat to village. They should leave it maybe about fifty yards away from the village and they can cook it there and eat it. I don't know it myself but I heard like that. And forth, about the mountain sheep, a woman should not eat the front part of mountain sheep leg and some part of ribs, and the head too. Sheep head a woman should not eat. I don't know. I never heard about anybody got sick but they believed it. Might be when the women ... , when the women eat the sheep's head ... she became blind, can't see nothing. That was the rule.

Another thing when ... a person died who has a family, they should not go into the house from outdoors. For the person losing the one family, they should not go in for about six months. They could tell by the moon among the old people, that all I know. They don't bury the body of the dead people. In the old days, just lying on the ground and cover over with caribou hide. But in the mountain where rock is ... they buried in the rock.

And then in old days when the mother and after the child was born, mother was died shortly after child was born, and that left the little child with no mother, dead mother. And hauled her ... , outside of the house, to dry place. And the little child keep on crying from the dead mother. She died during the winter time, very cold too, very cold for the child, living ... , of course, but the child was crying and keep on crying. Finally keep on crying. And finally she comes to the village. try to talk to people

Taboos

I will talk a little about what I hear of the Eskimo in the early days before they knew about Christian religion. They had all kinds of laws about what people should and should not do. In the first place, they should never use new skin to make socks or mittens or pants or parkas during the fishing at the fishing hole. I believe sometime they died after they used new skin and this group always got sick. That is why they don't want to make any more mittens and socks or pants and parkas at the fishing holes during fishing time.

And another thing, when a man gets a wolf or wolverine, he should not drink from the family water bucket for four days if it was a male and five days if it was a female. This is another law of the old Eskimos. And third, when the people got a grizzly bear or a brown bear, they should not bring the fresh meat to the village. They should leave it maybe about fifty yards away from the village and they can cook it there and eat it. I don't know it myself but I heard it like that.

And fourth, about the mountain sheep: a woman should not eat the front part of a mountain sheep leg or parts of the ribs or the head. A woman should not eat a sheep head. I don't know why. I never heard about anybody getting sick but they believed it. It might be that if the woman ate a sheep's head, she became blind; couldn't see anything. That was among the Eskimo rules.

Another thing, when a person died, the family should not go into the house from the out-of-doors. They should not go in for about six months. Among the old people, they could tell by the moon, that's all I know. They did not bury the body of the dead person. In the old days, they just left it lying on the ground, covered over with caribou hide. But in the mountains, where there are lots of rocks, they buried the body with rocks (see Campbell 1972: pls. 2, 3).

And then in the old days, if a mother gave birth and died shortly after the child was born, that left the little child with no mother. And they hauled her outside of the house to a dry place, together with the child. And the little child kept crying. The mother died during the wintertime, very cold too, very cold for the living child of course and the child kept on crying and crying.

Finally, the child came to the village and tried to talk to the people who were trying to kill it. The little child was trying to kill. The little child and jumping around and jumping around like a football and the child landed from on his diaper never run ... just jump, jump. Little child landed on his diaper, and after that, somehow they worked it out and little child didn't see in the village. He went to very bright fire, they can't see no child in that. Except the flying fire, it is like charcoal in the fire ... charcoal in the wood. Somehow they stop the little child from jumping around, among the medicine men ... they must have had the power too and a little child bring around.

Arlvaloiruak's Lesson

Another thing in early days when a person died in the house and the family lived in the house of the dead man or women and one story talking about who was stay alone during the summer. He was single. His name is Arlvaloirak ... the spelling A-r-l-v-a-l-i ... o-i-l-r-u-a-k, Arlvaloiruak. After he stay alone during the summer towards in fall he is planning to looking for people somewhere ..., he must have known where about the people are. And after the snow ... freeze up the river, he got his sled and dogs. He was loading up his sled with summer caribou skin, cause the caribou skin is of some value to the old timers in early days for clothing. The story says he was camping several times before he found someone being around or tracks in the snow, camping in there several times. And then pretty soon he found some old tracks of man and he says to himself and pretty soon I reach some people, because he was lonesome during all summer. Then he camped at a river cause in the fall in the river, it is dangerous too ..., during the night, some part of the river, there is thin ice dangerous to break through the ice. That is why in the story he was camping and stay over night until the morning. And then early in the morning when it is beginning the day light over in the east he is loading up his sled and fix up his dogs and started. Pretty soon he found the village ..., but he don't see no fresh tracks.

He saw several houses all right, over in the river side. And then pretty soon Arlvaloiruak could hear noise from the house up there ..., singing, like this ... I could sing his song ... (singing song). That meaning all the words of that song, Arlvaloiruak you are not be living very long. But Arlvaloiruak he never get scared ... when he see

jumping around and jumping around like a football, landing on his diaper, never running, just jumping and jumping. The little child landed on his diaper and after that, somehow they worked it out and the little child wasn't seen in the village any more. He became a very bright fire and the people couldn't see any child in it, except for the flying fire; the child was only like charcoal in the fire, charcoal in the wood. Somehow, the medicine men (*aŋatkut*) stopped the little child from jumping around, they had the power to stop the little child from jumping.

Arlvaloiruak's Lesson

Another story. In the early days a person had died in the house and the family lived in the house of the dead man or woman. There was a man who stayed alone during the summer. He was single. His name was Arlvaloiruak (Alvaluiḷiruaq).

After he stayed alone all summer, toward fall he was planning to look somewhere for people—he must have known about where the people would be. So, after it snowed and the river froze up, he got his sled and dogs and loaded up the sled with summer caribou skins, which were of value to the old timers in the early days for making clothing. The story says he camped several times before he found signs of someone having been there. Pretty soon, he found some old tracks of a man and said to himself, "Pretty soon, I will reach some people," because he was lonesome, having spent the summer alone.

He camped at a river for the night because the river could have thin ice and it would be dangerous to break through the ice. That is why in the story, he was camping and staying overnight until morning. Then, early in the morning when it was beginning to get light in the east, he loaded up his sled, fixed up his dogs, and started out. Pretty soon he found the village but he didn't see any fresh tracks. He saw several houses all right, over on the riverside. Then pretty soon, Arlvaloiruak could hear singing coming from the houses up there—singing like this [Paneak sings]. The meaning of the words of that song were "Arlvaloiruak, you are not going to live very long." But Arlvaloiruak did not get scared. He saw the people and the man who was singing up there.

He went to the house where the noise was coming from and it was pretty dark. He couldn't see anything

the people who was the man who was singing up there. He went to the house where the noise came from and he says that he is going to house … and he, it is pretty dark, he can't see nothing. And then Arlvaloiruak would say … "too dark I can't see nothing … The voice answer him … "too dark around here – too dark around here And then Arlvaloiruak, he want to feel that men and women was speaking from in this house. Pretty soon he could feel the very frozen nose or the person, frozen nose. And then Arlvaloiruak was scared. He went out running towards his dogs. He is looking back and saw the big fire started rolling towards him, like a big ball, like a big boulder, rock, but it was a big … and rolling towards Arlvaloiruak and slowly …

Arlvaloiruak was doing up his dog team wanted to go home. But he was slower than the big fire … , rolling – rolling fire. Almost big fire catching Arlvaloiruak who was pushing the sled. Then he throw one of his mittens to the big fire … rolling fire. Then, my gosh, the fire is stop. And burning up the mittens. And he was quite aways before it burnt it all his mittens. The big fire after burned up all Arlvaloiruak mittens start again chasing Arlvaloiruak.

And when it come near to Arlvaloiruak, he threw another his mittens. He make the fire stop. Arlvaloiruak was work hard and pushing his sled and sweat too because he was pushing the sled and scared same time and dogs scared too. But and rolling fire a little faster than dog team traveling. And after the fire burned all up Arlvaloiruak's mittens and same things … started chasing, following Arlvaloiruak trail. And coming close again. And Arlvaloiruak threw his outer parka, he take and feed it to the fire, rolling fire. Fire burning and screaming at same time and screaming just like a fighting dogs, fighting other dogs. Arlvaloiruak couldn't understand what the screaming, what the fire screaming. And it was a while before the fire start chasing again … , and then same thing. Next time the fire comes close near to Arlvaloiruak he drop all the load of caribou hide. When the fire almost catch him, he threw one caribou hide at a time. He almost emptied up his sled but his home is a quite aways yet. And he was sweat, sweat and pushing his sled because in case his dogs get tired and dogs pretty tired. But a no way to stop cause the fire might burn Arlvaloiruak his dogs and sled. He was not very far. He only had one skin to threw to the fire. And when it very come close to him, he threw one skin again. And he was pushing his sled all he could and sweat

and said, "It's too dark. I can't see anything." And the voice answered him, "Too dark around here, too dark around here." Then Arlvaloiruak wanted to feel the man or woman who was speaking in the house. Pretty soon he felt the very frozen nose of the person and then he was scared. He ran out toward his dogs. Looking back, he saw a big fire rolling toward him like a big ball or a big boulder, rolling slowly right after him.

Arlvaloiruak was hitching up his dog team, wanting to go home, but he was slower than the big fire rolling toward him. The big fire almost caught Arlvaloiruak, who was pushing his sled. Then he threw one of his mittens to the big, rolling fire. Then, my gosh, the fire stopped and burned up his mitten and he got quite a ways away before the mitten was burned. And then it started to chase Arlvaloiruak again.

When it got near, again he threw another one of his mittens and once more he made the fire stop. Arlvaloiruak was working hard, pushing his sled. He was sweating and scared and the dogs were scared, too. But the rolling fire was a little faster than the dog team and after it burned up the second mitten, it started chasing Arlvaloiruak again.

It came closer and Arlvaloiruak took off his outer parka and threw it to the rolling fire. The fire was burning and screaming at the same time, screaming just like fighting dogs. Arlvaloiruak couldn't understand what the fire was screaming. It was a while before the fire started chasing him again—then the same thing, when the fire almost caught him again, he threw out one caribou hide at a time. He almost emptied his sled but his home was quite a ways away yet. And he was sweating, sweating, pushing his sled because his dogs were pretty tired. But he couldn't stop because the fire would burn him, his dogs, and his sled. He was not very far from his house. When the fire came very close to him he threw it the last skin he had. And he was pushing his sled as fast as he could and he was sweating and sweating.

Then he reached a little moss house and he sneaked in without unharnessing his dogs. The fire kept on coming, roaring and splashing a lot of snow, and burned up Arlvaloiruak's sled and all his dogs; then it began to go in after Arlvaloiruak and burned up his skin door. Arlvaloiruak was waiting, he had no way to stop the fire anymore. The rolling fire at the door started singing, singing and burning at the same time, and

and sweat. And then he reaches a little moss house and he was sneaking to this house without unharnessed his dogs. And the fire keep on coming – roaring – roaring and splashing lot of snow. And burned up all Arlvaloiruak's sled and dogs. That burning fire took all Arlvaloiruak's dogs and sled and began to go in to after Arlvaloiruak, to burned up his skin door. And Arlvaloiruak waiting, got no way to stop the fire anymore … waiting for the fire. And the rolling fire at the door started singing, singing and burning same time …, and singing Arlvaloiruak … (singing song) …, that meaning you could not live very long. Then Arlvaloiruak and pissing on … pissing on the fire … by gosh the fire was, fire was putted out right away, soon after Arlvaloiruak was pissing on the fire, no more fire. Arlvaloiruak was very tired and go to sleep. And after that, he told all the story where he had the trouble. When he met somebody and told all about when the person die in the house they should not live in the house, or not living in the house … without that carrying out. And from that time, nobody leaved a dead person in a house anymore after that time.

singing, "Arlvaloiruak, you have not long to live." Then Arlvaloiruak started pissing on the fire and, by gosh, the fire was put out right away. No more fire.

Arlvaloiruak was very tired so he went to sleep. And after that, he told everybody the story of how he had the trouble. When he met somebody, he told them that when a person dies in a house, they should not live in the house without carrying the dead person out. And from that time, nobody ever left a dead person in a house anymore.

Scary Story

———

Hello Jack … I just fixed up the recorder up and I grease it with vasoline inside and cause the noise is funny, just like it is nervous, nervous noise.

A good number of families went down to Pt. Barrow to live in 1905. And we are still together three families of us, there is Frank Rulland's father and May Kakinya's father and us. May Kakinya's parents had to stay and old fellow grandfather of May Kakinya too. And that old fellow had all kinds of stories … I should learn what he is telling about the old people. That old fellow he had fun … yeah, he was fun with me and he had some kind of colored plugs on his lips. While and he tried to hand it over to me in my mouth and so I could have a long life like his. But I don't like it, but he was too strong. And he hand it over to my teeth and file it … and finally his plugs split and then he began to sad, he was sobbing. He knew he would die before too long, and he says, "I don't like to be in the starvation of my life but nothing can get help. And we are separated from the groups and my parents have to stay for summer in the mountains and May Kakinya's parents had to stay too

Scary Story

———

Hello, Jack [Campbell]! I just fixed the recorder. It had a funny noise like it was nervous so I greased it with Vaseline inside.

A good number of families went down to Pt. Barrow to live in 1905. Three families of us stayed together [on the Arctic Slope]. There was Frank Rulland's father, May Kakinya's father, and us. May Kakinya's parents had to stay, and her old grandfather too. That old fellow had all kinds of stories—I should learn about the old people from his stories. That old fellow was fun—yeah, he had fun with me. He had some kind of colored plugs [labrets] in his lips and he tried to put them in my mouth so I could have a long life like his. I didn't like it but he was too strong and he put the plugs over my teeth and filed them. Finally his plugs split and he became sad; he was sobbing. He knew he would die before too long and he said, "I don't like to be in the starvation of my life but there is no help."

We separated from the groups and my parents had to stay in the mountains for the summer. May Kakinya's parents had to stay too (see Chapter 4). Her old grandfather and old fellow grandfather of May Kakinya is still alive in that time which is making me scared. And one time down at (Kalatagiak) when the moon began to get darkness and then I went over to Frank Rulland's house. Of course I go into the house and the old fellow screaming, make a lot of noise.

Parent of All Mosquitoes

———

Parent of all mosquitoes are discuss all about problem to their bunch of childrens in early of June after had them in all winter long in special room they had for Store. Cannot go out during cold weather winter month. Too cold for you kids.

Wait sonnys & daughters. Time is not quite right. Too early – too cold you maybe freeze to die. Father shut the door. Never mine sonny & daughters, I'll open the door for you when time come.

Father we pretty tired. Let us go out & pretty hungry for blood we cry, we are sleep for all winter, no sir papa. Crying in loud, lift the big ball shape. The house big as earth size and all of mosquitoes lifting up & down & sound like thunder roar.

Papa and mama was told kids all about situation if any danger do not come near.

I, Sure enough first if any oily things is very danger from stuck cannot come off only have to die if any ones of you landed oily things.

II Second if open fire is very dangers

III Third do not come near to a man & women if puffed smell like rotten shd- sting!!

IV All the childrens say we will & very happy & laugh jump up & down

V Papa and Mama was told them time is come. Go ahead & go all over the country

VI Come back kids in middle of August or earlier. Kids was replied yes papa & mam see you in later on

VII Kids was so happy flown & sing all the song & covered whole world. And chilly summer it was and

VIII Spenting in all over earth no sleep many of them was died in oily especially when Eskimos oiling their

IX *Umiak* &Kayak & Mukluk & many other – oily in cooking pot & many of them died in open fire perhaps no ones seen before come to the end and killed by human being. Burned them down

was still alive at that time and I was afraid of him. One time down at Kalutagiak (Qalutiaġiaq) (Map 3) when the moon was dark, I went over to Frank Rulland's house, and when I went in, the old fellow was screaming and making a lot of noise.

Parent of All Mosquitoes

———

In early June, the parents of all mosquitoes (Figures 10 and 11) were discussing problems with their many children after they had been in a special room for all winter. "You cannot go out during cold winter weather. Too cold for you kids."

They said, "Wait, sons and daughters, time is not quite right. It is too cold; you maybe freeze to death." Father shut the door. "Never mind, sons and daughters, I'll open the door for you when the time comes."

The young mosquitoes said, "Father, we're pretty tired and pretty hungry for blood. We have slept all winter, let us go out." Crying out loud, all of the mosquitoes began lifting, flying up and down in a big ball shape, as big as the earth. They made a sound like thunder.

Papa and Mama told the kids about all the dangerous situations.

1. Oily things are very dangerous. You can get stuck in them and then will die.
2. Open fire is very dangerous.
3. Do not come near to a man or woman if [they] smell like rotten shd—sting! (?)

All of the children said, "We will [obey]" and were very happy and laughed and jumped up and down.

Papa and Mama told them, "The time has come. Go ahead and go all over the country. Come back in the middle of August or earlier." The kids replied, "Yes, Papa and Mom; see you later on."

The kids were so happy and flew and sang all the songs and covered the whole world. It was a chilly summer and they spent it all over the earth with no sleep. Many of them died in oil things, especially when Eskimos were oiling their *umiaks* (*umiat*) or kayaks or mukluks or cooking oily things in the cooking pot. Many of them died in the open fire, which they had never seen before, and were killed by human beings in this way.

In the fall in middle of August most of them going home to parent.

Papa & Mama ask them question & said are you lost many of your brother & sister? But no ones would give right answer. Everyones shook his head & look one another. Finally one said do not know, point out in other side of the big crowd, must be know better over there. No! One was said, oh we maybe loose about five kids. Ha ha, I, laugh one, I was get out from five peoples ha ha. That meaning he was got away from five fingers as he called five peoples.

In the fall, in the middle of August, most of them went home to their parents. Papa and Mama asked them questions and said, "Have you lost many of your brothers and sisters?" No one would give the right answer. They all shook their heads and looked at one another. Finally, one said, "I don't know," and pointed to the other side of the big crowd. "Someone over there must know." One said, "Oh, we maybe lose about five kids." "Ha, ha," laughed another. "I got away from five people, ha, ha." He meant that he got away from five fingers which he called five people.

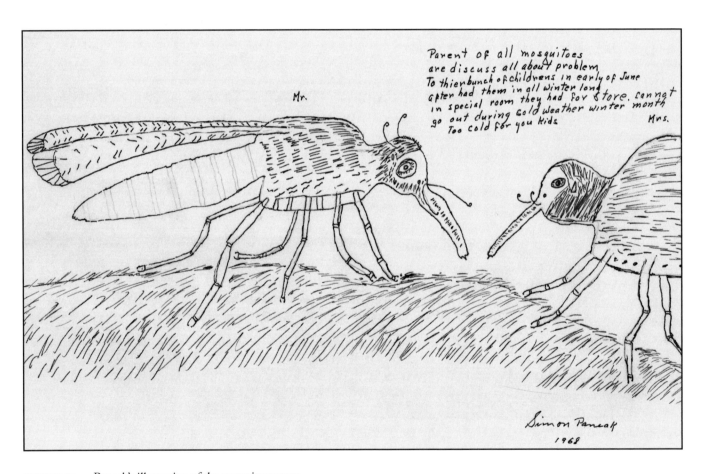

FIGURE 10   Paneak's illustration of the mosquitoes story.

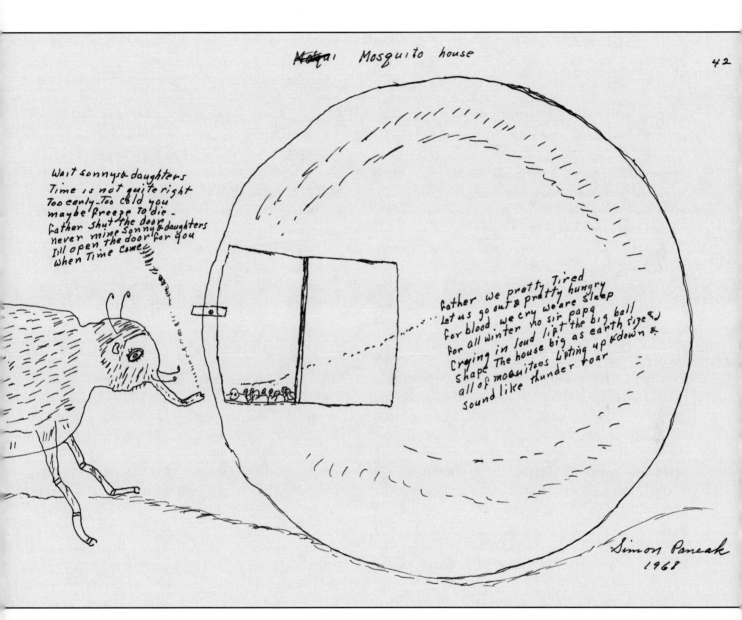

FIGURE II   Paneak's illustration of the mosquitoes story.

The Story of Mouse

An early days there was a family of Mouse in long warm Summer and having only two young Kids mice and two kids was growing fast bigger & bigger in every day & night. And papa & mamma was so busy in by night re-built old house they have & cleaned & put new bedding with Soft dead grass for winter living quater. And also making new cellar for stored up Maso – Legrice roots & pile up green leaves for Winter food Supply. And two lonely kids was so lonesome in most of times. Of course, papa & mamma was taught them how to be behaf and watch from enemies too many was hunt for mices – Short eared Owl – Arctic white Owl – Rough legged hawk, Marsh hawk, Duck hawk – Pigeon hawk – Gyfalcon hawk & Arctic Shrike and erman – weasels – all the foxes – wolverine – wolfs – grizzly bears and others too many etc.

No fun for two kids. And one in evening after papa & mamma left the kids at home & told them not go away. Watch all the times. When enemies come, hide in the hiding room. One kid told other kids, Said how we going to have fun. And look around near by hole and see dead wood laying on the ground and other dead woods. And think & think situation and finally told other. Come on kids help me kids on this carrying the dead wood. And other was saying for what! Go ahead, come on, you will see soon we after put over to laying wood on the ground, soon we put across way on top of the dead wood. And other kids is follow what other kids was wanted. And other kids call other kids, stay here on other end of the log – All saw how could be fun. And 1 be on other end & other kids does not know what gone a be done. Started jumb under willow tip having big green leave and started up & down and on – that was lots of fun. And soon after fun one was crying in loud voise. Oh Oh! I touch heaven or sky and earth or ground. Ha-ha he laugh when he touch willow leaves by his top head saying heaven & earth. And from mice human learned, has learned how to play See-Saw, Atchakisak.

The Story of Mouse

In the early days, in the long, warm summer, there was a family of mice (Figure 12) who had only two young kids who were growing fast and getting bigger and bigger every day and night. Papa and Mamma were very busy at night rebuilding their old house and cleaning and putting new bedding of soft, dead grass in their winter living quarters. They also made a new cellar to store maso-legrice (*masu*) roots [*Hedysarum alpinum*, a common Nunamiut food plant] and piled up green leaves for their winter supply.

The two little mice were lonesome most of the time. Of course, Papa and Mama taught them how to behave and to watch for enemies—short-eared owl, arctic white owl, rough-legged hawk, duck hawk, pigeon hawk, gyrfalcon and arctic shrike, and ermine, weasels, all the foxes, wolverine, wolves, grizzly bears, and others, too. It was no fun for two kids. One evening, Papa and Mama left the kids at home and told them not to go anywhere, to watch at all times and when enemies come, hide in the hiding room.

Now one kid said to the other kid, "How are we going to have fun?" So he looked around near the hole and saw dead wood lying on the ground and [he] thought and thought about the situation and finally told the other, "Come on, kid, help me carry this dead wood." And the other said, "For what?" The first replied, "Go ahead, come on, you will soon see. Over the dead wood lying on the ground, we will put one across the top." And the second mouse did what the first mouse wanted.

Then the first mouse said, "Stay here on the end of the log and I will be on other end." All saw it could be fun, and started jumping up and down under the willow that had big green leaves—that was lots of fun. And soon, one cried out in a loud voice, "Oh! Oh! I touch heaven or sky and earth or ground." "Ha-ha," he laughed when he touched the willow leaves with the top of his head, saying, "Heaven and earth." And this is how humans learned, from the mice, to play seesaw, *atchakisak* (*aatchikisaaq*).

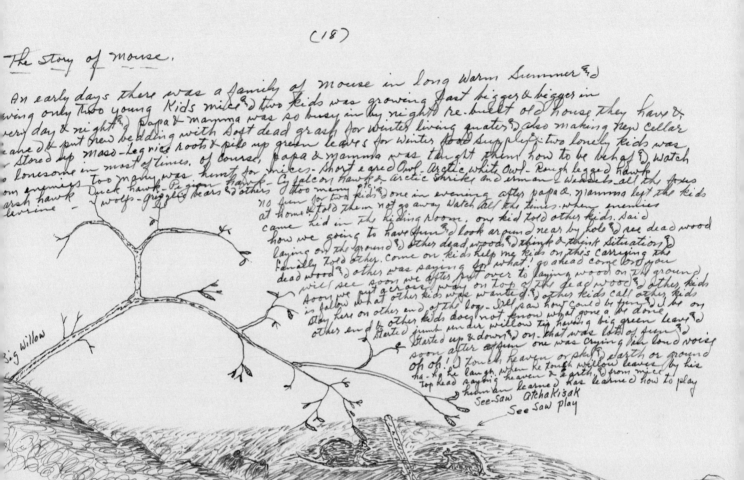

FIGURE 12   Paneak's illustration of the mouse story.

THE HUNTING TRAIL

Except for their dogs, the Nunamiut lacked domestic food plants and animals, surviving instead by foraging for whatever their tundra homeland offered in the way of wild food sources. Because edible wild plants were so few, and in general so unsustaining, Nunamiut subsistence was based overwhelmingly on hunting and fishing (Figure 13). Fishes, caught both in open water and in holes cut through winter ice, were so important that neither in good times nor bad (see Chapter 4) could the Nunamiut have survived without them. Mammals were even more important, and among them the caribou (the wild North American reindeer) was the paramount food source.[1]

Firearms were introduced to the Nunamiut early in the latter half of the nineteenth century, and by shortly before 1900 flintlock and percussion cap trade guns—whose smooth bores would accommodate anything from lead balls to gravel—had been replaced by modern repeating rifles (Figures 14 and 15; also see Chapter 3). Thus, by 1900, the year of Paneak's birth, the rifle had become the principal Nunamiut hunting weapon. During those same turn-of-the-century years, the Nunamiut became involved increasingly in the fur trade, bartering furs for white man's commodities at scattered trading posts (Figure 16) or aboard ships of the Yankee whaling fleet in the sea ice off the Arctic coast (Map 2, and Chapter 5). And while fur animals were killed with both native techniques[2] and steel traps, rifles were used for the same purpose, as Paneak describes in the following pages. The term "hunting" then,

as it is used here, includes the pursuit of furbearers as well as its more fundamental role in food getting.

In Chapter 4, Paneak relates how, weak from hunger, Nunamiut hunters went off on forlorn and often fruitless searches for game, desperate searches in the face of starvation, and in parts of this chapter we are told of going hungry. But with the sometime exceptions of soldiering and sailoring, few professions hold the romance of hunting. Fishing, as I have noted, was essential to Nunamiut survival, and could be fun as well, but fishing carried with it very little in the way of romance. Hunting, on the other hand, was grand sport.

Small boys embarked on their hunting careers by throwing sticks and stones at birds and ground squirrels. I recall the eight-year-old who, knowing of my interest in Brooks Range fauna, brought me a white-winged crossbill (rare on the tundra) that he had killed with a rock. When, at the age of twelve or fourteen, a boy shot his first caribou or sheep, his parents invited the whole camp to share in the feast.

Another of my personal recollections of the lure and lore of hunting is that of the first day of the incredible 1961 fall caribou migration (Figure 17). In the evening, after the hunters had used up their ammunition, they gathered in a dilapidated U.S. Army squad tent to reload empty rifle shells, and as they took turns at the camp's only reloading tool, there was a mood, a spirit in that old tent that is nearly impossible to describe. These Nunamiut were hunters in the best and most ancient sense of the word, and that morning, after scouts had brought news of the approaching herd, the hunters had scattered out,

FIGURE 13   A Nunamiut couple, with their baby in its mother's parka hood, start off in search of game in the mountains bordering Anaktuvuk Pass. They will be out for a week, hoping to find caribou or sheep in the high country. Photograph by JMC, 1957.

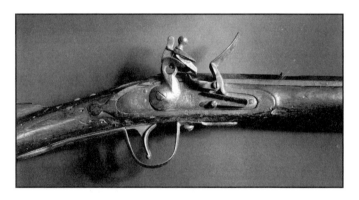

FIGURE 14   This .58-caliber flintlock Northwest Gun (see Hanson 1955) was manufactured in England in 1862, expressly for trade with Indians and Eskimos. Quite possibly it is of the same model as that described by Paneak as having come down the "Mighty MacKenzie River." In his First Flintlock story he says that probably it was traded at Fort McPherson (a Hudson's Bay Company post on the Peel River). From the bottom of the trigger guard to the top of the small knob on the hammer, it measures five inches. Howard Rodee Collection. Photograph by JMC, 1998.

FIGURE 15   For most of the first fifty years of the twentieth century, breech-loading Winchester repeating rifles, especially those designed for the Winchester .30-30 cartridge, were Nunamiut favorites (see Campbell 1998a:23). By 1950, many of these old reliables had been replaced by smaller calibers of higher velocities, but a few remained in the Nunamiut camp. This Winchester .30-30, an 1894 model, was purchased by Campbell at Anaktuvuk Pass in 1957. From the bottom of the trigger guard to the top of the hammer it measures four and one-fourth inches. J. H. L. Whiteley Collection. Photograph by JMC, 1998.

lying in ambush across the route of the caribou. Now was the time for telling the story, and much of the following narrative shines of that same mystique.

This chapter includes tales of both the old days, as told to Simon by his elders, and, beginning in the first decade of the twentieth century, his own experiences. [All stories in this chapter are from Paneak's taped narratives. I have provided their titles.] His first account tells of traditional Nunamiut techniques of snaring, trapping, and impounding without the use of modern steel traps and rifles. Then he talks of how as a boy he learned hunting, fishing, and trapping from his elders, and he tells us further of his adult experiences—hunting with his close friends and compatriots, Elijah Kakinya and Frank Rulland. And finally, with astonishing detail, he relates the history of rifles among the Nunamiut.

FIGURE 16   (Right) James N. Crouder, the white trader at the now-deserted riverine town of Old Bettles. Here, with one of his young sons, he is displaying two sled loads of wolf and caribou hides brought in over the ice of the John River by Nunamiut hunters living at Chandler Lake. Photograph by Veree Crouder, 1947.

FIGURE 17   The vanguard of the incredible migration of tens of thousands of caribou through Anaktuvuk Pass in the fall of 1961. The animals shown here are cows with their calves, typically leading the way from one seasonal pasturage to another. Photograph by JMC.

Early Times and Ways

Right now I begin to talk about what I learn about the trapping and hunting, sheep hunting, caribou hunting and moose hunting and all the north animals. All the animals we learn about it, how to get it or tag it or sneak it to every animal because our parents or father or forefather teach us how to be. And by that time old people were talking about their hunting and trapping and how to set the trap and how to snare the animals and I learn because I was interested. Interested to learn because my parents were kind of poor living, sometimes, not all the time too. Sometimes my father getting rich, sometimes he is getting poor. My father when he is getting rich, he helps out the poor people, live for nothing. And I learn quite a bit from my grandfather who stayed with us and way back in the 1912 for all winter and my father's father name is Anushela. And he set a trap, he set the steel traps and get a few red fox and one white fox over in the mountains there in Akmalik. And he also set up rock deadfall because Jesse repaired the old timer stone deadfall. Jessie repaired it and set it a lot of deadfall in every valley of the mountains in the Brooks range. In every creek there are several deadfall that we could found anywhere. And especially over in the Killik Valley, Okokmilaga, and Chandler Lake and here over in Anaktiktuak and here in John River and everywhere all the way over to Galbraith Lake and way over to Sagawon River. But I hear according to people who was talking about the; they couldn't stand around much east of Sagawon in the early days. That was in my grandfather's time I guess or before and every marmot hole had a deadfall … too many of them. I learn because my grandfather was teaching me how to set trap and deadfall and other things for catching a marmot. And my parents and even my mother knew how to set the stone deadfall for getting a marmot and ground squirrel. And also when they don't have snares, my mother sometimes when they found a good rock to set deadfall for a ground squirrel, and she get it.

Early Times and Ways

I begin by telling how I learned about trapping, and about hunting sheep, caribou, and moose, and all the northern animals. Our fathers or forefathers taught us how to sneak up on every animal. The old people would talk of hunting and trapping, and how to set traps and snares, and I learned because I was interested. I learned because sometimes, but not all the time, my parents lived poorly. Sometimes my father was rich and sometimes he was poor. When he was rich he helped out the poor people for nothing.

And I learned quite a bit from my grandfather, my father's father, whose name was Anushela (Nuisillaa), and who, back in 1912, stayed with us all winter. My grandfather set steel traps, and that winter he got a few red foxes and one white fox over in the mountains on Akmalik (Agmaalik) Creek (Map 3). And he also set rock deadfalls, because Jesse Ahgook (see Campbell 1998a:23) had repaired the old-time stone deadfalls. Jesse repaired them, and set deadfalls in every valley of the mountains of the Brooks Range. On every creek we could find several deadfalls, especially in the Killik Valley, Okokmilaga (Uqquumilaat), and Chandler Lake, here on the Anaktiktoak (Anaqtiqtuaq) River, on the John River and all the way over to Galbraith Lake and way over to the Sagawon River [a tributary, and a shortened version, of Sagavanirktok (Saġvaġniqtuuq); Map 3]. But I heard from the people who were telling about it, that in the early days you couldn't live much east of the Sagawon.[3]

That was in my grandfather's time, or before, I guess, when every marmot hole had a deadfall, too many of them. I learned this because my grandfather was teaching me how to set traps and deadfalls and other things for marmots. And my parents, even my mother, knew how to set stone deadfalls for marmots and ground squirrels, and sometimes when they didn't have snares, when my mother found good rocks, she [even] set deadfalls for ground squirrels, and got them (see Campbell 1998a: pls. 34, 46).

Coast people, they make snares from wood stick and young walrus skin. Is good and tough to bust the snares. The snares for moose, caribou mountain sheep, I know how to set it myself, how high the loops are going to be setted, hold it by two willows. I know how to set it, I can use it myself. I get a few, caribous easy to snare right in the creeks where the caribou have their trail in the willows easy to snare. The sheep about the same easy to snare. When the sheep they come through there or follow the sheep trail right in the mountain or near the cliff or right in the creeks where the willow are. Even if no willow right in the edge of the cliff, the sheep always got in the snares very easily I can't see it, and but not many moose. But when they found the moose trail they set it and they capture moose by the snare. Frank Rulland set the snares for moose in 1949. He catch two moose alright by the snare. Up here no place to set snares for grizzly bears, but over in Noatak and Kobuk and where the spruce are they catch it by snares. They have to use heavy spruce to lift it up there by the snare right in the fork of trees. As I draw it in a picture some years ago in your book. They also set death fall out of our spruce, put a lot of weight enough to squish down that bear like wolverine. In the early, people know everything how to catch foxes, wolf, wolverine. They make everything; they have equipment everything. They catch fox by snares and I have picture in your book how to set the snare and a deadfall out of willows or spruce or rocks, also they make summer net for rounding a meat catch where the animal been eating they make a little snow house.

I never try snares for any of the foxes and wolf and they says that they used to snare them in the early days too and I know how and somehow I could learn from old people too. We learned it from our parents or grandfather because they were teaching most of the time, talking about the stories and I am talking about the hunting.

A long time ago all inland, they make a living, they catch caribou in the river in the Colville by the spearing in a kayak. But the early people love to stay in one lake more room for killing I guess, not like in river. And sometime when caribou herd come through before they beginning moving up by the sled and dog team, they set the corral too for caribou. When there was a plentiful enough to go around during all the winter they had to stay otherwise they had to go in up to mountain to live better. And catching better wolverine and wolf by the rocks and deadfall and snare better too for caribou and sheep.

The Arctic Coastal people [the Tareumiut] made snares from wood sticks and young walrus hide. It is good, and it is tough for the animals to break these snares. I know how to set snares [of caribou hide] for moose, caribou and sheep, and how high the loops should be set, held by two willows. And I have used them myself, getting a few caribou in the creek bottoms where they are easy to snare on their trails through the willows.

Sheep are nearly as easy to snare, either on their mountain trails near cliffs or when they come down to the creeks where the willows are. Even when there are no willows [growing naturally] on the edge of a cliff, the sheep are caught easily in snares [with willows that have been brought up from the creeks]. I have not seen these sheep snares, and I have seen only a few for moose. But in the old days when the Nunamiut found moose trails, they caught them with snares. In 1949, Frank Rulland caught two moose with snares. Up here, [on the tundra] there is no place to set snares for grizzly bear, but over on the Noatak (Nuataaq) and Kobuk (Kuuvak) rivers, where there are spruces, grizzlies were caught with snares. For catching grizzly bears they had to hang their snares from the forks of heavy spruce trees, and some years back I drew a picture of this in your [sketch] book (see Campbell 1998a: pls. 44, 45). They also made deadfalls out of spruces, putting on enough weight to squish down the bear, like a wolverine [deadfall]. In the early days the Nunamiut knew everything about catching foxes, wolves, and wolverines, and they made all of their equipment from their own [native raw materials].

They caught foxes with snares, and I have pictures in your [sketch] book of how to set snares and deadfalls with willows, spruce trees, and rocks (see Campbell 1998a). Also, in summer they set nets [for foxes or wolverines] around their meat caches where these animals were feeding, and in winter they set traps at the meat caches in little snow houses. I never tried snares for foxes and wolves, but I learned from the old people how they used to snare them in the early days. I learned from my parents or grandfather, because they spent a lot of time teaching me.

A long time ago all the inland Nunamiut killed caribou in the Colville River by spearing from kayaks, but the early people liked better to spear them in certain lakes, where there was more room for killing, I guess. And sometimes when the caribou herds came through before the people were traveling by sled and dog team, they set corrals, too, for caribou (see Campbell 1998a: pls. 35, 36). When one

FIGURE 18   A view of a part of the caribou pound at Chandler Lake shown in Campbell 1998a: pl. 35. Like the question of who or what lies buried in the little hill (Figure 30 and Chapter 4, n. 6), the origins of this double-lined stone fence remain obscure. According to Elijah Kakinya (Grant Spearman, personal communication 1999), it was built by Indians. Simon, on the other hand (herein), and Rausch (1951:191) describe it as a Nunamiut type. Photograph by Grant Spearman, 1985.

Talking about how to make fences over in corral for catching caribou. And fences for near the lakes, double line fences work all right. Caribou don't like to come near to the fences because double line is something like a moving too when we walking in the side of the double line and other, second, whatever you call it, second line of fences something like a moving, a skin on top, tied up, tied up to a little stick on top of the fence, pile it up with a deadhead or piece of ground. During time over in Chandler Lake we had a shovel, much easier than old timer, but they don't have a shovel like we have. They have shovel for snow all right, but not very good for digging. They were digging with caribou horn handles, with whales or antlers foot. They says in the early days that they had ice chisel to make a hole in the fishing hole through the ice with the caribou horn and walrus tusk. And they have got to be careful with it digging in the ground, sometimes in the rivers, sometimes I hit to have no water just only gravel in the ice. Know how is too frozen solid to the bottom but the old timers know the water in the early days. They know how even we could tell ourselves. And over in the fishing hole which is not frozen too solid to the bottom, and we know that this is like, this is a water underneath this ice. And we could tell by the cracks in the ice because our grandfather or parents or father told us what kind of cracks look like.

We know how to set the traps and over in windy valley, along arctic coast, that is where there is a lot of wind over there and you know how to cover with old granulated snow. Granulated snow is much better than new snow bank because new snow bank is no good after it gets frozen

of these hunts, either by corralling or water driving, produced enough caribou to go around, to last all winter, the people stayed nearby. Otherwise, they had to go up into the mountains to live through the winter, where there was better trapping of wolves and of wolverines with deadfalls, and where caribou and sheep could be caught better with snares.

They told me about how to make fences, corrals, for catching caribou, and for snaring caribou near lakes, and how to make double-line [stone] fences near lakes. Double-line fences worked well (Figure 18). The caribou did not like to come through these double lines because the lines had little sticks in them with pieces of moving [fluttering] hide on their tops. The sticks were held up with deadheads [rocks] or pieces of sod [and the caribou were thereby diverted into the lake or into the heart of the corral?]. When we lived over at Chandler Lake we had a modern shovel [for digging pieces of sod, for example]. This made it much easier than it was in the old days. Then, the people had snow shovels all right, but they were not good for digging. They dug with whalebones, or antlers.

The old people told me that in the early days they made fishing holes through ice with caribou antlers or walrus tusks, and that in rivers they had to be careful not to dig holes in ice [covering gravel, rather than deep water]. They knew, too, those places where the ice was frozen solid to the bottom. The old timers knew the water, and we learned it too, where to find fishing holes that are frozen solid to the bottom. We knew the holes where

up, no good. And that granulated snow never gets spoiled for quite a while unless a snow buried in some places or strong winds blow off the cover, off steel traps.

And they are very clever too the old Eskimo because they learn. They only living by doing it and that way we learn. But right now, all these young people never did learn because they were in school. We got no time to teach them, even when we told them about the hunting and fishing like we doing it, they never could learn before they could see it. That is why our young people almost lost the old timer culture, cultures, whatever you call it, culture about nature. Like right now they are learning how to be in the high school or school. In the school they learn among young fellows, same thing with the way we learn and do it and see.

I remember one time lynx came along and they let him go ahead and come and they could shot at the one lynx right close to shoot with by old black powder .44-caliber rifle. And May's mother is good shot. And crazy dogs saw it and go after the lynx and the lynx run very fast, but the dogs were very fast running too. And catch the lynx before too long. And then a bunch of dogs were right at trying to bite this lynx. But they couldn't stand his sharp claw I guess, because we follow my father. We knew where they were, the dogs were going around the lynx and some of the dogs holler. They were scared and we took them near the lynx. And I could see where the lynx, they grab the dogs by the side of the dogs and then with one arm. And the dogs try to get away from the leg but she was grabbing the lynx and the lynx was still watching the other dogs come near. And by gosh, if only one dog has left screaming because lynx claw went through the skin, right through the skin. And so when we went through my father shot the lynx. Then in the beginning of my learning how to be an Eskimo, Eskimo way.

And we got to learn by ourself too quite a lot. Because when I was young there was no wolf at all around here and I became hunt caribou or sheep or moose and no wolf at all. And after we come back from Arctic coast in 1936 or '37, we try and come near to wolf and by gosh, it was very hard. Very hard to fool a wolf and before I learn a little bit. When I learn a little bit by myself, and getting better all the time and finally sometimes I fool him and come into my view and good enough to shoot you know. I fool him with my walking stick and rifle and it is sticking up above my head. But I can't stand up cause he could recognize me because the wolves are smart sometimes and the people are shoot-

there was water underneath the ice by the cracks on its surface, because our grandfather, or parents, or father had told us what to look for.

We know too, how to set traps in Windy Valley [location unknown] on the Arctic coast. There is a lot of wind over there, and we cover our traps with old, granulated snow. Granulated snow is much better than new snow, because a bank of new snow will freeze up [and freeze the traps]. And granulated snow will not get spoiled in this way for quite a while or unless a strong wind blows the cover of snow off the (?) steel traps.

But right now, all of our young people do not know these things because they have been at school. We have no time to teach them, and even when we have told them about the old ways of hunting and fishing, they did not learn them because they had not seen them. That is why our young people have nearly lost the old-time knowledge of nature. Right now they are learning what is taught in high school, and they are learning by being among young fellows, and seeing and doing the way we learned [but about different things].

I remember once when a lynx came toward us, and they, the older people, let him come ahead so they could shoot it at close range with the old black-powder .44-caliber rifle. And May's mother was a very good shot. But the crazy dogs saw it and went after it, and the lynx ran very fast, but the dogs were faster and before long caught it. And the whole bunch of dogs were trying to bite the lynx.

But they couldn't stand his sharp claws, I guess. We knew where they were, and I followed my father and found the dogs going around the lynx, and some of them were hollering. They were scared, but we took them to the lynx, and I could see the lynx, with one arm [leg] grabbing the dog by its side. And the dog was trying to get away from that leg, and was grabbing the lynx at the same time. And the lynx was watching the other dogs close in. And by gosh, one dog was left screaming because a lynx claw had gone right through its skin. And when we came up my father shot the lynx. That was in the beginning of my learning how to be an Eskimo; the Eskimo way.

And one has to learn quite a lot on his own, too. When I was young there were no wolves around here at all, and I hunted caribou, sheep, and moose. And after we had come back from the Arctic Coast in 1936 or '37, I found that it was very hard to come near a wolf. Before I learned a little bit, it was very hard to fool a wolf. But little by little I taught myself, getting better all the time, and sometimes

ing before and they are getting smart easy. But some wolves is like dog; they don't pay no attention to come around to hunter. But some are smart wolves, they are very hard to fool them. When I had my walking stick and rifle both and set up on top of my head and I saw them and I holler like a caribou. And I with my hands, I scratching the ground to make a sound like a caribou kicking the snow to reach the caribou lichens. And by gosh, it works all right and the wolf they always come around and I fool him that way, but I have to holler like a caribou, (caribou noise) like this. That is why the wolves come near to the hunter.

Another thing, in a flat country, no way to fool him. And I am crawling, crawling on the ground instead of standing. And then the wolf was looking at me. Before they started them on to me, I was in any old direction. I was crawling around and slowly, I don't need to make it fast, just slowly. And then the wolf after they gather together, howling and they begin to come around to me. But they never come together at once, one by one that is the trouble, I can't shoot them all in a bunch. And then foxes, colored fox is easy to call him and like mice noise. I can't understand why a wolf and was going after me when I was crawling on the ground, that must have think it was polar bear or brown bear or was walking around in the winter times and I understand like that. Because they were always coming around to me, even two of us. One time Frank Rulland and I, we were find the wolf packs and there were six or seven wolves in the bunch and we got no way to come close to shoot. And then soon enough, we started crawling to watch them and they see us already. And they watching us when we are crawling and they lay down. And they watch us already and they watching us when we are crawling. And they started walking around slowly one by one. And then we got two wolves at that time because some of them are quite a ways behind the two wolves and we can't get them, too hard to shoot.

And the foxes, well, don't know about the men who call them like the mice noise. They are very easily come around like a little young pups. And we called them like tried to be a mice noise. Like this if I could make it, Jack (squeeky mouse noise) like this. And always every fox can hear this they come along, we got it.

I would fool a wolf, and get close enough to shoot, you know. I would fool him by sticking my walking stick and rifle above my head [like antlers]. But I would not stand up because he would recognize me. Wolves are smart sometimes; they get smart easily when people have been shooting at them.

Some wolves are like dogs, they don't pay attention to hunters, but others are smart and it is very hard to fool them. When I would see them I would hold my walking stick and rifle over my head, and holler like a caribou. And with my hands I would scratch the snow, like a caribou kicking the snow to reach the caribou lichens.

And by gosh it works all right, the wolves will always come around when I fool them that way, but I have to holler like a caribou [here, on tape, Paneak hollers like a caribou]. That is why the wolves will come near the hunter. Another thing—in flat country there is no way to fool him. There, instead of standing, I crawled and crawled on the ground. And then the wolves are looking at me, and to make them begin to come toward me, I crawled slowly in every direction; I did not need to make it fast. Then the wolves gathered together, howling, and began coming toward me, but they never came together as a pack. They came one by one, and that was the trouble, because that way I couldn't shoot them all in a bunch.

And then foxes; it is easy to call colored foxes [all foxes except the arctic fox are "colored foxes"] by making mouse noises, but I do not understand why the wolves were coming toward me when I was crawling on the ground. They must have thought I was a polar bear or a brown bear walking around in the winter time, because they were always coming toward me, even in the winter time. One time Frank Rulland and I found a wolf pack, and there were six or seven wolves in the bunch, but we could not get close enough to shoot. So we started crawling, watching them, and they saw us. And they watched us as we were crawling; then they lay down and watched us. And then they started walking around slowly, one by one, and then we shot two of them, but we did not get the others because they were quite a way behind those two and were out of range.

And then the foxes—well, I don't know [just how, in the old days] the men called them up with mouse noises, but they come easily, just like little [dog] pups to mouse noises, and in my day we called them by trying to make [this sort] of noise. If I can make it, Jack [Campbell; followed by a high squeak]. And always, every fox that hears it has come along, and we have got it.

My Hunting Life Begins

Our dogs were up and pulling for many miles without much to eat and also my parents are pulling, a very slow traveling, pulling a very heavy load, the sled, only had one good size of sled. Then we stay in that Ory Lake for several days, I don't know how long, it might be a couple weeks. And then my parents started to move towards north again because my uncle was down at the mouth of the Itkillik. He has enough flour and some oil we know. But I don't expect much fish. And then my father was looking around and all over in that area, but no caribou. And my father got no time to set the traps because in case of not enough food staying in one place. He decided to see colored fox, I think. Then in the morning my parents and I get down to our skin huts because shortly after knocking down and loading up to the sled, my gosh, three caribou showed up from north towards us. And there was three big bulls heading towards us and my father was takes his rifle and waits for them. He got them all those three. My gosh, we had a lot of meat. And then my father was never take rest, looking around for more caribou because caribou was showing up from north. And he was out looking around and by snow shoes and telescopes spotting the country, but no caribou. No more caribou. And then when he had enough to go around by traveling and my parents start to move again. And, by gosh, we were slow moving and I was not walking always at that time and I was kind of little too small I guess. And then we camped, I guess, in one or two camps before we reach two families. There were three families there but Itchuruk, he died some time after freeze up and Kanok and a relative and Alak, they were just there in one place. And we got down there and we reach him by night and my parents left our sled after they tired of pulling. They walked down to the people, and they look around three miles before we found the people. And then they had enough to go around. And they said a few caribou west of Colville not very many. And sister was born in that time, I don't know what month, that was in 1909.

They stayed at one fishing place in Colville about approximately thirty miles below Anaktuvuk mouth in the Colville. Then the next day my father get our sled with three dogs and bring all the things. And then we stayed with Alawak cause the Alawak wife is Swalik mother, is my father's first cousin. They told us to stay there, but my

My Hunting Life Begins

Our dogs were up and pulling for many miles without having had much to eat. My parents were pulling also. It was very slow traveling as they pulled a very heavy load on the good-sized sled. At Ory Lake we stayed for several days, maybe even a couple of weeks, I don't know. Then my parents [and I] started to move towards the north again because my uncle was down at the mouth of the Itkillik (Itqiḷiq). We know he has enough flour and some oil but I don't expect much fish. My father was looking all around in that area, but no caribou. And my father has no time to set traps because we have not enough food to stay in one place. I think he decided to look for colored foxes. Then in the morning, my parents and I took down our skin huts and shortly after knocking them down and loading them on the sled, my gosh, three caribou showed up, coming toward us [from the north]. There were three big bulls heading toward us and my father took his rifle and waited for them. And he got all three. My gosh, we had a lot of meat. But my father did not rest, he was looking for more caribou to show up from the north. He was out on snowshoes looking around with his telescope,[4] spotting the country, but no caribou. No more caribou. And then because we had enough to go around while traveling, we started to move again. But, by gosh, we were moving slowly. I was not always walking at that time; I was kind of little, too small I guess. We camped in one or two camps before we reached two families. There had been three families there but Itchuruk (Itchauraq) died some time after the freeze up. And just Kanuk (Kanuq) and a relative, Alak (Alaq), were there in that place. We got there at night. My parents left our sled after they got tired of pulling and walked down to the people. They had to look around for three miles before we found them. Then they had enough food to go around. The people said there were a few caribou west of the Colville but not very many. My sister was born at this time—I don't know what month—but this was 1909.

Our family stayed at one fishing place on the Colville River, approximately thirty miles below the mouth of the Anaktuvuk. Then the next day my father got our sled with the three dogs and brought all our things. And then we stayed with Alawak (Aalaak) because his wife was Swalik's (Suvałiq's) mother, who was my father's first cousin. They told us to stay there but my mother wanted to go down

mother wanted to go down to brother. And then after three days we start again. And I don't know how lots of white foxes and colored foxes. I don't know how much they do, two families go after foxes that winter. And when we reached another families down here. Named head of the families name is Tauktuk. Then two couples, young couples, stay with them. I never see them before and they coming from up Mackenzie River or somewhere from up there and anyway stayed up in Taukutuk. He had a good size of a sod house, framed with willows. There is plenty of room for us. He has got a lot of fish to live with and few ptarmigan. No caribou down there but there is more white foxes down there. And some men catch a few down where the Taukuk are. After about a week maybe then we start again. And then we reach the Panuliuk family and then they were inviting us to have lunch. They are staying over at the mouth of the Itkillik and then my uncle, not very far. About two miles, I guess. They went up the Itkillik River and found them. That evening we found them. There is two houses there, two sod houses. My uncle and two families, brothers of course, Tumicuk and Kanikuruk, they were staying in the one house. And some of the two families I think, they say went to Pt. Barrow by dog team of Ugulak and Paniuk, the youngest brother to Mychuk and (?). And then we stayed down there towards in the spring. They got a few white foxes coming in from north and by that time trapping season is not closed. And nobody knew about the law in that time about the trapping seasons. My gosh, a lot of fox was in the evening when we are staying outdoors and play in the calm wind, or rather we hear some white foxes barking from all over the place sometimes, because the white foxes, they are in mating season, that is what they are barking for. And then sometimes in May, my parents have to move back up to Anaktuvuk mouth and to get their skin boat up there. And way up, first I catch one Ptarmigan, the very first I catch. My parents get a few white foxes on the way and my father, of course, shoot the rifle. He said it was a .30-50 caliber Winchester and use the black powder. He was reloading his own bullet, melted lead first, and then he load it. That must be pretty cheap, shooting in that time.

Some bunch of families stay at the mouth of Anaktuvuk, old Morry Maptigak and Arctic John, he is pretty good sized boy at the time and my father got a lot of geese and swans and some of the ducks, scaup ducks and loon. There are three kinds of loon down there, one (?) loon and pacific loon and yellow bill loon and few blackbill loon in this

to her brother. So then, after three days, we started again. There were lots of white foxes and colored foxes that winter, and the two families went after them. I don't know how [well they did]. Then we reached another family. The head of the family was named Tauktuk (Taktuk). Two young couples I had never seen before were staying with them. They had come up from the Mackenzie River (Map 1) or somewhere up there and are staying with Tauktuk. He had a good-sized sod house framed with willows so there was plenty of room for us. He had got a lot of fish to live on and a few ptarmigan. There were no caribou down there but there were more white foxes, and some men caught a few down where the Taukuk family was.

After about a week, maybe, we started off again and when we reached the Panuliuk (Paniulak) family, they invited us to have lunch. They were staying over at the mouth of the Itkillik River, and my uncle was not very far from there—about two miles, I guess. We went up the Itkillik River and found him that evening. There were two houses there, two sod houses. My uncle and two families, brothers Tumichuk (Tumitchaq) and Kanikuruk (Kaniquraq), were staying in one house. And I think they said some of the two families went to Pt. Barrow using the dog team of Ugulak (Uġullak) and Paniuk, the youngest brother of Mychuk (Mitchuk) and (?). We stayed down there until the spring. They got a few white foxes coming in from the north. At that time the trapping season was not closed; nobody knew the law on trapping seasons. My gosh, there were a lot of fox. In the evening, when the wind was calm and we were playing outdoors, we could hear white foxes barking from all over the place. This was because they were in the mating season. This was why they were barking. Then, sometime in May, my parents had to move back up to the mouth of the Anaktuvuk River [where they had left their] skin boat. And on the way up, I caught my first ptarmigan. My parents got a few white foxes on the way, my father, of course, using his rifle. He said it was a .30-50 caliber Winchester [that] used black powder. He reloaded his own bullets, melting the lead first. It must have been pretty cheap shooting.

A bunch of families stayed at the mouth of the Anaktuvuk River. Old Morry Maptigak and Arctic John, who was a pretty good-sized boy. My father got a lot of geese and swans and some of the ducks, scaup ducks and loons. There are four kinds of loon down there, one (?) loon, Pacific loon, yellowbill loon, and a few blackbill loons in this area. My, we had a lot of meat that spring because

area. My, we have got a lot of meat that spring because the small family. I am alone, my own, my sister is a very little young kid, about one year old, I guess. And then after the people are gone, my parents walked down to our skin boats, put up the cover skin of the boats rather and we was floating along the Colville. We didn't find no people even down at the usual places. They are already gone and then we never find no people till we reach Niklik. In Niklik they were settled down already for Pt. Barrow Eskimos, they were coming up along the Arctic coast and they were coming to meet the eastern Eskimos. They were bringing a lot of flour and sugar and rice and roll oats I guess, but there is no milk in that time. I don't carry no milk, no lard. They use seal oil when they cook, making donuts, seal oil or whale oil.

In these days, my parents and most of those over to the Niklik River, which is runs into the Bay of Niklik, which they call it a fish river and the Eskimos call it Alikpik. And then a lot of fish ever since drying up a lot of fish in that time, because they had fish net. A lot of fish – white fish, herring, and smaller white fish and humpback and some few salmon. And then my father plan to stay out there in the Fish River for the winter and we, my parents were going up the river.

Where we was up in the river, some Pt. Barrow – three – four – skinboats coming up to catch up with us. And stay with them, and my father and all the men they could go and look around for caribou, because a caribou skin is very valuable in that time after the caribou herd they never come back from the east. And my father got around twenty or more caribou in that time and coast people get a few but not much. My uncle got around ten. My father is biggest man and he catch the caribou. Then Pt. Barrow Eskimos told my parents to go down to Pt. Barrow to live. And because seven people died there from the starvation, and recently. They wouldn't want their relatives to die on the starvation. And my parents moved down to Pt. Barrow, follow along in skin boats. And way over in Arctic coast, Pt. Barrow Eskimos are gathering in Cape Simpson Bay. There is sailing two mast schooner, is crowded can't get them out. They are trying to get them out but they never make it because east wind drifting them into the beach, water was getting too low too along the Arctic coast too and the northeast wind. And then we, a big bunch of us, I can't even remember the Pt. Barrow Eskimo, and Panelak and Tumichuk and finally wind calm down and rise up and they took the anchor of the schooner to sink it over in

our family was small. [There was me] and my little sister, who was a young kid, about one year old, I guess. After the other people left, my parents walked down to our skin boats and pulled off the cover, and then we were floating down the Colville. We didn't find any people, even at the usual places. They had already gone and we didn't find any people until we reached Niklik (Niġliq) (Map 2, and see Chapter 3). At Niklik they were settled down already, waiting for the Pt. Barrow Eskimos. They [the Tareumiut from Pt. Barrow] brought a lot of flour and sugar and rice and rolled oats, but they had no [canned] milk at that time; no milk and no lard. They used seal oil or whale oil when they cooked, making donuts.

In those days, my parents and most of the other people at the Niklik River [which runs into the Bay of Niklik] called it a fish river, Alikpik (Iqalukpik). They caught and dried a lot of fish because they had a fish net. Lots of white fish, herring, a smaller white fish, humpback [white fish], and a few salmon. My father planned to stay at the Fish River for the winter and so we traveled farther up the river. While we were in the river, three or four Pt. Barrow skin boats caught up with us and we stayed together. My father and the other men went out to look for caribou because a caribou skin was very valuable at that time since the caribou herd had never come back from the east. My father got around twenty or more caribou at that time, and the coast people got a few but not many. My uncle got around ten. My father was the biggest man [best hunter] and he caught the caribou. Then the Pt. Barrow Eskimos asked my parents to go down to Pt. Barrow to live. Seven people had died there (see Chapter 4) recently, of starvation, and they wouldn't want their relatives to die of starvation. So we moved down to Pt. Barrow, following along in our skin boats. Way over on the Arctic coast, the Pt. Barrow Eskimos were gathered in Cape Simpson Bay (Map 2). There was a two-masted schooner there that they are trying to get out [of the ice] but they couldn't make it because the northeast wind kept pushing them toward the beach. There was a big bunch of us—Panelak (Paniulak) and Tumichuk and I can't remember [the names] of the Pt. Barrow Eskimos. Finally the wind calmed down and we took the schooner's anchor and dropped it about twenty to thirty feet away from the ship. This was a good-sized, two-masted sailing ship, belonging to Charlie Brower, an old-time whaler (see Brower [1942] 1994). We finally pulled the ship out and then later in the evening, there was another two-masted schooner coming down from the

about twenty – thirty feet away from the ship. Good size two mast sailing ship and these belong to Charlie Brower an old time whaler. Finally pulled them out the ship and then after that, in the evening there was another two mast schooner coming down from the east in calm weather. My gosh, it is very fast moving. That was a gas engine powered schooner. That it belong to (?) after he has been around over at the Flaximan Island for a big expedition up there, up to the mountain. And my gosh, it makes me surprised and when the moving very fast without sail and mast.

We came down to Pt. Barrow and my parents have relative down there or partners. And stay with the partners down there at Pt. Barrow and my gosh, they were very happy people. And they got one whale, just before we get down there. I try and eat some *maktuk* but I could not swallow it, too strong. Unless I cook *maktuk* and meat, I could eat little but not much. I don't even eat the seal meat, too strong for me, I can't swallow it. Then just before freeze up, one of the boys killed one little boy with a .45-70 caliber and my gosh, it makes me scared because I watch that when he shot the boy on the face. And we stayed up there at Pt. Barrow, what they call it, about twelve miles east of Pt. Barrow Village at the present time. But right now no more people to live up there, nobody lives up there at the point anymore, no people. And watching, Pt. Barrow whole crews going out. They got a lot of whale. I think they said that they caught around seventeen or eighteen whales. And the whale bones or baleen they are selling over in the whaling ship for Charlie Brower, bought them of course, and some of them are three Eskimo companies they are rich too.

And then my parents get tired to stay on Pt. Barrow, that is pretty poor living that way. They love animals, inland animals, that are better eating than sea animals, and we went back to stay at the Fish River and my uncle went back too. Went back to Colville, were not many people. They say they all went up to east where most caribou used to be near Barter Island, Demarcation Point and Hershel Island. And only a few families left. They all left and not us, all the people went up east and in 1910 and 1911 we came up here after my father trapped a lot of white fox down at Fish Lake. I got a white fox too in that time, first I catch. It seems to be a lot of white fox around but my father got not much traps, my uncle got a few too and at first I learn how to set traps for fox. And no caribou over there. Before it freeze up my father walk up and stay away for a couple weeks maybe. They have got around ten

east in calm weather. My gosh, it was moving so fast! It was an engine-powered schooner that belonged to (?). He had been over at Flaxman Island (Map 2) on a big expedition up the mountain. My gosh, I was surprised to see the ship moving so fast without sail and mast.

So we came down to Pt. Barrow and my parents had relatives there or partners with whom we stayed.[5] My gosh, they were happy people. They had got one whale just before we got down there. I tried to eat some *maktuk* but it was too strong, I couldn't swallow it. Unless I cook *maktuk* and meat, I can only eat a little. I don't even eat seal meat, it is too strong for me; I can't swallow it.

Then, just before the freeze up, one of the boys killed a little boy [both of them probably Tareumiut] with a .45-70 caliber and my gosh, it scared [me] because I watched when he shot that boy in the face. We stayed up there at Pt. Barrow about twelve miles east of the present-day Pt. Barrow Village. And nobody lives up there anymore. I watched whole crews going out. They got a lot of whales. I think they said that they caught around seventeen or eighteen whales. The whale bones or baleen they sold to Charlie Brower on his whaling ship. And there were three Eskimo companies, and they were rich also.

Then my parents got tired of staying at Pt. Barrow, that is a pretty poor way to live. They love inland animals—they are better eating than sea animals—and so we went back to stay at the Fish River together with my uncle. There were not many people there. They said [the rest] all went east to where most of the caribou used to be near Arey Island, Demarcation Point, and Herschel Island (Map 2). And so there were only a few families left. And then they all left, but not us. All the people went up east, and in 1910 and 1911 we came up there after my father trapped a lot of white fox down at Fish Lake [location unknown]. I got a white fox too, at that time. The first I had ever caught. There seemed to be a lot of fox around but my father did not have many traps. My uncle got a few too and it was then that I first learned how to set traps for fox. But there were no caribou there. Before freeze-up [of the sea ice] my father went walking, and stayed away for a couple of weeks. Inland, they had got around ten caribou, so we were able to have a parka and pants and mittens and socks and we had a nice winter that time.

In 1911, we came up here to [Anaktiktoak (Anaqtiqtuaq), near Tuluak (Tulugaq) Lake, Map 3] where my father found enough mountain sheep to keep us all winter. In the spring, sometime near April, we moved down to Tuluak

caribou and over inland. And we have a parka and pants and mittens, socks – like that you know – so we have a nice winter that time.

And then in 1911 we came up here over at Anaktiktuak and my father found enough mountain sheep over in Anaktiktuak to keep us all winter. And it was spring sometimes pretty near April and we moved down to Tulugak and over to the creek. And then we found one caribou, and now one bunch of caribou. They're all bull caribou, more than twenty I think. And no females, no cows. And my father caught twelve from that bunch, I think, my father got twelve and my uncle got eight. I was shooting caribou too, right close too, but never hit nothing. I was maybe nervous – can't get nothing. Then we going down to our skin boat and at the mouth of Anaktuvuk, mouth at Colville. And then we going to Niklik wait for Pt. Barrow Eskimo. And quite a bunch of them coming up and also Alok. And my grandfather came up and stayed with us for that winter. And then we went up and three families were. More caribou we found that time but I never got one yet. I had old .44-caliber black powder rifle that time and I was shoot some caribou but they never hit. And when we reached the mountain, by gosh, there was a lot of sheep. And first I catch a sheep, several of them with the .44-caliber. And towards spring, sometimes around March, my father want to move back to outside of the mountain line where there were more colored foxes. No wolves, but enough caribou, enough caribou around. Then we going, went over to Itkillik, and they said there was a lot of sheep over there too and some caribou too. And my father and I we got quite a few colored foxes in that time. And first I caught one wolverine that time. I was big man that time I thought. My grandfather, he got five or six colored fox, I think. He was very old, he can't hunt anymore. He had a trap run near the camp. And then he says he don't want to be with us anymore and would like to die over in the Kobuk area and over in the east, a nephew in upper Kobuk, to die over there where he can have a good coffin.

Then, here, every time we coming up to inland, more caribou, more moose too and no more starving, no more starvation. My parents bought a lot of flour and a lot of ammunition and they always bought more than they could haul up the river and on up the mouth of Colville. One cached down at Niklik and another at (?), too much to carry in a skin boat anyway. We went over to Killik and my gosh, a lot of foxes in that time. That winter I had a new .32-40 caliber and good rifle I have but I am not big

and over to the creek. There we found one caribou and then a bunch of them. They were all bulls, more than twenty, I think, and no females, no cows. My father killed twelve from that bunch. I think my father got twelve and my uncle got eight. I was shooting caribou too, right up close but I never hit anything. I guess I was too nervous to get anything. Then we went down in our skin boats to the mouth of the Anaktuvuk on the Colville on our way to Niklik to wait for the Pt. Barrow Eskimos. Quite a bunch of them came up, including Alok (Aaluk). My grandfather came up too, and stayed with us for that winter. We were three families now. We found more caribou but I still hadn't got one. I had an old .44-caliber black-powder rifle at that time, and I was shooting at the caribou but not hitting any. When we reached the mountain, by gosh, there were a lot of sheep and I got my first sheep and then several of them with the .44 caliber.

Toward spring, sometime around March, my father wanted to move back north of the mountain line [the abrupt north front of the Brooks Range], where there were more colored foxes. There were no wolves but there were enough caribou around. So we went over to the Itkillik where they said there were a lot of sheep and some caribou, too. My father and I got quite a few colored foxes at that time and I caught my first wolverine. I felt like a big man. My grandfather got five or six colored foxes, I think. He was very old and couldn't hunt any more. He had a trap run near the camp. Then he said he didn't want to stay with us anymore and wanted to die over in the Kobuk area to the east [west] where he had a nephew in upper Kobuk. There he could have a good coffin.[6] At that time every time we came inland, there were more caribou and more moose, too, and no more starving, no more starvation (see Chapter 4).

My parents bought a lot of flour and a lot of ammunition and they always bought more than they could haul up to the Killik River above the mouth of the Colville. They made one cache down at Niklik and another at (?). They had too much to carry in a skin boat. We went over to the Killik and my gosh, there were a lot of foxes at that time. That winter, I got a new .32-40 caliber. It was a good rifle but I was not big enough or smart enough at that time to know how to shoot or snare animals. I got a few sheep at that time, not very many caribou but some, and sometimes I got nothing. I guess I was twelve years old. Then we went back to our skin boat at the mouth of the Killik River. We saw only one caribou in that time and my

enough yet or I am not smart enough yet in that time to know how to shoot or snare animals. I got a few sheep, not very many caribou in that time, but some all right, I never get nothing. I was twelve years old, I guess in that time. Then we went back to our skin boat at the mouth of the Killik River in the Colville. The only caribou we saw in that time, my father got it, one big bull. And then we were floating along in the Colville after the ice is clearing up and, my gosh, we found quite a few caribou right above The Umiat. And we got in enough caribou, that was in June. And I learn more about the trapping over in Killik, in 1913. I catch one silver gray fox, which is very big prize. My father bought me a .30-30, a new .30-30 rifle and, my gosh, a good rifle, long range … pretty revolver and powerful. And I was a good shot in that time.

And then we got up three families of us and by the Chandler River, going by boat, and skin boats and then we had winter over near Chandler Lake. And by gosh, I got quite a few colored fox. And I chased them around and chased them around and I shot them and I got another silver gray which has a big price on it. And then my father bought me another new rifle again, this time an automatic, better rifle yet I have. And then, I believe that was 1914. When I got down to Bettles and I, we met a lot of mining people near Crevice Creek. And I try and talk and in English but myself. And (?) says, well we cannot understand a thing. That was awful time we had. Can't understand nothing. And then we met several families of Eskimo, Kobuk people of course. Two stores down at Bettles, enough people around, good-sized town that time, Bettles.

father got it, a big bull. Then we were floating along in the Colville River after the ice cleared up and, my gosh, we found quite a few caribou right above Umiat. That was in June, and we got in enough caribou. I learned about trapping over on the Killik in 1913. I caught one silver gray fox which was a big prize. My father bought me a new .30-30 rifle and, my gosh it was a good rifle, long-range, and powerful. And by then I was a good shot.

And then the three families of us went up the Chandler River in our skin boats and wintered over near Chandler Lake, and by gosh, I got quite a few colored foxes. I chased them around and chased them around and I shot them and I got another silver gray which had a big price on it. And then my father bought me another new rifle, this time an automatic, a better rifle than I had ever had. I believe that was in 1914. When we got down to Bettles (Map 2) we met a lot of mining people near Crevice Creek. I tried to talk English myself but they said, "Well, we cannot understand a thing." That was an awful time we had. Couldn't understand anything. Then we met several families of Eskimos, Kobuk people, of course. There were two stores down at Bettles and enough people around. Bettles was a good-sized town at that time.

Rifles

According to people talking about in the early days, we don't know how long ago, probably the early 1800's, probably and one flintlock coming east. Flintlock gun which is ignited by stone flints and put a little powder on the spoon, on the top of the barrels and black powder ignited by the stone and burned and fire going down to the chamber, to powder already loaded with a slug and that is why they could shoot something or animal in early days. And one is coming down from east through Fort McPherson, what do you call it, river up there ... Probably carried by somebody from outside shortly after that ... muzzleloader with a little primer. This time we were a lot better than flintlock. Then muzzleloader being around in Alaska and everywhere, I guess ... and everybody had several different kinds of barrels. And some of them were a little smaller and some of them larger, two kind I am sure ... The muzzleloader much better than flintlock, they says anyway, I don't know much better. Those flintlock can ignite in the windy on a little hollow on the top of the gun. Flintlock gun which is ignited by the flint and the powder explode down to the little hole down in to the powder. The flintlock gun could explode the powder down there first and push him up, the slugs whatever you call it.

Then I don't know how long they have the muzzleloader, some double some single barrels and after that shells like a .22, no primer in it. I think somebody bring it up, probably an American. I think, (Ramidish), rifle ... caliber is pretty near like old .44-44 and that is long range can reach a long distance. Primer shells which you call, which is carried in the magazine fifteen shells, and they call it by Eskimos a (kimalik) (akimialik), which is carrying a magazine of fifteen shells. What we found an empty case of the rifles and they were very short, even shorter than old .44-caliber but could not to reload because no primers. No primers in the cartridges and some people write a letter couldn't catch anymore shells for the rifles. And then after that, shortly after that, .44-caliber, .48 is black powder rifle show up, very expensive, and very expensive for the type .44-caliber too. They says the bullet can carry good, a day without drop much for long distance shot. They says very, very good rifle, this is .44 is having primer, much better than (?). Then I don't know how long the people had it before they know about the old Winchester, Winchester brand, I guess, Winchester model. And they

Rifles

According to the older people, in the early days, probably the early 1800s, a flintlock gun came in from the east. A flintlock is ignited by a stone flint. You first put a little powder on the spoon [pan] on top of the barrels, and this black powder ignited by the stone. [The flint held in the jaws of the falling hammer when the trigger is pulled] sends a spark down into the chamber containing powder and a lead slug [that has been rammed down the barrel from its muzzle]. And that is how you could shoot something, or an animal in the early days. And that first flintlock came down from the east from Fort McPherson near the [Mackenzie] River probably carried by somebody from the outside (see Chapter 3, The Story About Flintlock Gun, and Figure 14).

Shortly after that came muzzleloaders with little primers. They were a lot better than flintlocks, and these muzzleloaders [became common all over Alaska] and everywhere, I guess, in several different kinds of barrels [calibers]. They were much better than flintlocks [although I never used them myself]. They could fire even on windy days, because the igniting powder was contained in the cap, while the flintlock is ignited by the flint [whose spark reaches down to the powder in the chamber] through the little hole, and the exploding powder would then push the slug or whatever out of the flintlock's barrel.

I don't know how long the [Nunamiut] had [cap and ball] muzzleloaders, and after that came [breach-loading rather than muzzle-loading calibers like the .22, whose shells] had no primers in them, [and which were used] in both double and single barrel [guns]. I think that probably an American whose name was Ramadish (?) brought in a larger caliber [breach-loading] rifle that was nearly like the old .44-44, a long-range gun. It had a magazine that held fifteen shells [cartridges] and in Eskimo it was known as a *kimalik*, or *akimialik*, which referred to its fifteen-cartridge magazine. We once found a case of empty shells of this caliber, and they were very short shells, shorter even than the old .44 caliber, but we could not reload them because they had no primers.

And some people wrote a letter to the [white trader supplier] asking why we could not buy shells anymore for this caliber. Then shortly after that the .48-caliber black-powder rifle showed up. It was very expensive [and so was the .44 caliber]. They say that the bullet would carry all

could reload. They have a reloading outfit like they had to melt, make one bullet for the .44 rifle and they had to buy only reloading outfit like a, like a lead and black powder and a primer.

And shortly after that they have a short kind of caliber. They have a very common .45-70 caliber, cannon, I call it, Winchester .45-70 big one. Another thing is a .38-60 caliber, I think is much faster than the .45-70, longer shells. I know my father had one and they says that some of them larger caliber single shot, which is carry a long ways – long distance shot, single shot, big rifle.

Same thing with the .45-70 but the shells is twice as much longer as the .45-70 and nobody told me about the caliber. I don't know what kind of number is the single shot, single shot rifle, this is long distance you could reach. My father's uncle, Kanayuk his name is, I never know when, but my father was talking about and all the people. And he had one. He could reach a long range, he could take an animal for a long distance. He knows how to raise the side, I guess, they only more important how to raise the side pair side. Then .38-55 Winchester, another very common rifle use black powder and lead bullet. Another thing, some around 1910, people had down at Pt. Barrow, small caliber. And then shortly after that we know about the rifle, .32-40, pretty near like the .30-55 but it is a little shorter and narrower. After that, all kinds of caliber began to show up after 1920, .30-30, .25-35, 30 Remington and 35 Remington, all kinds of them. And the first I knew .22 special in 1910. Not very many, the only one I saw, owned by one of the boys who is down in Pt. Barrow . . .

day without much drop. They say that this was a very good rifle, this .44 with primers, much better than what we had before. Then I don't know how long it was before the people found out about the old Winchesters. And they could reload those shells. They had a bullet mold for the .44 rifle, so they had to buy only a reloading outfit, and lead, and black powder and primers.

And shortly after that they got a shorter [smaller ?] kind of caliber. Then the .45-70 caliber—a cannon, I call it—was very common. This was the Winchester .45-70, a big one. Another was the .38-60 caliber, which I think was much faster than the .45-70 with the longer shells. I know that my father had one, and they say that some of those larger caliber were single-shot rifles, and would carry a long ways. It was the same thing with the .45-70 single shot, but the shells for these other rifles were twice as long as those for the .45-70, although no one told me their calibers. I don't know when, but my father's uncle, Kanayuk (Kanayuq), had one of those long-range single-shot rifles, and he could kill an animal at a long distance. He knew how to raise the sights.[7]

Then there was the .38-55 Winchester, another very common rifle using black powder and lead bullets. Around 1910 the people [Eskimos] down at Point Barrow got small-caliber rifles, and shortly after that we knew about the .32-40 caliber whose shells were pretty much like those of the .30-55, but a little shorter and narrower. After that, after 1920, all kinds of calibers began to show up: the .30-30, .25-35, .30 Remington, .35 Remington, all kinds of them, and the first I knew of the .22 special was in 1910. There were not very many of them, and the only one I saw was owned by one of the [Tareumiut] boys down at Pt. Barrow.

TRADE

Evidence of trading—both for life's necessities and for its desirables—appears abundantly in north Alaska historical and archaeological reporting. Eskimo oral histories, and published observations of the first white men to explore Alaska north of sixty-six degrees north latitude (Map 1), document aboriginal trade routes and trade rendezvous in Alaska, and across the Bering Strait as well (among other references, see Gubser 1965; Ray 1975; Oswalt 1979; VanStone 1984; and Burch 1998). And archaeological evidence demonstrates that such commerce, both internal and transcontinental, reaches back to remote antiquity.

The testimonial data relative to early north Alaska barter have to do with the recovery of artifacts (including "flint" and other raw materials of manufacture) whose types or sources were obviously derived from other regions (see as examples Larsen and Rainey 1948 and Giddings 1964). Among such evidence are artifacts from sites in traditional Nunamiut territory whose ages span collectively several thousand years, including faunal remains, varieties

of stone, and artifact types from sources scattered across the northern regions of both continents (Solecki 1951; W. Irving 1953; Campbell 1962). Then, for protohistoric and later decades, and referring now to the central Nunamiut area only (from the valley of Chandler Lake eastward to Itkillik Lake; Map 3), data from numerous old camps support and enhance Paneak's stories of Nunamiut commerce (see Campbell 1972).

EARLY TRADE

The first of Simon's trading accounts is his narrative of Alaskan-Siberian commerce as it prevailed before the arrival of seafaring white men.[1] As he says, he learned this story from his parents, but its attention to the details of places, tribal names, and items of trade imply accuracy, even though it is derived in its entirety from oral accounts passed down through several generations. And of interest is that it is not contradicted, indeed is supported, by the findings of the modern writers cited above.

Early Trade

Finally, I begin to try recording about the old stories you asked for, but God knows, no time for me to find a place to recording there are too many children of course, in my house during all summer … caribou is healthy and fat so we have a pretty good meat supply for this winter and we have early snow up here, early our landing field is closed heavy snow covered it up, up to hips around here. Today is November seventh.

Early people trade with Siberian native and they buy Siberian goods like a green leaf tobacco and reindeer skin especially spotted skin is look lots better for outside parka and outside for outer pants for early people. For nice beautiful mukluk, make out of reindeer, spotted or white color knee boots and short boots that is beautiful for the early people in the early days, way before my grandfather time. According to what everybody was talking about it, about the early people … and story say an old people custom cannot sell reindeer hide with the leg. They have to cut the leg off from the skin shortly after butchering and the skinning before drying out. All skin ready to sell as separate legs according to custom in old way on Siberian side. And buy also Siberian wolverine skin. The early Eskimos liked Siberian wolverine skin than Alaska wolverine – more white strip and a long hair and bigger.

No one talking about beads until later on. The early green leaf tobacco, pack it up in spring reindeer skin to make it so two person can handle by ropes. Rawhide or regular ropes, never mention what kind of made up ropes they put it, but they say ropes anyway.

And early people across the Bering Strait by skin boat in the early summer. And according to story only few men across the Bering Strait during the winter time. After the freeze on the ocean they take a walk. It's not dangerous, I guess, to me anyway, but with kayak kind of dangerous if broken out the ocean some may get lost easy, but they make it. Some strong people I guess not like us. They

Early Trade

Finally, I begin trying to record the old stories you [Campbell] asked for, but God knows there is little time for me to find a place to record because there are too many children, of course, in my house all summer. The caribou are healthy and fat, so we have a pretty good meat supply for this winter, and we have early snow that has closed our landing field and is hip deep around here. Today is November seventh [1970].

The early north Alaska Eskimos traded with Siberian Eskimos for Siberian goods like green leaf tobacco and reindeer skins, especially spotted skins because they looked a lot better for outer parkas and pants.[2] Those spotted or white-colored skins made beautiful mukluks, both knee boots and short boots, that were beautiful to the early Eskimos way before my grandfather's time. According to the old stories, in those early days there was the custom that reindeer hides could not be sold with the leg skins attached. Shortly after butchering they cut the legs from the hides, then skinned and dried them.

According to this custom, in the old days the leg skins were sold separately on the Siberian side of the Bering Strait, and the Alaska Eskimos liked Siberian wolverine skins better than those from Alaska. (Except where noted, all locations mentioned in this chapter are shown on Map 2.)

The Siberian skins had more of a white stripe, and had longer hair and were bigger. According to the stories, there were no glass trade beads until later on. The early green leaf tobacco, traded into Alaska from Siberia, was packed in spring reindeer skins. Each such bundle was roped so that it could be handled by two people. The old stories don't mention whether these were regular ropes or were of rawhide.

And the early Alaska Eskimos crossed the Bering Strait in kayaks in early summer, but according to the stories only a few men crossed in the wintertime. They cross the Bering Strait in the winter time pretty often, according to story one day walk.

King Island old timers village over there, what they call it in Eskimo Ukiuvakmiut, that meaning for their biggest winter settlement. We believe that is King Island people did not move around for all winter that is why they stay, they were settle down in one place without moving, Ukiuvakmiut. And Cape Prince of Wales and called by the early people, Kingikmiut, name meaning the village is located in a high place. And Diomede Islander people called Imakling that meaning those people who live in the ocean all the time or in the water, that meaning to early Eskimo, Imakling.

And St. Lawerance, first people call it by Eskimo, Ungarikmiut, that meaning for these bodies in the short, south Eskimo. These three, four places, those people, those people come to Kotzebue every summer after they get a trip over to Siberian Eskimo, must have a meeting place over in Siberia too. And all these people moving all Siberian goods and several boat, *Umiak*, of course, take a trip to Kotzebue in every summer for exchange.

From Alaska in the Kotzebue, flint, like arrowhead and spear head, knife and ulu and some arrow already made and bow. People buy them ready made in exchange for whatever people like to buy. And spruce split already ready to make bow, bundled up ready for to make arrows too. They bought it because in those days tools not very easy to make before the white man make or sell axe or adze. Before, probably, they worked very hard to split up the spruce with jade or flint, but they can't help it, they know how to do it, and trying hard, I guess.

Exchange they call it I guess because nobody know, nobody know about the money. But they know how much it would cost every item in every group – from

walked across on the ice after the ocean froze [in the fall], and to me, anyway, it does not sound dangerous, but the kayak crossings sound kind of dangerous. If the ocean was broken [stormy] some kayaks might get lost easily I would think, but they seemed to have made it. They were strong people, I guess, not like us. They pretty often crossed the Bering Strait in the wintertime, and according to the stories it was one day's walk.

The old-time King Island Eskimos, known as Ukiuvakmiut (Ukiuvagmiut), had a village on that island. Their name means "biggest settlement," in which they lived all winter without moving. Then there were the Prince of Wales Eskimos, whose name was Kingikmiut (Kiŋigmiut), and to the early people [it] meant that their village was located on a high place. And there were Diomede Island Eskimos, called Imakling (Imaqłiq), a name meaning that they lived all the time on the ocean, or in the water.

The St. Lawrence Island Eskimos were known by the first (early) Eskimo name as the Ungarikmiut (Uŋariġmiut), meaning that their bodies were of the short, southern Eskimo type. And the Eskimos from those three or four places came to Kotzebue every summer after they had [crossed the Bering Strait] to trade with the Siberian Eskimos, where there must have been a trading place too. And all of these American Eskimos carrying their Siberian goods in several boats, *umiak* (*umiaq*), of course, came to Kotzebue each summer for exchange.

At Kotzebue [interior north Alaska Eskimos] brought flint, like arrowheads and spearheads, knives, *ulus* (women's knives; Figure 19), and some arrows and bows already made, and bundles of split spruce ready for making bows and arrows. These were bought [by the coastal Eskimos] because in those days, before the white man's axes and

FIGURE 19   An *ulu* or *ulo*, the traditional Eskimo women's knife, and the Nunamiut name for a famous lake in central Nunamiut territory. This example was made by Elijah Kakinya for his wife May from walrus ivory and the blade of a handsaw. Length of its blade is five and one-half inches. Photograph by JMC, 1998.

Pt. Hope, in Eskimo name spelling, Ektikigagamiut, and Kivalikmiut, almost like Kivalina, Noatakmiut, who live over in Noatak in two groups is the location or the people staying among the Noatakmiut – in early days, Noatakmiut call it who is living up in upper Noatak River and down there in lower which is in settlement (in which they live right now) Napaktukmiut, they call it right now Noatak Village, Napaktukmiut who in the forest or trees, same of the Noatak Eskimos but the settlement is different, that's all.

In the quarries where spruce wood or trees, good find and stay where the spruce are – Kobukmiut and Seligmiut. These two groups, dialects, sound and meaning were about the same probably only splitted from each other. And Kungnimiut and Kuralikmiut about the same dialects in the language the sound probably only split to get Tarigmiut or the Kotzebue.

All the groups come together to Kotzebue for exchange every summer from all over the place … and those people have a nice time together among the old people, way before … in Alaska nobody know Russian or American.

In those days my parents were taking about the early people … the early people good number, they try to figure around 7,000 people along the Brooks Range from Itkillik, Ulo Pass, of course, all way over at Howard Pass a lot of people in those days, before the people would die out through out the country.

adzes, [sharp] tools were not easy to make. Probably, the interior Eskimos worked very hard to split up the spruce with jade or flint, but they could not help it. They knew how to do it though, by trying hard I guess.

They called it exchange because nobody knew about money. But every group of Eskimos knew the cost (value) of every item. There were the Eskimos from Point Hope whose Eskimo name was Ektikigagamiut (Tikiġaġmiut), and the Kivilikmiut (Kivalliġmiut), almost like Kivalina (Kivaliŋiġmiut), and the Noatakmiut (Nuataaġmiut) who lived over on the Noatak River, in two groups (bands). In the early days the group living on the upper Noatak were called Noatakmiut, and down lower, the people in the settlement in which they live right now, and is called Noatak Village were known as the Napaktukmiut (Napaaqtuġmiut). This is in the forest, and the people were of the same (tribe) as the upper Noatak Eskimos; their settlement was different, that's all.

Places that provided wood (artifacts) from spruces or other trees were favored by the Kobukmiut (Kuuvagmiut) and Seligmiut (Siiḷivigmiut) who lived where there were spruces. The sound and meaning of these two groups' dialects were about the same, but split from each other— and the dialects of the Kungmimiut (Kaŋiġmiut) and Kuralikmiut (Kurraliġmiut) were about the same, but had split to get Tarigmiut (Tareumiut) or the Kotzebue (?).

Every summer all the Eskimo groups came from all over the place to trade at Kotzebue where the old people had nice times together. This was way before north Alaska people knew Russians or Americans. My parents said that in those early days there were good numbers of Eskimos. They (my parents) figured that there were around 7,000 [Eskimos] living along the Brooks Range from the Itkillik River and Ulo Pass (Map 3) all the way over to Howard Pass (Map 1).[3] There were a lot of people in those days before they died out throughout this country.

Trading North To The Arctic Coast

And the men fishing, after this freeze up when this silver salmon, we can't understand why when they are coming down from above, they are very, very tiny and beautiful silver fish ... silver salmon and they say that after they are spawning up in the river somewhere they come back with a new kayak, I don't know for sure myself ... but Eskimos talking about like that.

And all the women they were about the same busy, making mukluks, kamik of course, mukluks is a kamik, and mittens and sock, alexi. Nunamiut women know how to make mukluk too out of seal skin ... but they say a needle is not very good, bone needle and bone thimble made out of sheep legs. They make it in the place of thimble, they make out of sheep legs bone and caribou horn too. They make a lot of thimble to sell and bone needle out of caribou legs and end legs that is little piece of the little bone, slimmer one for needle. They are solid bone.

Some people are or women make new parka and one seen them sand powdered sand that is finished of the tanned skin, and make the skin thinner and softer too. They leave it all white nothing else but white. They use this powdered white sand, really fine ones and people wear the parka without the outside parka it look very white nice. In the early days no calico material of course.

In those days they got to be nice and clean every week cause some people got a lot of louses, mostly coast people who are not moving all the time by the dogsled during the winter time.

Among the Nunamuit not really bad some having lice all right but not all of them cause they know how to fight lice. During the winter time in cold weather they bring sleeping bed and mattress and blanket which is made out of skin, they freeze it and then shake it out and pound it with a stick to trap all the lice. My parents anyway shortly after meeting is over down at Niklik lousy, lousy people, but when we coming up in the river and we had some lice too. But after the freeze up all lice disappear, altogether ... Now lice is in the earlier, the coast people had to sell to inland.

The coast people have all the time make seal skin poke ... Nunamiut would like to have that for mashoo, grass roots, also for filling with the berries, cloudberries ... Axsiavik for winter supply. They had it for change in diet during the winter time, also mashoo and cloudberries

Trading North to the Arctic Coast

The Nunamiut men fished after freeze-up in the fall when the silver salmon, we can't understand why, are coming back down [the river] from up above. They are very very tiny and beautiful silver fish, these silver salmon,[4] and it is said that after they have spawned up in the river somewhere they come back with new kayaks. I don't know this myself for sure, but that is what Eskimos say.

And the women were keeping busy too, making mukluks (*kamŋgich*) and mittens and socks (*aitqatit* and *aliqsiich*). And the Nunamiut women knew how to make mukluks too out of seal skins (as well as caribou skins). But they say that the needles were not very good (?), that the old bone needles and bone thimbles were made from the leg bones of sheep, and caribou horn [antler] too. The thimbles were made in place of [metal] thimbles. They made a lot of thimbles to sell (trade), and bone needles out of caribou leg bones too. At the end of caribou leg bones there is a little piece of bone that is most suitable for a slim needle. These needles are solid bone.

Some women used powdered sand in making new parkas from tanned caribou skins, and this made the skins thinner and softer too. The powdered white sand left the skin entirely white, and people wore these fine parkas without the outside parkas because they looked so fine and nice. In those early days there was no calico material of course.

In those days the parkas had to be kept nice and cleaned every week because some people got a lot of lice, especially coast people (Tareumiut) because in winter they were not moving all the time by dogsled. Among the Nunamiut lice were not really bad. Some had them all right, but not all of them, because the Nunamiut knew how to fight lice. During the cold weather of wintertime they brought outdoors their sleeping beds, mattresses, and blankets [of caribou] skins, and after these had frozen they shook them out, and pounded them with sticks to trap [kill] all the lice. This is what my parents said anyway, that shortly after the meetings were over down at Niklik the people were lousy, and when we [the Nunamiut] were coming back up the Colville River we had some lice too, but after freeze up they disappeared altogether. In those earlier days lice were in the goods the coast people traded inland.

The coast people always made sealskin pokes that the Nunamiut liked for storing mashoo [licorice] roots (Figure

mixed together. Mashoo legrice roots cleaned, washed in water and cooked, boil in water for an hour and put it away in whale oil or seal oil. It freezes for all winter. Delicious food and sometime mixed with blueberries and cranberries added cloudberries akpiks carried in sled when traveling in winter. Sometime leave in where *umiak* but in ground digging before ground freeze up. Make cellar, save from animal eating and in spring when owner going back is a delicious.

And the Pt. Barrow people had the raincoats for parka out of uguruk intestine and also for carrying water inside the parka during in cold weather, so the water won't freeze. They also use it for carry little oil whenever they move around by walk for surveying the land. Seal oil or whale oil for winter supply for light for lamps, other use for oiling boots and for greasing boats, boat they dry up after they were in wet ground and water, they have to keep dry and put grease on.

What some people want to have very difficult to have over inland, then in early days they want to make a partner. When they want to make a partner or a fellow got to give something without any charge at least with the only they began the partner together but the one fella got to give something without charge that's why they got the partner everyone of them. And what I have seen myself, when travelers come from Niklik they bring you flour and molasses and I have seen two kinds of tobacco in those days and chewing tobacco too.

20) and also for filling with cloudberries, *aqpiich*, for a winter supply. They had these for a change in diet during wintertime, and also mashoo and cloudberries mixed together. The *mashoo*, or legrice, roots were cleaned, washed in water, boiled for an hour, then put away in the bags in whale or seal oil to stay frozen all winter. This was delicious food; sometimes blueberries and cranberries were added to the cloudberries, and the Nunamiut carried it on their sleds when traveling in winter.

Sometimes the Nunamiut left these bags in the ground [at the places where they cached their *umiat* for the winter]. They would dig cellars before the ground froze [so that after freeze-up the bags were protected from] animals. And when the owners got back in the spring this food was delicious.

And the Pt. Barrow Tareumiut people had rain parkas made of *ugruk*, bearded seal, intestines, and also for carrying water inside the parkas during cold weather, so the water won't freeze. They also used *ugruk* intestine bags for carrying a little oil when they walked, scouting the land. Seal or whale oil was used in winter for lighting their lamps, and for oiling boots and greasing boats. Boats [or boots?] dry out after they are used in wet ground and in water, and they have to be dried and greased.

Some of the coastal products that the inland, Nunamiut, people wanted were very difficult to get in the interior, so in the early days the Nunamiut wanted to have partners among the Tareumiut. When a fellow

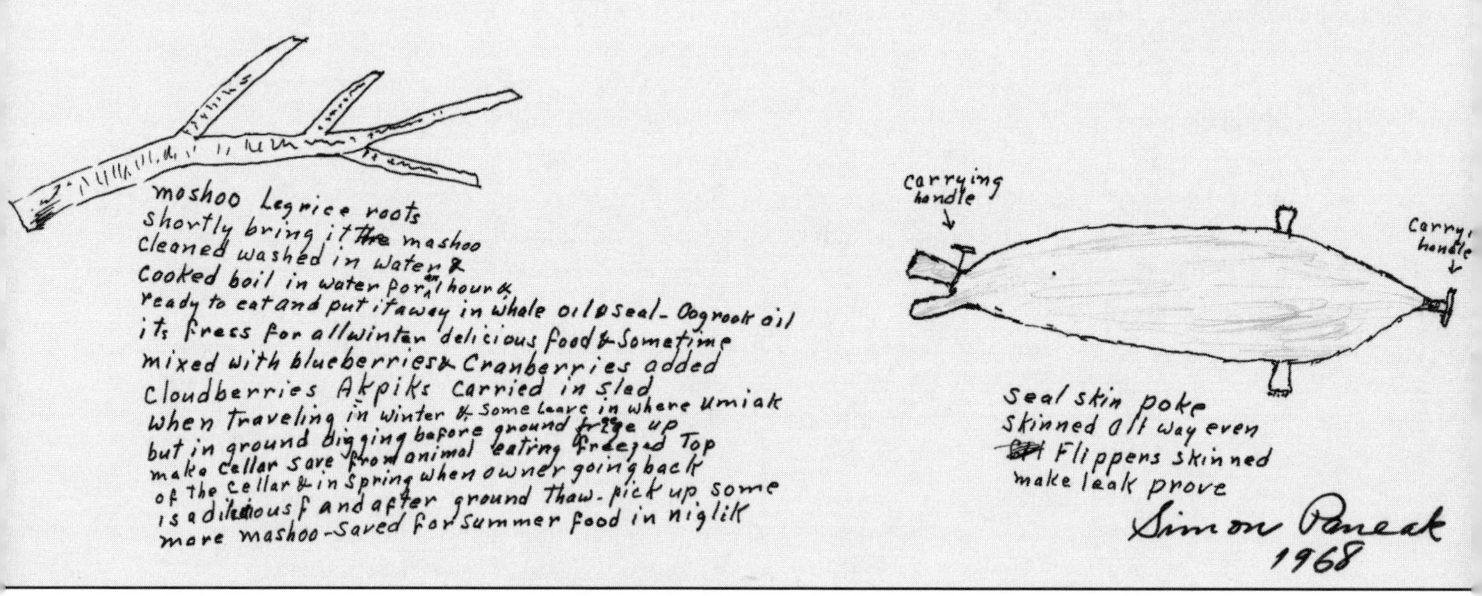

FIGURE 20   Paneak's illustration of food and food storage.

Tobacco two kinds, one is a black navy tobacco and it is colored black and it is packed up around the 50's, I guess, put in wooden box. The other is a light color, brown. They call it sand tobacco. They said that it is real good tobacco, the sand, they say better smoking than black navy tobacco.

wanted to have a partner he had to give a free gift to the other fellow, at least at the beginning, and that's how every Nunamiut got a partner. And I have seen myself that when the Nunamiut travelers came up from Niklik they brought flour and molasses, and in those days I have seen them bring two kinds of [smoking] tobacco, and chewing tobacco too. The two kinds of smoking tobacco were a black navy (colored black), packed in about fifty tins, I guess, in a wood box. And the other was a light brown color—they called it sand tobacco, said it was real good, and better smoking than the black navy.[5]

The Eighteenth and Nineteenth Centuries

Turning to more recent times, the following stories relate primarily to the nineteenth century, although four of them, or their parts, may refer to the 1700s. Russian iron pots possibly reached central Nunamiut territory before 1800, and the same goes for the north Alaska introduction of flour; the first flintlock on the Kobuk River; and parts of Trading North to the Arctic Coast—the latter of which, however, has nothing to do with Russians.

We are on firmer chronological ground with the Story About Nunamiut Eskimos, which on internal evidence spans from about 1875 to 1905. While by 1875 the Nunamiut had acquired certain modern artifacts (see Gubser 1965), their culture remained substantially intact, so we learn in the first part of this account of their traditional routes and techniques of travel, and of native artifacts of barter. Then we are told of Nunamiut immigrations to the Arctic Coast and of other related adventures.

Similarly, First Made a Wooden Stove obviously has a late nineteenth century setting (note reference to Point Barrow and schooners); the Niglik flintlock may be assigned an earliest date of 1840;[6] and Paneak writes that the First Bright Light arrived in 1905. With the exception of Trading to the Arctic Coast, each of these seven stories provides insight into the reception of white man's goods, and as regards the two flintlocks we are delighted to read of the abiding traditional powers of Eskimo divines.

Rivited Iron Pots

Early people like to move around by dogteam, by sled. It is not very easy. Myself I go through lots of time during my life from my boy hood. Then they, some of them, the man had to travel around during the winter time and over in the Brooks Range try to sell what they have to, whatever they have to sell. … they make a profit make some more things to sell like down at Kotzebue, like down at Point Barrow, like down at Niklik, like up in Collinson Point. The people love to travel and sell whatever they have to sell. They make a profit, especially towards the spring people run out of tobacco, that is more important for the old people in the early days. And later on they mention it what here, Siberian people to sell rivitet cooking by the pot. Rivited pail, Utkushik call it, Utkushik cooking pot – Utkushik, spell it Utusik…. Cause in early days before knew about iron pot thay have to make cooking pot out of clay which is pick it up from mud salt where the sheep used to lick.

…rivited cooking pot and some knives traveled by the Bering Straight, some of the white man make things. And pans too out of iron, but they were a very expensive to early people, but they bought it. And we found several rivited pot over in Chandler Lake.

Riveted Iron Pots

The early Eskimos liked to move around by dogsled. It is not very easy, and during my life, from boyhood, I traveled this way a lot. In the [old days] some of the men traveled around this way in the Brooks Range during wintertime, trying to trade whatever they had to sell. They made a profit by making things to trade at places like Kotzebue, Point Barrow, Niklik, and Collinson Point. The Nunamiut loved those travels, and they made a profit, especially toward spring, when the Nunamiut ran out of tobacco [which could be got at the coastal places just noted]. Tobacco was more important to the old Nunamiut people in the early days.

And the old stories mention that later on [the Nunamiut] got riveted cooking pots (Figure 21) traded from Siberian people. These pails were called *utkusik*—cooking pot—because in the early days, before the Nunamiut knew about these iron pots they had to make cooking pots out of clay from the salty mud that the sheep used to lick. Riveted cooking pots, and some [metal] knives, some things made by white men, traveled to Alaska across the Bering Strait. And these included pans too, made of iron, which were very expensive to the early Nunamiut, but who bought them. And we have found several riveted pots over at Chandler Lake.

FIGURE 21   Riveted iron buckets of the kind described by Simon were among the first Czarist Russian trade items to reach central Brooks Range Nunamiut territory. This much used and mended example includes holes repaired with pieces of hammered lead, and it may well have begun its journey across north Alaska some two hundred years ago. Nine and one-fourth inches tall, it was found by Campbell in 1956 at a nineteenth-century Nunamiut encampment on the shore of Chandler Lake. Photograph by Peabody Museum of Natural History, Yale University, 1963.

The Story about Nunamiut Eskimos and others Eskimos Probably in last part of early 18 century probably 1870 or later than this

———

First the man name are Iklangasaluk and his 3 sons with they name are from older Turatcheak – Inualurak –Auksakiak and their wife and childrens. And other two family listed their name as follow first Silatkutak and Kunulak & their wife & childrens. Jessie Ahgook is little boy stayed with his grandfather Eklangasaluk and Jessie Ahgook father Nigaaluk stayed in upper Noatak river. And all those bunch Iklangasaluk party are stayed for winter in Canning river. There were many game large number of Caribou and many Mountain Sheeps – Wolfs – Wolverine and Colored foxes. According to story was telled they have caught many furs, must be lots of White Arctic foxes but arctic fox skin worth Nothing Much. Among Eskimos no place to sell Arctic fox skin they catch. And those Eklangasaluk party went back to their *Umiak* in the mouth of Canning river late in the spring probably last part of May & hunt seal. Many seal there report and soon as ocean ice clear up trip down to Niglik or to Nunamiut where Nunamiut waiting for Point Barrow – Utkiaguikmiut those who come up along the coast by Skin boat – *Umiak*. And Iklangasaluks party are bring very good news about good country. About many animals they found, by that times Coast Eskimos does not bother much inland Eastern Eskimos stayed near Barter Island in The Map Named Arrey Island few miles west of Barter from there up near Demarcation Point and Herschel Island.

Iklangasaluk party going up on Colville R. with bunch of Nunamiut by *Umiak* and haul their *Umiak* over to Noatak and met their relative & friend bring very good news all about they had found. And many Eskimos was interested and many family desire and planning to follow Iklangasaluk party by next winter & Summer. And Ikangasaluk party went down on Noatak soon after river ice clearing up down to Kotzebue Sound.

Sisaulik The Camping place of Noatak peoples & Hunt white whale – Beluga when they catch by Kayak spear them after driven to Shallow water. Butchered Save the meat & blubber & *Maktuk* and Cooked by boiling water Store in Seal skin poke for winter food.

Story About Nunamiut Eskimos

———

A Nunamiut man named Iklangasaluk (Iglaŋasaaluk) had three sons whose names from oldest to youngest were Turatcheak (Tuurratchiaq), Inuralurak (Iałuuraq), and Auksakiak (Aqsiataaq). All three had wives and children, and they and two other Nunamiut men, Silatkutak (Siḷatqutaq) and Kunulak (Kunullaq), and their wives and children, traveled with Iklangasaluk. Jesse Ahgook (see Campbell 1998a:23) was then a small boy and lived with his grandfather, Eklangasaluk [same as Iklangasaluk above], while Jesse's father Nigaaluk lived on the upper Noatak River [in Noatagmiut (Nuataaġmiut) Eskimo territory].

The Eklangasaluk party wintered that year on the Canning River, where they found much game: caribou, sheep, wolves, wolverines, and colored foxes. They trapped a lot of furs, and they must have seen many white, arctic foxes [a creature of sea ice and saltwater shores], but their skins were not worth much [apparently because at that time there was no white man's market for them]. Late in the spring, probably in late May, the Iklangasaluk party retrieved their cached *umiat* (plural of *umiak*; the large, open, skin-covered boat of the Eskimos) at the Canning River mouth and went seal hunting. There were many seals, and later, when the sea ice moved offshore they sailed and paddled their *umiat* to Niglik (see Spencer 1959:199 205; Gubser 1965:178, 179; and Campbell 1998a: pl. 19 for descriptions [and other spellings] of this trade center).

Near Niglik, there were other Nunamiut who were waiting for the Pt. Barrow people, the Utkiagvikmiut (Utqiaġvigmiut) (band of the Tareumiut; Spencer 1959: 3), who would come to Niglik by *umiak* along the coast. And Iklangasaluk's party brought very good news about the Canning River country and its abundant game. By this time there was no longer quarreling or fighting between the coastal Eskimos and the inland eastern [Nunamiut], some of whom were now living along the coast from Arrey [Arey] Island, near Barter Island, to Demarcation Point and Herschel Island.

Iklangasaluk's party, with another bunch of Nunamiut, then traveled by *umiak* up the Colville River, and from there hauled their boats on dogsleds to the Noatak River valley, where they met relatives and friends, and told them the good news about all they had found in the Canning

After The Meeting is over in Kotzebue and Noatak peoples going up on The Noatak river stayed in Aniyaak in upper Noatak river until late April. Many family started across Northern Brook range probably by Howard Pass to upper Colville R. & big group is in the Mouth of Itivelik on Colville R. waiting for river ice floe clearing. And after the ice gone and floating along in Colville and Met other group Eskimos at The Mouth of Killik on Colville & had enjoyed Meeting – dances and other trick many game. And Continued travel and Met another group at The Mouth of Anaktuvuk on Colville. And another happy together they had. Met relative & friend and in that times family of Utukak Eskimos go along with them after had Met in the Mountain in Near Howard Pass.

Same peoples any how only different is stayed like Noatak & Utukak Kangianik the Upper Colville River. Killik – Anaktuvuk call themselves Noatakmiut, Utukakmiut, Kellikmiut, Kakmalikmiut – or Anaktuvukmiut Same laung-guages Not too much different Sound about the Same.

Umiak Frame only when a haul in over land.

They are big crowd in Niglik – the gathering place for Early Eskimos waiting for Utiagvikmiut – The peoples of Point Barrow.

And then have a potlach and have a Kayak & boat races and pulling by fingers & arm pulling & Severals kind of rustling and running races & high kicking and high jumb and Severals kind of trick game and foot Ball play and dances being in every night After play all day long and Exchanced. And put near every man have own partner for years & years and among women have partner also.

Inland Eskimos purchase all land animals skin, Stone made a like Sandstone for oil lamps and flint – double edged flint knives & Ulu – Spear head – Arrow head Scrapper head. Valcano glass – Bone & horn Cutter and hair Cutter. The Volcano glass are found in west of Killik East of Itivelik river. And An Barrow Eskimos has stock of all sea animals skin & oil & *Maktuk* and pre-paired already made for Exchanged – water light Mukluk – change boot – knee boots - hip boot – Oogrook hide – Oogrook Raw hide line & young Walrus skin lines for pulling *Umiak* in Colville river and bundle of made Snares – one bundle is 20 Snares - Seal skin lines for Snow Shoe lashes and other uses.

After The Meeting are come part and by the times of Iklangasaluk in that Summer by that times Nigalok follow his father Iklangasaluk and when come a part Many family

River region. And many of the Noatagmiut were inter-ested, and planned to follow the Iklangasaluk party the next winter and summer. Meanwhile, after the ice broke up on the Noatak River, Iklangasaluk's party boated down to Sisualik [Selawik], the Noatak Eskimos whaling place on Kotzebue Sound.

There, after the animals had been driven into shallow water, they speared belugas (the small white whales) from kayaks; boiled the meat, blubber, and *maktuk*, and stored them in sealskin pokes for winter use. After the meeting was over in Kotzebue Sound, and the Noatak people had gone up the Noatak River, the Nunamiut stayed over in Aniyaak (Aniyaaq) [Aniuk River], on the upper Noatak, until late April. Many Nunamiut families crossed the Brooks Range, probably via Howard Pass, to the upper Colville where they met a big group of Eskimos at the mouth of the Etivluk (Itivluk) River, waiting for the Colville River to become clear of winter ice.

After the ice was out, they floated the Colville, meeting another group of Eskimos at the mouth of the Killik with whom they enjoyed visiting, dancing, and games. Farther down the Colville at the mouth of the Anaktuvuk River they met still other Eskimos, again enjoying their com-pany, and finding here relatives and friends. On much of this journey from the upper Noatak the Nunamiut were accompanied by a family of Utukak Eskimos (Utuqqaġmiut) from the Utukak River, whom they had met in the mountains near Howard Pass, and who differed very little from the more eastern Nunamiut.

Then there were the Nunamiut from the Killik River, and today some of the Anaktuvuk people call them-selves Killik [when Anaktuvuk Pass village was settled in 1949, some of the Nunamiut came from the Killik River; see Rausch 1951:154; Solecki 1950:150], the Noatak-miut, Utukakmiut, Kellikmiut [the above-noted Killik people] and the Kakmalikmiut (Qagmaligmiut)—or Anaktuvukmiut (Anaqtuuvagmiut), who spoke the same languages that were not much different and sounded about the same. [The Noatagmiut were a distinct tribe; the others were Nunamiut bands.]

How an *umiak* frame is hauled overland (Figure 22).

The Eskimos [whose travels and friendly encounters Paneak has described above] made a big crowd at Niglik as they awaited the arrival of the Pt. Barrow people, Utiagvikmiut. When they arrived all of the people held a big potlatch, in which there were kayak races, finger

follow Iklangasaluk party. And go along with Barrow Eskimos who was taking trip in along The Arctic Coast as far as Collinson Point – Nuvuak – the other gathering place in old days – Eastern Eskimos usually coming to Collinson Pt. located West Barter Island waiting for Barrow peoples and Indians peoples usually coming down from inland by dog pack walking to Meet Barrow people for Exchange – trading.

By that times had said when a big group arrived in Collinson Pt. one of the Indian man was get mad & sad when he recognized some man from Anaktuvuk. Of course, Indian man father was killed by Anaktuvuk man in the last war in Near Tulugak. Almost war break (declared) but Never Make Some how. Among Indian was scared because not enough man to fought by that times. Among Indian had only Musseloader gun not like Eskimo had rifles – 44 caliber Rimless & 44 caliber Rifle some having 20 shells in magazine holding it. By that times among Eskimo has Rimless Caliber 44 and 44 Winshester rifles.

All The Nunamiut beginning live on Mountain range and some coming down to Niglik to their relative & friend

and arm pulling contests, foot races, high kicking and high jump contests, several kinds of trick games [games of wit], games of kicking a ball, and dancing every night after playing all day long. Then partners exchanged gifts. Nearly every man had had a partner for years, and the women had partners, too (see Chapter 2, note 5). The inland Eskimos [Nunamiut certainly, but perhaps including the Noatagmiut and the Kovagmiut (Kuuvagmiut)] had all kinds of land-animal skins, and sandstone for oil lamps, flint for double-edged flint knives and *ulus* (see Figure 19), and for spear, arrow, and scraper heads. And the inland people had volcanic glass [obsidian] for cutting bone, horn, and hair. The volcanic glass was found west of the Killik and east of the Etivlik rivers.

In exchange, the Pt. Barrow people had stocks of all sea animal skins, and oil and *maktuk*. And already manufactured and ready for trading, they had waterproof change (?) boots, knee boots, hip boots whose soles were of oogruk hide, and oogruk rawhide lines and young walrus skin lines for hauling *umiat* up the Colville River. They had bundles of manufactured (baleen?) snares, each

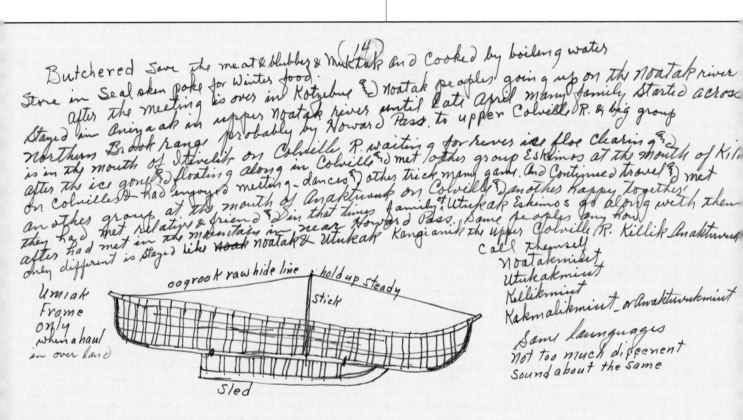

FIGURE 22   Paneak's illustration of overland transport of a boat.

bring more good news about good country they found and come back with their relative. More & more peoples moving up east and finally later in 18 century White Mans Whalers coming on Arctic Coast need Eskimo hunters furnashing all white man goods. And teach them how to drink whiskey thats the Eskimo loved and more & more peoples moved from all over Northern of Alaska. Many White Man ships had winter at Herschel Island and Several ships had wrek in Arctic ice probably some ship had no power must be sailing ship and Severals of them had power with Steam engine.

In some winter said round 20 ship had wintered in Herschell Island harper. That why all Eskimos moving up like Caribou migrating because more importand white man goods, while very hard to have white man goods in here in Brook Range.

On Whaling times. Severals whaling ships had wintered again in Herschel Island in some how heard about gold striken in Dawson and Klondike on Upper Yukon. In that times some Indian from Crow Flat in Near Old Crow usually coming down on Herschel Island Firth river, to buy what ever they need from Whalers.

Whalers trade and buy furs in those day. Silver gray fox skin are worth big for exchange & Cross fox skin worth better than Red fox skin. Red fox skin worth better than White Arctic fox skin, worth very little on White fox skin. Lynx worth Nothing and Marmots is very good worth to white man for parka's.

In those days among Sailor of Whalers heard gold rush being in Dawson & Klondike area and in by Night an among Sailor Crews was Sneaken to Ship cellars. Peoples pick out what they can use on the trail if they lucky to got away from Hercshell Island they are. They are from every ship. And Captain & Mates Never know till Sailors get away. No one knows in Herschel Island Village and Probably in among Sailors know each others what or about times to go by Night.

When a times come all the Sailors together and took Severals Sled – Eskimo sled rifles & shells and go by night to their stuff, which take the stuff before or head a times. And said few Eskimo family stayed in Mainland and took a Eskimo dogs away from Eskimos and tell them if they do not let go their dogs they would fought them or kill them. So Eskimos let go their dogs and took Eskimo Clothes Socks – Mitten Parka's and others.

And One Eskimo man coming on the Firth river (the called by Eskimo Herschel river). And met the bunch of

bundle containing twenty of them, and sealskin lines for snowshoe lashings and other uses.

After the meetings at Niglik adjourned, Iklangasaluk, followed by his son, Nigaaluk, and many other families joined the Pt. Barrow Eskimos in a trip eastward along the Arctic Coast. They traveled as far as Collinson Point—Nuvuak (Nuvuaq)—which was the other (Arctic Coast) gathering place in the old days, and where more eastern Eskimos, in addition to interior Indians, came down to the coast, walking and with pack dogs, to trade with the Pt. Barrow people.

When the big group from Niglik arrived at Collinson Point, an Indian man got mad and sad when he recognized a man from Anaktuvuk. The Indian's father had been killed by an Anaktuvuk man (or men) in the last war at Tulugak (Tuluak Lake, Map 3; see Gubser 1965: 44–47, and Chapter 4, this book), and another war might have resulted right there at Nuvuak if the Indians had not been outnumbered by the Eskimos. Further, the Indians had only muzzle-loading guns, while the Eskimos were armed with repeating rifles: .44-caliber rimless, some having magazine capacities of twenty shells. By then the Eskimos had .44-caliber Winchester rifles (see Logan 1959:136–39).

The Nunamiut began living in the mountains [in the Canning River region?] and when coming down to Niglik they would tell their relatives and friends about what good country they had found. More and more Nunamiut moved eastward, and later in the eighteenth [actually, nineteenth] century white man's whaling ships began arriving on the Arctic Coast, and Eskimo hunters provided them with food. The white men taught the Eskimos to drink whiskey, which the Eskimos loved, and more and more Eskimos moved to the Arctic Coast from all over northern Alaska. Many ships wintered at Herschel Island and several were wrecked in the sea ice. Some of the whaling ships were sailing vessels only, and others had auxiliary steam engines.

In some winters there were as many as twenty whaling ships wintering in the harbor at Herschel Island, and that is why all the Eskimos moved north to the coast like migrating caribou. White man's goods had become very important, but could not be had in the Brooks Range. During those whaling times, several ships wintering at Herschel Island somehow heard of the (1897–98) gold strikes at Dawson and the Klondike, on the upper Yukon River. In those times, Indians [Kutchin Athapaskans]

Sailors traveling on the Firth river up and took whole things he had full of Caribou Meat and gears and his dogs he was Scared walk days to Herschel Island and Soon after the Eskimo man telling News about the bunch Sailors had going up on The Firth river heading South. And All The Captain of whalers together and Make a plan Chase them up. And send two first Mate of the ships and took Several Eskimo mans. Started off soon after ready but cannot catch until quite of way up in Mountain Valley, of course, those Sailors had lots of dogs they took from Eskimos.

And when come close from An Among Sailors – fire with powerful 45-70 Government to the Chasers. Could not catch them in first place and in second times Among Sailors Started Shoot back again and Mate tell his Crews – Eskimo's go ahead shoot the Sailors. And said two sailors was kill and some sailors wave hand up and Mate told his Crews stop to shoot and some sailors climbing up to Mountain like wolfs. They let them go and took back a sailors who was hands up and others Sailor across the country by foots and found indians in South side of Brook Range. And 2 Indian man take them over to Dawson & Klondike or to where early white mans discovered pure gold – Gold rush in wilderness. And few years after Sailors across the country from Herschel Island and two man was come on whaling ships and both are nice friendly to Eskimos friend and bought things from the ships as gift free to Eskimos friend. Both are having wear Suit a Clothes must be gotten rich in gold rush – Dawson or Klondike and both are not like a before in Herschel Island by that times when a bunch of Sailors desired to got away from Whalers in Herschel Island.

One of Whaling Ships have caught 60 Whales (Bowhead) in two Summer Season the biggest catch than any other whalers. Whale bone or Baleen is very good worth to Eskimos in Pt. Barrow Must be very good money in outside and in later I heard at $15.00 a lbs. The end of the story.

from [Old] Crow Flats came to the coast via the Firth River to trade with the whalers [and perhaps the Indians brought the gold strike news].

In those days whalers were also traders and fur buyers. Skins of the silver fox were worth a lot in trade; those of the cross fox were worth more than ordinary red fox skins, which in turn were more valuable than those of the white, arctic fox. Lynx skins were worth nothing, but marmot skins, for making white man's parkas, brought good prices.

When the whaling crews heard of the gold rush in the Dawson–Klondike area they began sneaking at night into the ships' cellars [holds] and picking out what they would need on the trail if they were lucky enough to escape from Herschel Island. These sailors were from every ship, and neither the captains and mates nor the people in the Eskimo village on Herschel Island knew about the desertions until after the sailors had got away. Only the sailors who were part of the plot knew when they would leave.

When the time came, the deserters took several sleds and went by night to where they had been caching their stuff. There were a few Eskimo families living on the nearby mainland, and the sailors took their dogs, threatening to kill the Eskimos if they would not hand them over. So the Eskimos let them have their dogs, and the sailors also took the Eskimos' clothes: socks, mittens, parkas, and other items.

Then the sailors went up the Firth River, called by the Eskimos Herschel River, and met an Eskimo man from whom they took everything: caribou meat, gear, and dogs. The scared man walked for days to Herschel Island, where he told the news of the bunch of sailors heading south up the Firth. Hearing this, all the captains of the whaling ships got together to plan how to catch the sailors, and accordingly, first mates from two of the ships, accompanied by several Eskimo men, soon started after them.

They did not catch up with them until they were quite a ways up in the mountains, but of course the sailors had a lot of dogs they had taken from the Eskimos. And when the pursuers finally came close, the sailors began firing at them with their powerful .45-70 Government [U.S. military rifles; see Chapter 2]. Then the pursuing men came close a second time, and the sailors again fired at them, and the mate, commanding, told his crew—the Eskimos—to go ahead and shoot at the sailors, which they did, killing two of them. Several of the others put their hands in the air and surrendered, and were taken back to the ships, and the mate told his crew to stop shooting, while some of the sailors were escaping by climbing the mountain like wolves. The mate and his men let them go, and those who escaped went on foot, and found Indians on the south side of the Brooks Range. Then two Indian men took them to Dawson and the Klondike where white men had earlier discovered pure gold, creating a gold rush in the wilderness.

A few years after the sailors had deserted across country from Herschel Island, two men arrived back on whaling ships, and both were friendly to their Eskimo friends, and brought free gifts from the ships. Both were wearing fine suits of clothes, so they must have gotten rich in the Dawson-Klondike gold rush, and neither of them behaved as if they had ever before been on Herschel Island, when they were members of the bunch of sailors who deserted.

At this later time, one whaling ship visiting Herschel Island had caught sixty bowhead whales in two summer seasons, more than any other whaling ship had taken. Whalebone, baleen, was very valuable to the Eskimos at Pt. Barrow. It must have sold for very good money on the outside [the contiguous U.S. states and territories], where, I heard later, it sold for $15.00 a pound. The end of the story.

The Story About Flintlock Gun in Two Country One is in Niglik and Other in Kobuk

———

First one Flintlock gun coming down in Mighty Mackenzie River probably from Fort McPherson on Peel River the earliest settlement for Indian and white peoples.

One of the Eskimo bought the Flintlock gun with all the slug and gun black powder and then one of the man from Point Barrow bought that gun. The man's name are Umikluk. The man must be rich man in Barrow and he is collecting early white man goods and said he also have alcohol and learned how to light the alcohol in his pointer (finger). And in next summer come along again from Barrow he take along his flintlock gun. And he was, he was fooling Nunamiut in Niglik. By that times Nunamiut does not know flintlock gun. Before must be heard but did not see. And the man show them how on this powerful gun and shoot for long distance must be aimed away up

The Story about Flintlock Gun

———

The first flintlock gun (see Figure 14) seen by the Nunamiut came down the mighty MacKenzie River, probably from Fort McPherson [a Hudson's Bay Company Post on the Peel River not far above its confluence with the MacKenzie; Map 1]. Fort McPherson was the earliest Indian-white settlement in those regions.[6] An Eskimo had bought the gun with its slugs and black powder, and had then sold it to a Pt. Barrow Eskimo man whose name was Umikluk (Umigluk), who must have been rich because he accumulated white man's goods, including alcohol [most likely wood alcohol for use in lamps and small stoves, but possibly high-proof whiskey, rum, or gin]. This Pt. Barrow man had learned to light his finger after dipping it in alcohol [which burned so briefly that he was not harmed].

The next summer he came to Niglik with his gun, with which he astonished the visiting Nunamiut, who by that time must have heard of flintlock guns, but who had never seen one. He showed them how, by aiming it way up in in the air when shoot for long distance and landed river in water big splashing white, and Nunamiut is earache and scared. And he was told Nunamiut, if he wanted kill all off from far off, which is the bow and arrows could not reach. And he keeping shoots in every day or shoot somebody sled runner and his slug plug go through make a hole. And finally one of shaman get tired to hearing big noise like a thunder he ask him – can you handed to me? The shaman name is Alunikrurak and then Umikluk given to him. Perhap the Alunikrurak wanted to see unusual things. And then Alunikrurak was nicely look over and over and then tip his finger in over his mouth and smear at the mouth of the gun and he given back to owner. And Umikluk try to shoot but the flintlock won't go off. No fire in this gun. And then Umikluk pay all the flint from Nunamiut but the gun cannot fired at all and Umikluk was helpless. And one morning Alunikrurak was told him if he do not try to scare peoples his gun would alright in normally. And Umikluk say yes – and I would never, and he tried out again shoot alright.

One more Umikluk has fooling Nunamiut with alcohol. He was light the Eskimo oil lamp and place a cup (iron cup) put little alcohol – he called water but he bought a power from Tanig – whitemen. Even good Eskimo shaman would not see Tanig power is absolutely different. And then all Nunamiut come over to him and see what the man doing. Everybody come together and watch the men doing. And Umikluk was screamed make all the noise he could make and he was calling – Tanig Kain – Tanig Kain Come on white men – Come on. He tip his finger pointer into cup of water and light in burning oil lamp and he say watch my finger are burning the flame would give no harm on my finger. And everybody was suprising because the common river water was burn. By that time no one has matches to start fire, only Eskimo has fire drills and pyrite stone.

One flintlock gun are bought by one of Kobuk man in Kotzebue. The first man has flintlock gun. And in that times a family was stayed in upper Kobuk river live on fish and said the family from Sismorof in Eskimos called – Sangmaliakrumiut. And the people of Kobuk or Kobukmiut usually go down by skin boats – *umiapiaks* – the meaning real skin boats to Kotzebue the gathering exchange place for early Eskimos from all over, Western Eskimos and Nuatak – Kobuk – Silivak – Kivalena – Pt Hope – Kangik (candles) – Sismorof – Deamede – King Island – Wales and Sepearean.

the air, this powerful gun would shoot long distances, with its balls landing in the river with great white splashes, and scaring the Nunamiut, and giving them earaches. He told the Nunamiut that if he wanted, he could kill at distances far greater than bows and arrows could reach, and he kept shooting every day, even shooting a hole through someone's sled runner. Finally, one of the Nunamiut shamans got tired of hearing this big noise like thunder, and he asked the man if he could hold the gun. The shaman's name was Alunikrurak (Aluniġruuraq), and Umikluk gave it to him.

Perhaps, thought Umikluk, Alunikrurak wanted only a close look at this unusual thing. But after Alunikrurak had looked it over nicely, he touched the tip of his finger to his mouth, and then, smearing the muzzle of the gun, he gave it back to its owner. And when Umikluk tried to shoot it, it would not go off. There was no fire in the gun. Then Umikluk bought from the Nunamiut all the flint they had, but the gun still would not fire, and Umikluk was helpless. Then one morning Alunikrurak told him that if he would not try to scare people his gun would work normally, and Umikluk agreed that he would not try to scare them, and his gun worked again.

Then Umikluk fooled the Nunamiut with his alcohol. He lit an Eskimo oil lamp and then poured a little of the alcohol into an iron cup. He called it water, but he said he had bought a power from a *taniq* [or *tanik*], a white man. Even a good Eskimo shaman could not see that a Taniq's power was absolutely different.

So the Nunamiut people came over to see what Umikluk was doing, and making all the noise he could, he began screaming, "Taniq, Kain; Taniq, Kain (Tanik, qaiñ—come on, white men, come on!) Then he dipped the tip of his finger into the cup of alcohol and lit it from the burning oil lamp, and he said, "Watch. My finger is burning but the flame will not harm it, and everyone was surprised because they knew common river water would not burn. At that time the Eskimos did not have matches, but only fire drills and pyrite stone for starting fires (see Paneak's drawing of a fire drill in Campbell 1998a: pl. 11).

Another flintlock gun was bought by a Kobuk man in Kotzebue Sound. He was the first man [in those regions] to own a flintlock. At that time there was an Eskimo family staying on the upper Kobuk River to fish, and it is said that this family was from Sismorof [Shishmaref] whose people were called the Sangmaliakrumiut (Saŋmaliaġrugmiut). The people of the Kobuk, the Kobukmiut, would go down to Kotzebue in skin boats—*miapiaks*—a term meaning real

In the family of Sismorof there was an old man. And then bunch of Kobuk Eskimos coming up on Kobuk River and knowing the family staying and one who has flintlock gun wanted to show to family and all the men are agree it one by one. Told the man go ahead and shoot, make the surprising and scared. And the man load his flintlock gun filling large amount gun black powder with big slug or shot. Fired make big noise and said – weather is sunny and clear and no wind at all.

The old fellow heard the big gun fire and told his family in very loud voice – air is bursted – air is bursted?? Sila – Sila - Kaaktoka?? And told his family stayed inside our house and the old fellow go inside his house he is last. He was afraid of the exploding. In earlier among Eskimos talk about exploding air could be in some day no one know when, just talking about. The old fellow is shaman and he begin doing his own power and idea, his own experience, and smear his house frame by his hand to make house stand stronger. And while he was doing this, Kobuk peoples arrived to where the family was and no one seen outside of the family. And the family of old fellow heard the noise of Kobuk peoples. Then the old fellow look through edge of the bearskin door – talo, and see and recognized Kobuk people arrived. And told his family come out with no fear. And the old fellow ask his friend about the big noise he hear and his friend was answered and told him the one has unusual powerful gun which is make big noise and can reach very long distance with heavy lead slug. And then the old fellow was so suprized on the wiber

And in few years after that most of the mans having Flintlock gun and Muslloader gun and third are 44 Rimless bored rifles &, forth 44 caliber & 45-70 government. And all kind of caliber rifles or black powder rifles and then others high power riflers used smokeless powdered first I know of 30-30 & 30-40 or 65mm & 32-40 & 22 Speacel rimless Shells and 25-35 22 high power 35 Remington & 30 Remington and others calibers.

skin boats (also *umiat*). Kotzebue was the gathering, trading place for Eskimos from all over: Western Eskimos, Nuatak (Nuataaq) [Noatak], Kobuk, Silivak [Selawik], Kivalena [Kivalina], Point Hope, Kangik (Kaŋiq) [Candles], Sismorof [Shishmaref], Deamede [Diomede], King Island, [Prince of] Wales, and Seperean [Spafarief].

In the Shishmaref family [who were fishing on the upper Kobuk River] there was an old man, and the man with the flintlock was among a bunch of Kobuk men who were coming up the river. They knew where the Shishmaref family were camped, and one by one the Kobuk men agreed with the gun's owner that they should surprise and scare the family. Accordingly, the owner loaded the flintlock with a big charge of black powder and a slug, or shot, and then he fired, making a big noise [like thunder], although it is said that the weather was sunny and clear, with no wind at all.

The old fellow heard the big gun fire, and in a very loud voice said, "Has the air burst? Has the air burst?" "Sila, Sila, Kaaktoka? (Sila, Sila *qaaqtuqhaa*!)" And he told his family to get inside the house, and the old man was the last one in. He was afraid of the explosion because there was an old Eskimo story that someday—no one knew when—the air would explode. The old man was a shaman, and he began using his own power and ideas and experience. He rubbed the house frame with his hands to make it stand stronger, and while he was doing this the Kobuk men arrived unseen.

But the old fellow's family heard them outside, and then he looked through the edge of the bearskin door, the *talo* (*talu*), and he saw and recognized the Kobuk people. He told his family that they could all go out without being afraid, and then he asked his [Kobuk] friends about the big noise he and his family had heard. They answered that one of them owned an unusually powerful gun that made the big noise, and that it could reach a very long distance with a heavy lead slug. And then the old fellow was so surprised. A few years after that most of the Eskimo men had flintlocks, then muzzleloader [percussion cap] guns, and [these were followed by rifles]: .44 rimless, .44 and .45-70 [center fire] government, as well as other calibers. [Then, in turn] there were rifles using smokeless powder, the first of them that I remember being .30-30, .30-40, or 6.5 mm, .32-40, .22 special rimless, .25-35, .22 high power .35 Remington, .30 Remington and other calibers (see Figure 15).

This is the Story about First Made a Wooden Stove

One of Nunamiut man his name is Nuisilaa. Probably had seen some stove in Pt Barrow or in some schooners. He is a first man maker of wooden stove. He is collecting empty can – black powder can. He is make shape like schooner, all rivited together. He make a tin can rivits. Possibly take good many cans and all Nunamiut found out after the unusual stove much easier than heating stone by open fire in out of door and one year after all Nunamiut has wooden stove.

Story About First Flour

Only one sack flour bought in Kotzebue by a man of Noatak probably from russian ship two masted schooner which is first show up first in over Berring Sea and an

Story About the Wooden Stove

A Nunamiut man whose name was Nuisillaa made the first Nunamiut wood-burning stove after probably having seen one at Pt. Barrow, or on [whaling or trading] schooners. After flattening and riveting together many tin black-powder cans, he built an effective stove, in the shape of a schooner (Figure 23). And when the Nunamiut people saw this unusual stove [which would burn small, arctic willows], and was much more convenient than heating stones in open fires, within a year they all had wood-burning stoves.

Story About First Flour

The first sack of flour [in Eskimo North Alaska] was bought in Kotzebue by a Noatak River man, probably from a Russian two-masted schooner from over the

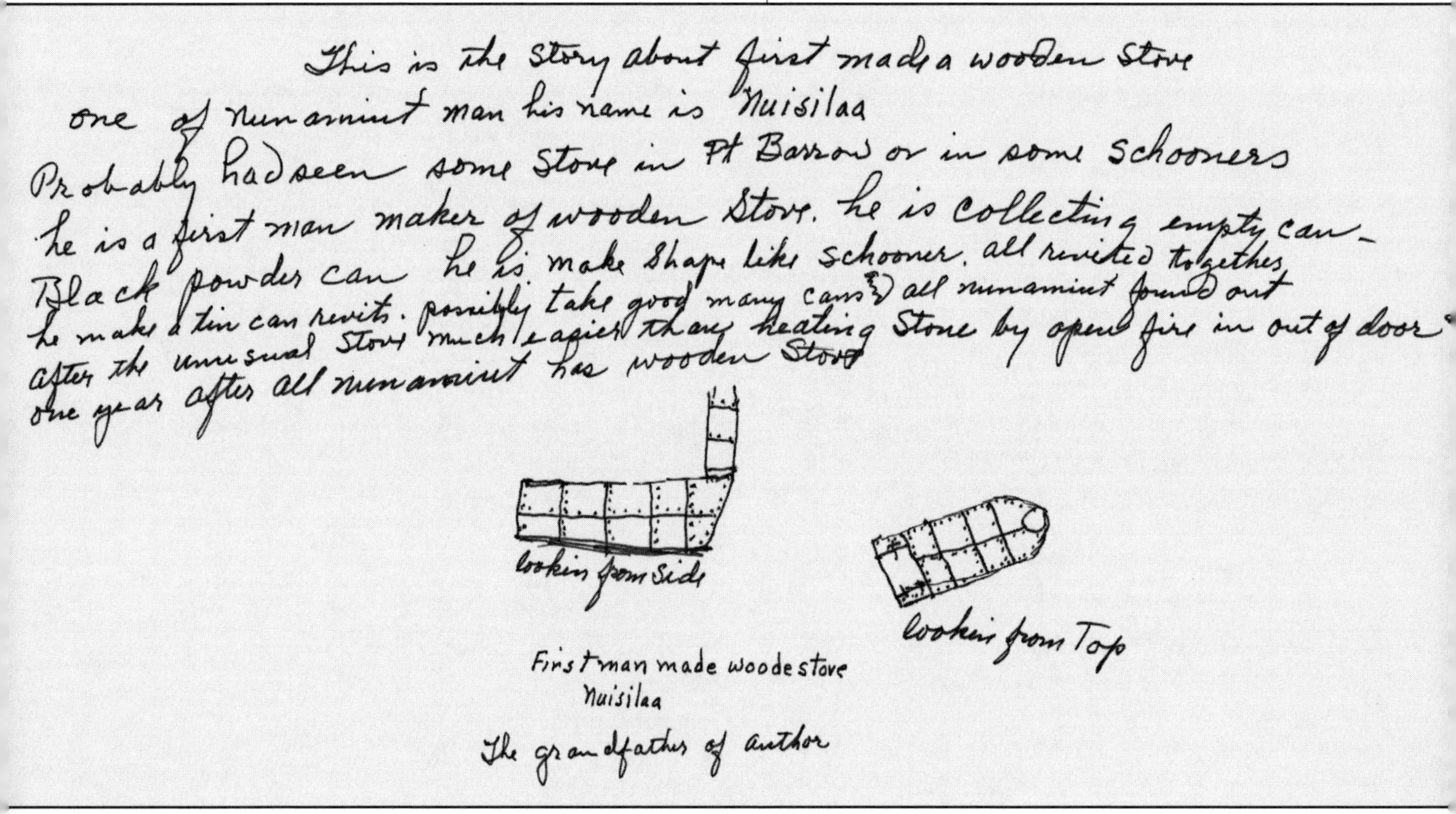

FIGURE 23 Paneak's illustration of the first Nunamiut stove.

among Eskimo learn how to cook & serve. They make a juice boiled in big Iron revited pail so every can have a drink while is hot like a drink meat broth.

By that times early in the fall probably in September after killing caribou in lake or in corrals enough food or more than can use or may have extra meat. And Noatak peoples sent two man as messengers to Killik peoples invited to Noatak. And had big potlach and happy together and many way playing but it is closing with epidemic flu. Many peoples died on the epidemic. By that times in potlach and cook whole sack-flour by many pail and said that was good to drink because mix with brown sugar and seal oil to taste. It might be pretty rough to sick peoples.

Bering Sea, and the ship's company taught the Eskimos how to serve it. They made a juice, boiled in a big riveted iron pail, and the men drank it like hot meat broth. In those times, the Noatak people, after killing more caribou than they needed in early fall lake drives or corrals (see Campbell 1998a: pls. 35, 36), sent two men as messengers to the Killik people, inviting them to a feast at Noatak. So they had a big potlatch and were happy together playing many games, but then they were struck by a flu epidemic and many people died. At potlatches in those days the people would cook a whole sack of flour in many pails. And it is said that it was a good drink when mixed to taste with brown sugar and seal oil, although it might be pretty rough on sick people.

First Bright Light
Came On Anaktuvuk River In 1905

———

By that time first I know kerosene lantern Gee, is really bright light owned by Konakrak the light wind do not put it off in out of door when in need, and all the man have a dinner in that skin tent (Itchalik) and all the man bring tool bag 4 wolverine head skin sewed together it make tool bag called in Eskimo (Ikligvik). All the making fish hook – fish lines out of Baleen (Shukak) and Snowshoe making and netting, make ladles – (Kayutak) – out of ram Sheep horn and ice chisel – (took) and other etc.

I wish we have light too but my parent are poor condition.

In the spring of 1905 or 1906 last caribous herds migrating toward east just by north of mountain lines and ever since caribous never come back and in later heard south wind bring in around Holahola river all the herds went by the valley and across the mountain range. Last for two winter 7 peoples died from starvations. Not enough sheeps for everybody in the mountains range. Not like today. Very few mooses in the north slope by that times. Not like a today. Nobody thought about airplane – no mail.

First Bright Light
Came on Anaktuvuk River in 1905

———

[Simon Paneak was five years old when in 1905 he witnessed the first use of a kerosene lantern on the Anaktuvuk River.] Gee, what a bright light the kerosene lantern gave (Figure 24), and even out-of-doors a light wind would not put it out. It was owned by Konakrak (Kunagrak), and all the men took it into a hide tent [*itchalik*], and each man carried his tool bag [*ikḷigvik*] that was made of four wolverine head skins sewed together.

In the tent they ate dinner and worked at making fishhooks [of antler or ivory], fish lines of baleen [*suqqaq*], snowshoes, netting, ladles [*qayuuttaq*] of ram horns (Figure 25), ice chisels [*tuuq*] and other implements. I wished we had a lantern too, but my parents were poor.

In the spring of 1905 or 1906 the last caribou herds migrated eastward, north of the mountain line [the north front of the Brooks Range], and they did not come back toward us, and we later heard that a south wind had taken them over to the Holahola (Hulahula) River, from which all of the herds went up that valley and across the Brooks Range. The caribou were gone for two winters and seven [Nunamiut] died of starvation (see Chapter 4). There were not enough sheep for everybody in the Brooks Range. It was not like today. There were very few moose on the north [Arctic] slope at that time, and unlike today, nobody knew about airplanes. And there was no mail.

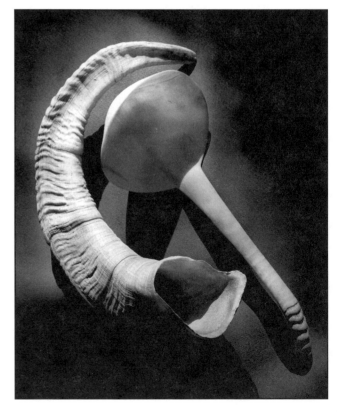

FIGURE 24 This ship's lantern (seventeen inches tall) was recovered in the summer of 1958 from the ruins of a log cabin on the upper John River. According to old-timers in the Koyukuk River village of Old Bettles, it was left behind by members of the 1901 Schrader expedition to the Arctic Coast (Schrader 1904, and see Paneak's "First Bright Light" story). Photograph by JMC, 1998.

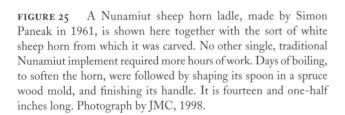

FIGURE 25 A Nunamiut sheep horn ladle, made by Simon Paneak in 1961, is shown here together with the sort of white sheep horn from which it was carved. No other single, traditional Nunamiut implement required more hours of work. Days of boiling, to soften the horn, were followed by shaping its spoon in a spruce wood mold, and finishing its handle. It is fourteen and one-half inches long. Photograph by JMC, 1998.

WAR AND HUNGER

The dark side of north Alaska native history is reflected in recurring episodes of warfare and famine. The latter resulted generally from the remarkably short far northern food chains, which contain few species of human food animals and even fewer of food plants, while war had as its principal causes economic stress of one sort or another, combined commonly with long-standing ethnic animosities.

WAR

Until recently, published accounts of north Alaska Eskimos contained very little on either intra-Eskimo warfare or on war between one or another Eskimo group (band or tribe) and their Athapaskan Indian neighbors. In fact, as noted by Burch (1974), nineteenth and early twentieth-century reporting (by both civilian and military writers) typically ignored the subject or left the impression that at least in the regions treated in this book (see Map 2) the Eskimos were remarkably unwarlike when compared with most other Native Americans. However, beginning in the 1960s Gubser (1965), Burch (1974, 1998), Fienup-Riordan (1994), Bandi (1995), and Sheehan (1995) have revised our thinking concerning both the prevalence of late aboriginal and early historic war in Eskimo north Alaska and the idea that these people were pacifists. Paneak's war stories support the scholarship reflected collectively in the papers cited above.

Within a given north Alaska Eskimo band or tribe, murders, including deadly grudge fights, were resolved according to legal precedent (see Pospisil 1964). On the other hand, occasional intertribal killings of individuals—especially, it would seem, killings between Eskimos and Indians—were far less amenable to settlement, and carried with them the probability of continuing conflict. Both these sorts of incidental intertribal murders, and battles that qualify as actual war, are described below, the latter consisting of episodes in which an in-strength enclave of armed men essayed to slaughter as many of another populous or relatively populous assemblage as they could manage. Battles were planned, tactics were practiced in mock combat among friends (see War Games, below), and prisoners were taken only rarely.

In any given action (episode) the number of combatants and/or innocent bystanders involved varied from two or three dozen to perhaps one hundred individuals. Burch (1974:4), on the testimony of several north Alaska Eskimo informants, states that a war party numbered between ten and fifty men. Burch's informants' testimony supports the fact that in each action these figures were, of course, increased both by the size of the opposing military force—if there was one—and by the number of noncombatants.

As background, we begin Simon's accounts of armed conflict with a story of the mythic past involving foreign invaders; his remarks on old-time Nunamiut knives and arrowheads, including warheads; and his War Games, a Nunamiut equivalent of modern military mock combat.

Then, getting to the real thing, he relates an interconnected series of Eskimo-Indian encounters that begin and end with bloody massacres, but at the same time illuminate the sometimes most amicable of relations between these two quite different peoples. This saga, which involves several human generations, is followed by Eskimo-Indian incidental confrontations, and Simon finishes his war stories with detailed accounts of hostilities between north Alaska Eskimo tribes.

In War Games, Simon implies that in his youth he witnessed examples of this military exercise (which by then had lost its military significance). We assume that his other stories of armed conflict or confrontation describe events that occurred no later than the early nineteenth century.

Foreign Invaders

Another thing in the early days according to the old story talking about it, in very old days, shortly after glacier growing in over Alaska … After it melts, My! Too many enemies, everywhere. They could only fight them off and kill them. I don't know where from … That might be people from Siberia crossing the Bering Strait. That is where the too many enemies who were in Alaska, who were in the northern part of the Brooks Range, but you can't believe it, or you can't believe them or not according to the story they were telling about. That sounds like to me, the old Eskimo story, some stories are true, some of them are very hard to believe … cause among the Eskimo, they never write a book they just go by the story.

Stone Knives and Warheads

This is very, very, long time ago … I don't know what kind of knife they might use it … it might be flint … flint or chert … they could not be knife like we have right now … might have been funny knife but they could use it. Also they use some of the jade, jade stone, they use it for these because much easier to make it, not like flint. Flint only had when the men know how and chipping them and cracking them and making them arrow and arrowhead.

They say that there is two kinds of arrowhead, they used to make in early days. One is for warhead, for fighting, arrowhead whatever you call it and another one for caribou and grizzly bears and all that. That is warheads, they say had a little hook on the arrow and that is like very hard to pull it back just like white man's fish hooks, maybe.

Foreign Invaders

According to a story from the very early days, shortly after the melting of the glacier that had grown over Alaska there were too many enemies everywhere, and they [the Eskimos] had to fight them off and kill them. I do not know where [the enemies] came from. They may have been people from Siberia, across the Bering Strait, but anyway there were too many enemies in Alaska, and in the northern part of the Brooks Range. You may or may not believe this story. It sounds to me like [other] old Eskimo stories, some of which are true, and others hard to believe. This is because they were not written in books, but were [passed down by word of mouth].

Stone Knives and Warheads

I do not know what kind of knife [the Nunamiut] used a very long time ago. It may have been of flint or chert, but it could not have been the kind of [steel] knife we have now. It may have been a funny [strange-looking] knife, but they knew how to use it. And they had some knives made of jade (from the Kobuk River; Map 2), because it was much easier than flint to work. They had flint tools only in the days when the men knew how to crack and chip the flint and make it into arrowheads. They say that in the early days [the Nunamiut] made two kinds of arrowheads: one for war, and one for caribou, grizzly bears, and other game. The warhead was of flint, and had little hooks at its base (see Campbell 1998a: pl. 37), so that it was hard to pull out; just like white man's fishhooks, maybe.

War Games

An among Nunamiut has practiced how to be soldier by playing with folded mitten and ball. – Mitten, put stone in it make weight or make faster and hit harder and when mitten or ball touch a man, are quit and last to man and lost the game on one group. And start another game again. And Nunamiut are training, of course, how to be soldier like white peoples who learning in army, among young boys. Perhap old or middle age man taught them.

To the older people, more playing makes stronger, and build up young peoples muscle and run better and jump

War Games

The Nunamiut used to practice combat by playing with [skin] mittens containing stone balls that made the mittens travel faster and hit harder (Figure 26). They chose sides, and when a mitten or stone touched a man on the opposing side, he had to quit. Then, when one side's last remaining member was hit, that group lost the game, and they started over again. This training was like that of white people when they teach their young boys to be soldiers. Perhaps, similarly, old or middle-aged men taught the Nunamiut boys.

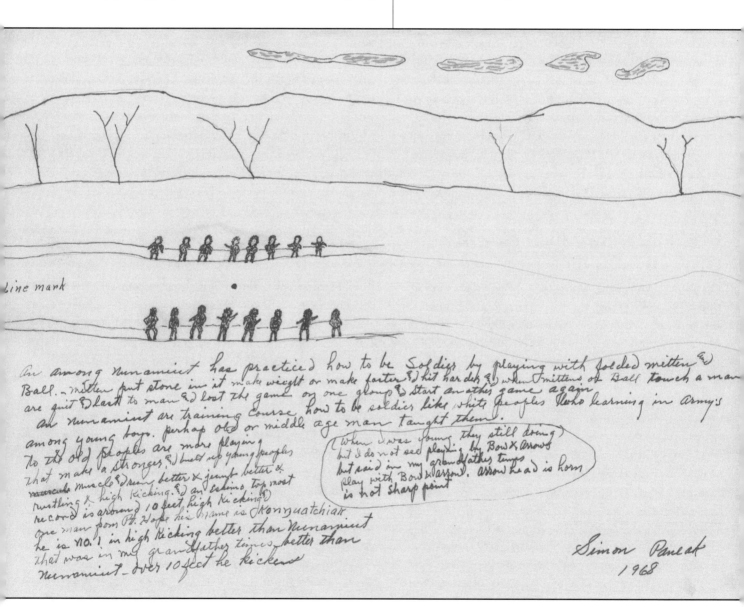

FIGURE 26   Paneak's illustration of war games.

better and wrestling and high kicking. When I was young, they still doing but I do not see playing by bow and arrows. But said in my grandfather times play with bow and arrow. Arrowhead is horn, is not sharp point. In my grandfather times one man from Point Hope is number 1 in high kicking – better than Nunamiut – over 10 feet he kicken.

The older people believed that more playing of this game; and running, jumping, wrestling, and high kicking, built up young people's muscles and made them stronger. When I was young the Nunamiut were still playing this game, but I never saw them using bows and arrows, with which it is said the game was played in my grandfather's time, although the arrowheads were of horn [antler], and without sharp points. In my grandfather's time a [Tareumiut] man from Point Hope (Map 2) was number one in high kicking. He was better than the Nunamiut, and could kick higher than ten feet.

Eskimos Against Indians

——

I was talking about old Indians who was raised over at head Noatak and Kobuk, just between there, nearby, you know where it is. According to story was talking about them, I don't know, we don't know or nobody, talking about how many years those Indians staying over in that area. This is a very, very long time ago but later on, somehow there was a mix up between Kobuk and the Indian because the Indians was jealous about the hunting grounds and Kobuk people can't stand without it too, because they want to hunt too, nearby.

And then there was kind of quarreling and they became enemies of each other. Finally they started to fight, killed one another and finally they began a big fighting and one at a time and then from generation to generation, they said that one time they almost kill all the Kobuk one group almost. Indians, there are too many in those too I believe … almost they kill them all off, the Kobuk people, but one fellow he was jumped off the fence and got away from that group, and Kobuk people had their fences … all around all their tents for during some time but too many Indians pulled them apart and found them, they were ready to fight with the bow and arrow they had bow and arrow already in that time.

And then one boy he jumped off the fence and he run away to get to another people from down below … and a bunch of Kobuk people going up to where the Indians are … they fought them off … Indians can't hardly stand it any longer and they beat it.

That is why they, I guess that not many men left they didn't want to stay where they used to live in that area and

Eskimos Against Indians

——

I am talking about old-time Indians who lived over between the heads of the Noatak and Kobuk rivers.[2] You [Campbell] know where it is. This was a very long time ago, and we don't know how many years those Indians lived in that area. Finally, there was a mixup between the Kobuk Eskimos and the Indians because the Indians were jealous of these hunting grounds, which the Kobuk people needed for the same purpose, and could not stand going without. So they quarreled, and became enemies of each other. Then finally, they began fighting and killing one another, and then there was big fighting, from generation to generation, until, it is said, one time the Indians killed nearly all of a Kobuk group [band]. There were too many Indians, and they almost killed all of the Kobuk people, but one Kovagmiut jumped over the fence [barricade, built of willows; Gubser 1965:44] and got away. In those days the Kobuk people had defensive fences all around their tents, but in this attack there were so many Indians that they pulled apart the fences and found and massacred the people, even though the Eskimos had bows and arrows, and were ready to fight.

But the one boy who had jumped over the fence ran and got more Kobuk Eskimos from down below [downriver]. So these Kobuk people went up to [the scene of slaughter] and fought off the Indians. The Indians were beaten so badly that they could not stand it any longer, and they left [leaving the disputed hunting grounds to the Kovagmiut].

After their loss to the Kobuk Eskimos there were not many men [Indians] left, I guess, and they no longer

over in upper Kobuk and Noatak in the mountain there. In these very old days, they love to stay in the rocks, they make rock house. My, seem to be a hard to cut the trees, they don't have an axe, an axe and saw, that's why they like to stay in the rocks during the summer time, Eskimo also like to make a stone house too, according to story they were telling, but natives they love it very much.

And Indians moving from there to the northern Brooks Range near Howard Pass, over there where the Eskimo and Nunamuit live too and stayed over there for a long time and same thing. When the Indian grow up they become a unfriendly people and jealous on the ground.

And Eskimo don't like it that way, they could kill all the animals, as much as they could catch but Indians

wanted to live in that area of the upper Kobuk and Noatak or on the neighboring mountains. In those very old days the Indians loved to dwell in the rocks [talus slopes or bedrock outcrops], where they built rock houses (Figures 27 and 28). It must have been very hard for them to cut trees because they did not have axes or saws, and that is why they liked to stay in the rocks during summertime.[3] According to the old stories, Eskimos liked to make stone houses too, but the natives [Indians] loved them especially.

When the Indians were defeated on the Kobuk River they moved from there to the northern Brooks Range near Howard Pass [well north of the forest] where the Eskimos and Nunamiut lived too.[4] And the Indians stayed there for a long time and the same thing happened again. As the

FIGURE 27 Grant Spearman examining one of several peculiar stone structures discovered by Campbell in 1959 on a tall hogback ridge overlooking the treeless upper valley of the John River. They are of a kind that the mid-twentieth century Nunamiut associated usually with Indians, or "Little People," rather than their own antecedents (see Figures 18 and 28). Photograph by JMC, 1985.

FIGURE 28 William T. Stuart at one of several subterranean stone structures on a slope above the east side of Tuluak Lake. Although this example seems obviously to have been used as a meat cache (note the bones on its floor), older Nunamiut informants claimed that these features were not of Nunamiut origin. Photograph by JMC, 1961.

hasn't … Indian they love to take a limit because sounds like to me they are smart people they don't want to kill all the animals in that where they, whatever they used to live, they thought it might be, they might have animals next year for future.

And then they stayed together some time over there in upper Colville, and some young guys or women married or got the wives from Indian and some Indians got wives from Eskimo and during they stay together for so many years and they said anyway, so many years, you know how long … and then they became unfriendly each other … sneaking, sneaking on each other, kills man, one another and then finally they begin to fight.

And in the fall after they build moss house near the lake there, over in the map lake … I don't have, I never have a map right here and too slow for me to do writing and telling old story. And then can not stay right over there and moving over towards east, like over in Killik and Chandler Lake and Akvalutak place, staying there for so many years and probably here in Anaktuvuk too.

It is not too very far from now on, that is in my father, grandfather time, not too long ago, it is only a little couple hundred years ago. They had to fight and big fights as I call it at the mouth of Itikmalak, what you call it, Itikmalakpuk, about five miles north of Tuluak, the mouth is where Indian lost war in that time to Eskimo. Somehow these old Eskimo are too smart, they hold them or somehow fight them off. They did wound two guys I hear, but both of them healed up, lived. Among the Indian lose over twenty or more, a lot of them, never mentioned how many cause there is no time to count them. Shortly after the fighting then Indian never bothered from that time on the northern slope. And afterwards they learn the Indian move over to the Chandalar area, no Eskimo can follow them.

Indians stayed longer they became an unfriendly people, and jealous of the hunting ground.

The Eskimos did not like the ways the Indians hunted because the Eskimos killed all the animals they could catch, while the Indians did not. The Indians liked to limit their killing because it sounds to me that they were smart people, who, wherever they lived, did not want to kill too many animals, so that they might have some for future years.[5]

The Indians and Eskimos stayed together over there on the upper Colville, and some of the Eskimo guys or women married Indians, and some of the Indians got wives from the Eskimos, and it is said that they lived together for many years until they became unfriendly with each other (Figure 29). They sneaked up on each other, and killed one another, and finally began fighting. Then one fall, after the [Eskimos and Indians?] had built moss [winter] houses on that lake over there that the Eskimos call [? Lake]—I do not have a map right here, and it is too slow for me to write and tell the old stories at the same time. The Eskimos would not let them stay there, and they moved eastward to the Killik River, and to Chandler and Akvalutak lakes, where they stayed for so many years, and probably here in Anaktuvuk too [Akvalutak Lake is immediately north of Chandler Lake].

It was not too long ago, in my father's and grandfather's time, a couple of hundred years ago, that they [the Nunamiut] had to fight the Indians, and they had a big fight at the mouth of Itikmalakpuk (Itiġmalukpak) Creek about five miles north of Tuluak Lake (Map 3), and there at the mouth of the Itikmalakpuk is where the Indians lost their war with the Eskimos. Those old Eskimos were too smart for the Indians, fighting them without losing any of their own people. Two of the Nunamiut men were wounded but healed up and lived, while the Nunamiut

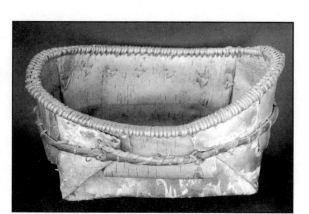

FIGURE 29 Nunamiut Eskimo–Koyukon Indian "borrowing" of native artifacts and techniques is illustrated by this elegant birchbark and willow basket designed for blueberry picking. Ten inches long, it is of typical Koyukon design but was made in the early 1940s by a Nunamiut woman whose family had taken up residence in Indian territory. Veree Crouder Collection. Photograph by JMC, 1998.

FIGURE 30 William Brown, National Park Service, and Grant Spearman, right, beside our exploratory 1961 excavation in the small hill that reputedly contains the bodies of Indians killed by the Nunamiut. The stone cairns were placed here by persons unknown following our 1961 expedition. Photograph by JMC, 1985.

I know over in Killik they had another fight, Indian lose about twenty people, twenty men. Eskimo lose six people, two or three women – four women and two men. Eskimo lose that much but Indian lose a lot of them.

In other words, according to story, way before Nunamiut fight Indians away from here. They probably get tired and scared and moving over to Chandalar area where Eskimo will never bother them anymore, but some groups, all the men, come back and try to attack the Eskimo several times but they never make it. They kill two persons all right when they coming back for fighting, they kill two Eskimos but they lost more than two. They probably got a few but they hide them somewhere and Eskimos never look for them and one came up to the Colville, the richest man among the Indians. And his name is Stacka, that is his name killed by one Eskimo.

Then some time later, in the winter time over in Killik, bunch of Indians together come to Killik they had fought some Eskimos and cause Eskimos never expect any more Indians come along in winter time and that is why Eskimo lost the one, and two fellows. Another place and another two, old fellow and two young fellows and young lady. And pretty soon Eskimo get tired of Indian and they only had to stay together, stay close together. They won't let people stay when people are living near the Indians cause Indians might kill them, some of the Eskimo, if there is not enough people.

killed more than twenty Indians; the precise number is unknown because there was no time to count them (Figure 30).[6] After that battle the Indians never returned to the northern [Arctic] Slope, and it was learned that they had moved to the Chandalar area where no Eskimos could follow them. [The Chandalar River and environs lie deep in Kutchin Athapaskan territory; see Map 1, and McKennan 1965.]

Then there was another big fight on the Killik River in which the Indians lost about twenty men, and the Eskimos [members of the Killikmiut band, presumably] lost four women and two men. The Eskimos lost that many, but the Indians lost a lot more. According to another story, long before (?) the Nunamiut drove the Indians from here [the Anaktuvuk Pass region], the Indians probably got tired and scared and moved over to the Chandalar area, where the Eskimos would not bother them any more. But some Indian groups of men went back to [Tuluak Lake] several times and tried to attack the Eskimos [Nunamiut], but they never overcame them. They killed two Eskimos all right, when they went back to fight, but they lost more than two of their own. The Nunamiut probably wounded a few more, but the wounded Indians hid somewhere, and the Eskimos never went looking for them. One of the Indians showed up on the Colville; he was the richest man among the Indians. His name was Stacha, and, he was killed, there on the Colville, by an Eskimo.

But Indians try to bust the sod house over in Killik and young fellow he kill thirteen or fourteen Indians when the Indians try to bust up the house. According to old timer, in the fall they used to ice up the house with the sod or gravel and mix it with the willows, little willows of course, over on the outside of the sod or moss. They put some gravel and willows and snow and then put the water on top of it to make an ice, let it freeze so the enemy coming in should not bust the house easily. That is why Indians lost a lot of men in that time in one house.

And another time, Indians come again, the men only for fighting and he was getting skinny and almost starving and they was skinny almost starved. They could not find any more Eskimos in that area and then finally, they almost starve. And then Eskimo found the men on way to go out to the Colville, late in spring sometimes in April. They told them not to come again anymore. If they want to come back to fight a later time, they could kill all them off right now. They told them like that and could have killed all of them Indians that time if they wanted but they says that they don't want to kill them anymore but they tell them like that, not come back again, if they are starving again, they kill all off so Indians never come back.

The Eskimo living over near where Indians are near Chandalar River, over near Arctic Village at present and over in the east of Arctic Village, over in Coleen, which is near porcupine country, Porcupine River and Sucker River over there; the Eskimos met there with all the Indians that were there. And nobody want to fight anymore because missionaries been around over in the Fort Yukon area by that time and so they are pretty nice to each other at that time.

One winter over on the Killik River, a bunch of Indians killed one or two Eskimos because the Eskimos never expected an Indian attack in the dead of winter. In those days the Eskimos became afraid of the Indians and began staying close together in groups, because if there were not enough Eskimos the Indians might kill them. I know of another fight over on the Killik River, when the Indians tried to bust up an [Eskimo] sod house,[7] but a young fellow [an Eskimo, again presumably of the Killikmiut band] killed thirteen or fourteen Indians when they tried to break into the house. An old-timer Eskimo once told me that in the fall the Eskimos used to ice up the outside of their sod or moss houses with sod or gravel, small willows, and snow. They would pour water on this mixture, and when it froze it provided protection from enemies. This is why on the above occasion the Indians lost a lot of men.

This same old Eskimo told me that the Indians came another time to fight, but that he, the old Eskimo, was skinny and almost starving, and so were the Indians. The Indians could not find other Eskimos to rob in that area [probably the Killik River region], and the Indians almost starved too. Then sometime in April, when the Eskimos were traveling out north to the Colville River, they found the Indian men and told them not to come back again. They told the Indians that if they had intentions of returning later to fight the Eskimos, the Eskimos would kill all of them right now. They told them just like that, and they could in fact have killed the Indians then and there if they had wanted to. They said that while they did not want to kill Indians any more, if the Indians were starving and came back again the Eskimos would kill them all. So the Indians never came back.

The Eskimos living over near [Kutchin] Indian territory—near the Chandalar River, Arctic Village, and east of Arctic Village near the Porcupine and Sucker River country [Map 2; Sucker River is a Porcupine tributary]—met with all the Indians who were there, and the two sides agreed that no one wanted to fight any more. This was because by that time missionaries had come to the Yukon River area and had persuaded the Indians and Eskimos to be nice to each other.

Eskimo Against Eskimo

They had a big fight near the mouth of the Colville. I believe I had marked it on the map in your book. I don't know for sure, but I thought, but I will mark it and I will write the name of the place where they had the big fight down there. Nunamiut fought with the Point Barrow coast people. Like both side lost a lot of good many men but the inland people win it all right. But they lost a lot of men too.

Another thing, another big fight over near Kotzebue, called Sheshalik, just east of Kotzebue Village. Of course, it is across the channel, I mean the bay, whatever you call it, bay. I could see the land above the Sheshalik place from Kotzebue. Not very far, about around ten miles I guess, I would say anyway, about that.

Another big place for fighting … they had a fight with the Pt. Hope people and they said that Pt. Hope lost their war with the Noatagmiut. Some other time they were talking about the big fight over in Pt. Hope too. They had the same groups from different places and went down to Pt. Hope. But the Pt. Hope people, they make some bone stakes on the ground. And the enemy never know where about they had put sticking up bones and ready to break when fellows were stepping on the bone. That way the Pt. Hope people is always winning the fight.

But outside of the Pt. Hope, the Point Hope groups lost a war a couple of times. I guess one was near the mouth of the Colville. And Pt. Hope groups, they coming up that time by the line. And Pt. Barrow Eskimo stay over on the island just west of Colville right near what they call Saktuina, on the map. Pt. Hope groups who were in that point, no way to go down to island. They got no boats, they are waiting for the people going up to the island, but they couldn't. Finally the group is starving, starving to death, that is bad business for them.

Eskimos Against Eskimos

The Nunamiut had a big fight near the mouth of the Colville. I believe I marked the place in your book [the sketchbook given to Paneak by Campbell; see Campbell 1998a: pl. 59). They fought the Pt. Barrow people, the Tareumiut, and both sides lost many men. The inland people, the Nunamiut, won it all right, but they sure lost a lot of men too.

There was another big fight, between Eskimo groups at Sheshalik (Sisualik), on Kotzebue Sound (Map 2). Sheshalik is just east across the channel, or bay, from Kotzebue village, and when I was visiting the region years ago I could see, from Kotzebue village, the land above Sheshalik at a distance of about ten miles, I guess.

Another big place for fighting was Point Hope, where, it was said, the Point Hope Eskimos [a Tareumiut band] lost their war with the Noatakmiut of the Noatak River. And there was another big fight at Point Hope, but that time the Point Hope people drove thin bone stakes into the ground. The enemy did not know where the stakes were hidden, and when stepped on they splintered. That way the Point Hope people won the fight.

But at other places, the Point Hope people lost a couple of wars, one of which, I guess, was near the mouth of the Colville River. That time, the Point Hope people came overland along the line [the mountain line, or the north front of the Brooks Range]. A group of Pt. Barrow [Tareumiut] Eskimos were camped on an island just west of the Colville near a mainland projection known as Saktuina (Saaktuiña) Point (Map 2). The Point Hope group occupied the point, but having come overland they had no boats with which to reach the island, and they waited in vain for the Pt. Barrow people to come to the mainland shore. Finally, because they could not get at the Pt. Barrow people's food, the Point Hope people were starving to death—a bad business for them.

Hunger

In these and neighboring regions native warfare ended effectively in the mid-nineteenth century. For example, the arrival of Anglican missionaries on the middle Yukon River in the early 1860s (Stuck 1920) resulted in a lasting truce between the Nunamiut and the Kutchin. But famine as a deadly scourge prevailed for one hundred more years. As late as 1958, anthropologists Elmer Harp, Jr., and Robert A. McKennan observed an Eskimo encampment in western Arctic Canada in which most of its members lay dead of starvation (see Campbell 1998a:31).

The following narrative contains Simon's eyewitness descriptions of the terrible starvation years of 1905–1907. That this story is told by a man who in 1905 was only five years old and who, in 1907, was short of his eighth birthday prompts us to wonder if, as Simon grew older, his recollections of those years were not annotated by his elders. But we should not jump to the conclusion that he did not personally remember most if not all of its events. Some of his testimony tells clearly of his own feelings of fear and hunger. And among the Nunamiut, as in all nonliterate societies, its members were taught from early childhood to learn and remember in detail the cultural and natural characteristics of their territory (for another Nunamiut example see Irving 1960:22–23).

Aside from its currency as a document of ultimate economic catastrophe, this story has value for what it says, specifically, about the Nunamiut subsistence round. Within the some 14,000 square miles in which the events occurred, Simon's family and others of his tribe traveled to particular localities in search of particular animals, localities known to generations of Nunamiut as harboring, usually in plenty or in abundance, this or that species of fish or mammal. In other words, even when quite literally the Nunamiut were on their last legs, they were not wandering randomly in search of something to eat, although for reasons unknown to them, and unanticipated, during those long months there was not nearly "enough to go around," as Simon would say.[8]

It is kind of difficult to remember all because it is quite a ways back. In 1905 I could remember in my memory 1905 as soon as I see the light, the kerosene light, my goodness, that is right. At that time, 1905 a lot of caribou in the spring. In May when we are down at Akmagolik and we stay alone. I don't know all of it, the people, a big bunch of people were going someplace, maybe a drying place. And my gosh, a lot of caribou, just like too many flock of geese or ducks. Then I and parents are drying up the meat too for summer supply of meat. And there just before break up over in Anaktuvuk River and cross over to the Tuluak Creek, we found father of May Kakinya and they had to stay for summer too instead of going down to Colville. And we stay alone. And we, my parents, they move around during the summer. Dog packing, we only had three dogs and I was walking little in the short time, but I couldn't keep up. I only had to ride on my father's back and then here we went over to Chandler Lake first. Then my father found quite a few marmot over there.

Marmot skin is very valuable to the Eskimo and all along the Arctic coast and sheep skin. On the sheep skin, he got a few, not much, I guess enough all right. But no caribou. All the time they were there they were expecting the caribou herd to come through from north or east, but there was no caribou all summer. And that time we live on

The Famine Years

It is difficult for me to remember all of it because it was quite a ways back. But I can remember 1905 in my memory because that is when I saw the kerosene light, my goodness, that is right (see Figure 24). At that time, 1905, there were a lot of spring caribou. In May we [Simon and his parents] were camped at Akmagolik (Agmaġulik) [an Anaktuvuk River tributary], and I remember a big bunch of people [Nunamiut] were going someplace, maybe to a caribou meat drying place. And my gosh, there were a lot of caribou at Akmagolik, as thick as many flocks of geese or ducks. My parents and I were drying caribou meat too, for our summer supply. Then, just before spring breakup of the Anaktuvuk River ice we crossed over to Tuluak Creek, near Tuluak Lake (Figure 31) where we found the father of May Kakinya, who with his family was staying for the summer too, instead of going down to the Colville River. But we camped and traveled separately, and we, my parents and I, moved around during the summer. Dog packing, we had only three dogs, and while, at the age of five, I could walk a little, I could not keep up, so I had to ride on my father's back. We traveled first to Chandler Lake, where my father found quite a few marmots.

Marmot and sheepskins were very valuable to Eskimos living along the Arctic Coast, and we got a few sheep-

FIGURE 31 Tuluak Lake, seen here as one looks east-northeast, figures as a prominent landmark and camping place in Simon's narratives, including his account of the starvation years of 1905–1907. Fed by large springs, it is four-fifths of a mile long, and to this day contains lake trout and other valuable native food fishes. Photograph by Stephen C. Porter, 1961.

sheep and fish, a lot of lake trout over in Chandler Lake there. A lot of marmots too and my mother know how to set a dead fall for marmot and my father too, they got quite a few marmot.

And in August, late August we went back to Chandler Lake. At a creek over there, it branches off the Willow Lake, about a few miles, we found May's parents. They are happy together in that time and then a couple of days doing some fishing in the stream above the lake. Pretty good fishing in one place about one or two miles above the lake in the river there. They also carry fish spear, got a lot of lake trout and greyling, enough to go around. Sometimes in the late September we had to come back to Tuluak Creek where our sled is. My father got one grizzly bear and then announced the word that there was another grizzly bear.

May's father and my father went after the bear and got it. And no caribou. They know how to make a living on the fish and the old fellow he make a fish trap over in the Tuluak Creek. Creek which is runs into the lake from the outlet off the Tuluak Lake and they got a lot of grayling and white fish down there. Enough to go around because they had a lot of meat there, from the spring meat, dried meat.

May Kakinya's father and us and we were waiting for travelers from the Colville that went down to meet the Point Barrow Eskimos, down in Niklik, cause we know that they will bring you flour or molassas and some other few items. When the travelers come up and my father and May's father bought some of what we need. And especially too our parents they love to have tobacco. Some families coming up, show up from the north, not very many, about five or six families. Taro family, Kayana family, Uguruk family, who else … let's see, I didn't say old Morey Map. That time he must have gone up to east by skin boat.

No, old Morey Maptigak is coming too. Six families and by gosh, we have a lot of fun, play together with the kids that time and then another bunch of our kids were coming up on the Colville. That was sometime in November and they spend around there for quite awhile, enjoy it together because of my parents and May's parents, they had a lot of dried meat, we keep it from spring supply and ling cod and white fish. And after the meeting is over we separate.

And my uncle, he is alone, his wife went by her parents, only my uncle alone coming up with us. I think he used two sleds that old guy, he is not old at that time. He is rich, a rich guy. Somebody, of course, helped him out,

skins, not many, I guess, but enough for trading. But that summer there were no caribou at Chandler Lake, even though we were expecting them to come through from the north or east. So we lived there on sheep and fish.[9] There were a lot of lake trout in Chandler Lake, and there were a lot of marmots around too. Both my mother and father knew how to set deadfalls for marmots, and they got quite a few of them.

In late August we went back to [this should read *from*] Chandler Lake to Willow Lake [Map 3, known in Nunamiut as Kanayyut Lake, and shown as Shainin Lake on modern maps]. (Except where noted all locations mentioned in this story are shown in Map 3.) And on a creek over there that flows into Willow Lake we found May's parents. At that time they were happy, living well, and for a couple of days they, and we, did some fishing in the stream above the lake. In that river there was pretty good fishing at one place a mile or two above the lake. They, May's parents, also had fish spears with which they got a lot of lake trout and grayling. Enough to go around. Sometime in late September we had to return to Tuluak Creek where we had left our sled. My father shot one grizzly bear, and then announced that he had seen another grizzly.

May's father and my father went after that bear and shot it, but still we had no caribou. They, May's parents, who knew how to survive by fishing, and the old fellow, her father, put a fish trap in Tuluak Creek, at the outlet of Tuluak Lake, and caught a lot of grayling and white-fish.[10] There was enough fish to go around because they had dried caribou meat too, that they had cached there after the spring hunt.

We, and May Kakinya's family, were waiting for Nunamiut travelers from the Colville River who had gone down to Niklik, in the Colville delta, to meet and trade with the Pt. Barrow Eskimos. We knew they would bring back flour or molasses and a few other items, and when the travelers arrived my father and May's father bought some of what we needed, and tobacco especially, because our parents loved tobacco. There were about five or six Nunamiut families who showed up from the north: the Taro (Taru) family, Kayana (Qaiyaana) family, Uguruk (Payauraq) family. Who else? Let's see, I didn't name old Morry Map (Figure 32). He must have gone on eastward along the Arctic Coast by skin boat.

No, old Morry Maptigak came too. There were six families, and by gosh, we had a lot of fun playing with

FIGURE 32   (Left) A mask of spruce wood and wolf and grizzly bear fur, made in the late 1950s by a Nunamiut man at Anaktuvuk Pass. Its facial details, including eyebrows and moustache, resemble closely those of Morry Maptigak, who the author met in the summer of 1956, and who, as an old man, died the following winter. Total height is fourteen inches. Photograph by JMC, 1998.

FIGURE 33   (Above) The summit of Anaktuvuk Pass, looking west-northwest, which today is occupied by the modern Nunamiut town of that name. For the past several thousand years this divide has served as a human and a big game route of passage through the Brooks Range, and as a place of habitation for numerous Eskimo and Indian peoples (see Campbell 1962). Here, in 1961, the Nunamiut camp of canvas tents and sod houses lies on the bend of Kayuk (Contact) Creek at mid-left. Photograph by Stephen C. Porter.

taking care of the other sled. And he had seven dogs. He come to us and stay with my parents when others separated. No caribou show up in that time. And my father got only one big old caribou in the fall and got a few mountain sheep down near Siksikpuk River. And then three families, we cross the Tuluak Lake over to Makaktuk and keep on going and make portage over to Chandler Lake.

And we spent around till January, I think. After that time we met Elijah's father, Puguruk. He came to us by walking and told us no caribou over in the south. And look like Anaktuvuk or Hunt Fork, he says that no caribou down there and had to come back down to north. And my parents and Puguruk, we traveled together and left May's parents. We left because May's father went out on the hills in the morning, and we traveled and keep on going following somebody's sled trail heading north and went down to near the mouth of the Anaktuvuk.

We stay there for several days. And our father and other older men, we know to scout, look around for caribou. And found some caribou, not very many over in Chandler River. All the men, they were walking across all the way over to Chandler River and they found a few over west of the Chandler River. They got a few, enough to go around, I guess. I don't know how many all the men got, quite a few I think, cause quite a few families and all the men came home with a little meat.

And my father and my uncle, they have a little meat on their back and soon after there was taking the rest of the one day. Then start to cross between the Anaktuvuk and Chandler River and into Chandler where they have to kill the caribou. And everybody, I don't know how long we settle down over there where they kill some caribou. I remember at that time that all the fishing hole, pretty poor. Not enough to go around for everybody that only got the fish by hooking, no open water at all, not even in spring. Water all frozen up, not many ptarmigan too. Not many ptarmigan that year, it makes a starvation winter.

And people starve all over in that area, over in Chandler River, and some of the families must have crossed the hills down to the Colville and find some more Caribou down there. And ourselves, my uncle and my father want to go up there on the Chandler River, and then my gosh, we found a big bunch of people over in the fishing hole, in Chandler River. Then we found my uncle's wife over there with her boy and my uncle's wife's mother and brother in that bunch.

the other kids. Then later, sometime in November, another bunch of kids [with their parents] came up from the Colville. We enjoyed their company, and they stayed around Tuluak Lake for quite a while because my parents and May's parents had a lot of dried caribou meat from the spring supply, and lingcod and whitefish. Then we separated.

My uncle, who was alone because his wife had gone to live with her parents, came along with us. I think the old guy, who was not old at that time, brought two sleds. He was rich, a rich guy, and had seven dogs, and of course someone else helped him by driving the other sled. He came with us, and stayed with my parents and me when the others separated. But no caribou showed up, and that fall my father got only one old caribou, and a few mountain sheep down near the Siksikpuk (Siksrikpak) River. Then three families of us crossed Tuluak Lake on the winter ice to (nearby) Makaktuk (Maġġaqtuuq) Lake, and kept on, making a portage overland to Chandler Lake.

I think we stayed in the vicinity of Chandler Lake until January. And after or during that time we met Elijah Kakinya's father, Puguruk. He came on foot, without dogsled, and told us that there were no caribou to the south. He had searched Anaktuvuk Pass (Figure 33) and as far south as Hunt Fork, and had then walked northward to Chandler Lake. Then my parents and I and Puguruk left May's family because May's father went out hunting on the hills one morning. We traveled north, following someone's sled trail down to the mouth of the Anaktuvuk, where we found other Nunamiut families.

We stayed there for several days while my father and other older men who knew how to scout went looking for caribou, and found some, not many, over on the Chandler River. The men walked, without taking their sleds and sled dogs,[11] all the way over to the Chandler, and found a few caribou not far west of that river. They got a few, enough to go around I guess. I don't know how many, but quite a few I think, because we were quite a few families, and all the men came home with a little meat [leaving the rest of the meat where they had shot and butchered the animals].[12]

And my father and my uncle had a little meat on their backs, and we rested for one day. Then we crossed by dogsled from the Anaktuvuk River to the place not far west of the Chandler River where they had killed and left the butchered caribou. We settled there, and ate caribou

Those people stayed together over in the Chandler River fishing hole. I guess they were doing fine in fishing because they could set their fish net, all net, over in the hole and go driving the fish into the net from both sides. A lot of suckers over there and white fish and grayling and some few arctic char. And they said some others were up in second fishing hole and we keep on moving up and we left my uncle's wife in that time, I guess he never tried to get back his wife.

At the second fishing hole we met Frank Rulland's family. Frank Rulland, he is not too big in that time too, he was just a boy, kind of a little bigger than I was. While we staying in that place, my uncle disappeared. He was walking towards the mountain, I don't know how long by snow shoeing. He don't carry sleeping bag, just one blanket that is all, because he has clothes with the caribou skin. He don't need sleeping bag. And then after that several days, my uncle came home and carried some marrow to me. Some meat.

And he says that he has got around twenty caribou up there near Castle Mountain, north of Chandler Lake. And we, my parents and my uncle started to where my uncle got some caribou up here, no worrying about starvation, I guess, after we reach my uncle's meat cache over in the Castle Mountains. A few caribou we got when we get up there. My father and uncle said that he has got enough to go around. Then sometimes in the last part of April, we go across over to Anaktuvuk because my uncle and my parents had left some skins or my uncle's stuff over in Anaktuvuk River, near Rooftop Ridge.

And then we got pretty tired after the pulling heavy sled. We only have, let's see, we have ten dogs, my uncle had seven and my parents had only three. And then my father walked up and looked for animals that were on a Rooftop Ridge and my uncle walked up river. And my uncle found May Kakinya's father and the old man, the grandfather of May Kakinya, both are dead. Already starving, already starving to death. And my uncle had come home and bring the bad news. He said that Changiuk they taught of me and the grandfather of May Ayunupuk and it was lying in a skin tent, *itchalik*.

Then after, in a few days someone come and see us, visiting us from down below and they says over in another river old lady and man starving, starve to death over there too. Starving to death, that was four people died in 1906 probably, nearly anyway.

for I don't know how long. I do remember that all of the fishing holes on that part of the Chandler River were pretty poor. There were not enough fish to go around for everybody. There was no open water at all, not even in the river's warmer springs, and the only fish caught were got by hooking through holes cut in the ice (see Campbell 1998a: pls. 28, 31). The water was all frozen up, and that year there were not many ptarmigan either. It made for a starvation winter.

And people [Nunamiut] starved all over in that Chandler River area. Some of the families crossed the hills down to the Colville, and found [or hoped to find?] some more caribou. And ourselves, including my uncle, decided to go farther up the Chandler River, and my gosh we found a big bunch of people [Nunamiut] at a well-known fishing hole in the river. Among the people at that fishing hole we found my uncle's wife with her boy, and my uncle's wife's mother and brother, all staying together.

I guess they were doing fine in their fishing because they could set their net across the hole under the ice, then drive the fish into the net from both sides (see Campbell 1998a: pl. 30). There were a lot of suckers in that hole, together with whitefish and grayling and a few arctic char. They told us that there were other Nunamiut up at the second fishing hole, so we moved up there, leaving behind my uncle's wife, and I guess he never tried to get her back. At the second fishing hole we met Frank Rulland and his family. He was just a boy, a little older than I. While we were at that place, my uncle disappeared. He went on snowshoes toward the mountains and did not carry a sleeping bag, just one blanket, because his clothes were of caribou skins. Then after several days he came back carrying some marrow, and some meat for me.

And he told us that he had got about twenty caribou up near Castle Mountain, north of Chandler Lake. And we, my parents and my uncle and I, started off for where my uncle had shot the caribou, and once we reached the cache of caribou meat in the Castle Mountains, I guess we no longer worried about starvation. [The two men] killed a few more caribou when we arrived there, and my father and my uncle said that they had then enough to go around among themselves and other Nunamiut families at the second fishing hole. Then, in the last part of April we traveled by dogsled back to the Anaktuvuk River because my uncle and my parents had left some skins or my uncle's stuff on the Anaktuvuk near Rooftop Ridge.

Then my father and mother do not like to go down to the Colville, they want to stay up in the mountains. So my father helped my uncle down, maybe one or two days helping him down. My father came home with one pack. And after my father came home, we starve on Anaktuvuk River. And we came to Depot Mound and found a skin tent and my father opened the bear skin door and I saw two guys lying just like asleep. Those are dead men. And then we passed and we keep on going.

And it was kind of pretty warm weather in that time, water was running already and way up. When we moving, pretty soon we meet the little dog team, on the river and they came to us and that was May Kakinya and her mother. They were starting for Colville, they had two dogs. And then my father wanted them to come back and stay with him for the summer because it was pretty late to be going down to Colville, almost break up the river and no way to go down to the mouth of Anaktuvuk River and Colville where the people are. Then when we got up to near Tuluak, we found more kids and one young lady ready to marry. That was Tukuk, the wife of old man Hugo, and another the wife of Jessie Ahgook and their brother. Then we come together and hunt the ground squirrels because there is a lot of ground squirrels over near Tuluak. And then we have enough food and then we went over to the Chandler Lake with the three kids. And then May's mother and May are separating from us and my father was telling them not to separate and but then, they don't mind I guess and go anyway.

And then we went to Chandler Lake by walking but then at that time I was riding on my father's back. Early in the morning I could walk all right but in the afternoon when I get tired I can't keep up with the grown up people. And when we get there, by gosh, tents right in the outlet of Chandler Lake. That was Elijah and his sister and mother. I got a lot of lake trout, and drying up some lake trout. Caribou, nowhere and my father got one mountain sheep, but it is pretty skinny, no fat at all, just like nothing, even very hard to cook.

My parents, Hugo's wife, and the wife of Jessie Ahgook, she is not grown full in that time but she is kind of big enough to hook some lake trout and they were hooking them everyday because nothing else to find the animal. My father didn't want to hunt anymore mountain sheep before fattening up. They got a lot of lake trout over in Chandler Lake but sometimes in June my father and Puguruk, they got around fifteen sheep. I guess,

Then we got pretty tired from pulling the heavy sled. Let's see, between us we had only ten dogs; my uncle had seven, and my parents only three. Then my father hunted up on Rooftop Ridge, and my uncle walked up the Anaktuvuk River where he found May Kakinya's father and grandfather dead of starvation. When he came home with the bad news he said that he had found May's father Changiuk (Saaŋiaq), who had taught me, and her grandfather Ayunupuk (Ayauniqpak) lying dead in a skin tent, an *itchalik* [the traditional Nunamiut caribou-hide dwelling]. Then, in a few days someone came to see us, visiting from downriver, and said that an old lady and a man had starved to death on another river. So that meant that in 1906 four people had died of starvation.

My father and mother did not want to go down to the Colville River, they wanted to stay up in the mountains, but my uncle wanted to go to the Colville, so my father helped him down the Anaktuvuk River taking one or two days. When my father came home he had one pack [of food?], and after he came we starved on the Anaktuvuk River. We started traveling, and when we came to Depot Mound we found a skin tent. My father opened the bearskin door, and I saw two guys (probably Changiuk and Ayunupuk; see above) lying just as if they were asleep, but they were dead men, and we kept on going.

The weather was getting warm, water was running already, and we soon met a little dog team on the river ice driven by May Kakinya and her mother. They had two dogs and were starting for the Colville. But my father persuaded them to stay with us for the summer, because it was too late to be going down to the Colville. The Anaktuvuk River ice was about to break up, and that would leave no way for the two women and their sled to reach the confluence of the Anaktuvuk and the Colville [where they wanted to join other Eskimos]. Then we, and May and her mother, traveled on up the Anaktuvuk River, and near Tuluak Lake we found more kids, and one young lady ready to marry. That was Tukuk (Tukkayak), who became the wife of old man Hugo [born in 1880], and another woman, the wife of Jesse Ahgook, and their brother. Then we camped together and hunted ground squirrels (see Campbell 1998a: pl. 34), because there were a lot of them near Tuluak Lake. So then we had enough food, and we went over to Chandler Lake with the three kids just mentioned. Then May and her mother left us. My father tried to persuade them not to leave, but they went anyway.

sometimes in the last part of June. They say that the skin is not too bad all ready.

And found a lot of sheep over on the lake where the sheep is licking the mud. We went up there sometimes in July. My parents don't want to hunt anymore mountain sheep, they want to hunt marmot. We are coming down and when we come down to the Chandler Lake, over in the south end of Chandler Lake, somebody build a fire up over in the outlet. The outlet of Chandler Lake because they were expecting their parents who were going to get the supply at the Anaktuvuk mouth in Colville. They bought it from river people. We, my parents put up the signal, build a fire and a lot of smoke out of the fire.

And that is the rule of the old timers, that meaning for happy, happy to be together, smoke signal. And when the people came up, they were very slow moving and we thought it might be a load of caribou meat. And I look at it and with a telescope, the dogs is a very slow moving and I think it is two or three dogs. And finally they went down to meet the people and I would like to too but they says you will never make it. You better stay here they told me like that. But I sad, I was sad because it is no fun for me to stay like that alone outside my parent's tent.

But I couldn't help it, I am too little. I guess when they came to us, got here, their dogs were very skinny, almost starving to death too. Then we all start to make a lot of grayling over in the river above Chandler Lake. One pool over there, a lot of big lake trout in there. My father caught them, spear fish and hook too so he had to keep his pole that he can not reach with his fish spear, got a lot of lake trout in there too. So they don't move around much because marmot season is a little early and the fur is not quite so good for using.

While we stayed in that place, Puguruk and his son, Elijah Kakinya come down by walking and there is a lot more sheep up there, he says, and no use to staying here. And all living on the fish alone. My father caught two rams from nearby too. And rams are getting fat already when he catch it. And my father says we want to hunt marmot. So my parents started to walk over towards east along the mountain line.

My parents separating from Puguruk and Elijah sometimes in first part of July. And we went back to Tuluak area where our sled is, we leave it when the break up about five miles north of Tuluak Lake. And my parents pick up some more equipment, especially my father's reloading outfit before we moving over to Siksikpuk, where the

We walked to Chandler Lake, and part of the time I rode on my father's back. Early in the morning I could walk all right, but in the afternoon when I got tired I could not keep up with the grown people. And when we got there, by gosh there were skin tents right at the outlet of Chandler Lake, and the people were Elijah Kakinya and his sister and mother. We got a lot of lake trout, and dried some, but there were no caribou. My father got one sheep, but it was pretty skinny, no fat at all, and was even very hard to cook.

My parents and I, Hugo's wife, and the [future?] wife of Jesse Ahgook, who was not full grown at that time, but was big enough to hook lake trout, were hooking them every day because they could not find other animals. My father didn't want to hunt any more mountain sheep before they had fattened up. They got a lot of lake trout in Chandler Lake, but then in the last part of June, I guess, my father and Puguruk shot about fifteen sheep whose hides were in fairly good condition.

They found a lot of them at a place on Chandler Lake where the sheep were licking the mud [at a mineral or salt lick]. We went up there sometime in July (?; see above), but my parents didn't want to kill more sheep, they wanted to hunt marmots. When we were coming down to the south end of Chandler Lake we saw that some Nunamiut had a fire at its outlet, because they were expecting their parents, who had gone down to the mouth of the Anaktuvuk to get supplies of food. And when we saw their fire we built one too, that produced a lot of smoke.

That was the old rule, a smoke signal meant for "happy to be together" times. And when the people who were returning from the north came up, they were walking very slowly because, we thought, they might be carrying a load of caribou meat. And I looked at them with a telescope, and saw that they had only two or three dogs. Finally my people and the others who were waiting went down to meet them, and I wanted to go too, but my parents told me that I would never make it, and that I had better stay behind, although I asked to go along, and it was sad for me because it was no fun to stay like that, alone, outside my parents' tent. But I couldn't help it, I was too little, and I guess that when the travelers reached us their dogs were very skinny, almost starving to death too [together with their owners]. Then we all began catching a lot of grayling in the river that flows into the south end of Chandler Lake. One pool there held a lot of big lake trout too, and my father caught them with both fish spear and hook, for

sheep is licking much, which they call salt lick. Anyway my father caught some, and forty sheep, I think, at that time. And he also catch two old caribou in August over there and one grizzly. And then they, my parents, we move it down to Siksikpuk to get some more marmot.

Because my parents knew all the country pretty well in everywhere, over in the Brooks Range or in the north slope, that is where I learn how to move around from my parents. And up there we went back to our sled and over in Tuluak and waiting for the people who was coming up on Anaktuvuk River from Colville. And we waited until the last part of November sometimes but then nobody showed up and my parents didn't want to wait anymore and we started back to where all our dried meat is.

And then when we got there my parents and making caches and over in the rocks so the wolverines wouldn't touch it. And so we keep moving by dogsled and we move over there towards Chandler Lake outside of the mountain line. That was a very slow, because we only have four dogs. In the spring my uncle gives us one his dogs, don't want to carry so many dogs with him while he is alone, because his wife is not with him, and she stay with her parents.

Then we went over to Colville and we camped there and wolf pack going after us and my father shot one, one of the six wolves and after that my parents hooked some big trout, especially my mother. My father keep on hunting and look for mountain sheep, no caribou, not even one caribou in the fall. That is funny country without the caribou.

While we were staying over there, after my father caught some sheep, quite a few, enough to go around, we, my mother and I, we are alone. Because my sister is too young, she is infant which is coming out in spring. I went to meet my father, walking. My mother and I, we hear the sound of man walking on the snow and we went over to meet my father. Usually I meet my father when I know he is coming back from out of his hunting. But this man I can't recognize. Big tall fellow, young fellow too, and I keep on and ask him, who are you? I am, I am me, he said, and he laugh at me, he never call his name is.

And then I was in front of him and he can't go around me at all. He was laughing so I ask him, keep on asking, how is his name. I want to tell my mother before that guy reach our tent.

And my mother hear our noise and she walked down to see us. And my mother was saying that he was old Morry Map. First time I met old Morry at that time. My mother recognized him because he was over here in Brooks

those he could not reach with his fish spear, and he got a lot of lake trout. So we did not move around much because the season was a little early for good marmot skins.

While we were staying at that place, Puguruk and his son Elijah Kakinya came walking in and said there were a lot of sheep up on the Siksikpuk River, and that there was no point in our staying where we were, and living on fish alone. So we left that place, and my father shot two white sheep rams nearby that were getting fat already. Then my father said that he wanted to hunt marmots, so my parents and I started walking eastward along the foot of the mountain line [in the direction of the Anaktuvuk River and Tuluak Lake].

We separated from Puguruk and Elijah in the first part of July [?], when we went back to the Tuluak Lake area and the place where at spring breakup of the river ice we had cached our sled. This was about five miles north of Tuluak Lake, and at that same place my parents retrieved other cached equipment, especially my father's rifle cartridge reloading outfit. Then we moved to the vicinity of a salt lick on the Siksikpuk, where over a span of several weeks my father shot about forty sheep, and where, in August, he shot two old caribou and one grizzly. From there we moved camp down the Siksikpuk.

This was to get more marmots in places where my parents knew we would find them. My parents knew pretty well all of that Brooks Range and Arctic Slope country, and that is how I learned about it, from my parents. From the Siksikpuk we went back to our cached sled near Tuluak Lake, and waited there for the Nunamiut who were supposed to be coming up the Anaktuvuk from the Colville. And we waited until the last part of November, but no one showed up, and my parents didn't want to wait any more, so we started back to where we had left all of our dried sheep meat on the Siksikpuk. When we got there my parents put the meat in [rock] caches so the wolverines would not get it, and then we kept moving by dogsled along the foot of the mountain line toward Chandler Lake. That was slow going because we only had four dogs. That spring my uncle had given us one of his dogs because he did not want to care for extra dogs now that he was alone because his wife had left him to live with her parents.

Then we went over to the Colville River and camped there, and a pack of six wolves came after us, and my father shot one.[13] After that my parents, especially my mother, hooked some big trout. My father kept on hunting, looking

Range before, before they went to near Barter Island with another Eskimo family, but old Morry stayed with his wife's father, Ikaksuk. Then old Morry stayed in late in the night and told us all about the news, Eskimo families and my uncle and his wife is stayed at Tuluak Lake to do some fishing, and towards morning he start to walk back to his family near Okokmilaga.

Then quite a few families went over to the John River and look for caribou, but there is no caribou there. Then we, my parents, go back to where they have dried meat, hide it over near a creek, not over in our camping place. And people was looking for our cache, but they couldn't find, because everybody was hungry. Big starvation is. And I don't remember, not very many ptarmigan either, all fishing is very poor and there is a very big starvation again in the second starvation.

And we went over to there to my uncle who stayed at Tuluak Lake and they have lost all the dogs, pretty near. Only two of them left. And then we went down to Anaktuvuk River to where my uncle left some whale oil, some flour, and some sugar and some molasses and some rice and some mush. We went down and with two whole sled loads of skins my parents had during the summer. My father bought some stuff cause my uncle has a lot, enough to go around for extra to sell. And got a lot of reloading for black powder, rifle in that time.

We went on and found May and her mother, Panuluk, and young guy taking care of his step-sister. And they do some fishing down there and got a little fish and sometimes enough to go around, have a supper. And further out along near Rooftop Ridge down at that, where the fishing pools are, they have to look for ptarmigan down there. And setting a lot of snares and my father had a lot of shells for old Winchester .44 caliber. He has reloading outfit and makes his own bullets for the gun and we shoot a lot of ptarmigan, enough to go around. And we had arrows a little, from my uncle.

And we also have our little sheep fat what left over from my parents taking us through the summer. And then my uncle was going down to Anaktuvuk mouth and to use a skin boat. He only have two dogs and my parents finally help him to get down to Colville. And when we went down my uncle had fifty pound sacks in the pack of flour. And 250 pounds in the brown sugar, I like it in the time like candy. And we are all right.

A big bunch of them had to camp the same place. And quite a few of them and pretty soon we hear of three more

for sheep, but in that region there were no caribou, not a single one that fall. It was a funny region, without caribou. While we were staying there, and after my father had killed quite a few sheep, enough to go around, my mother and I were left alone while my father went hunting because my sister was too young, she was an infant who had been born that spring. My mother and I heard the sound of a man walking on the snow, and I walked out to meet my father. Usually, I went to meet him when I knew he was coming back from hunting, but I did not recognize this man. He was a big, tall fellow, young too, and I asked him, "Who are you?" But he laughed at me, and said, "I am me"; he would not tell me his name, and then I was in front of him, and I would not let him go around me. He was laughing, and I kept asking him his name, because I wanted to tell my mother who he was before that guy reached our tent.

My mother heard our noise and walked out to us, and she said that he was old Morry Map (Maptigak) and that was the first time I met him. My mother recognized him because he, who was a Nunamiut, had lived in the Brooks Range until his family, together with another Nunamiut family, had moved out to the Arctic Coast to live near Barter Island (Map 2), but old Morry stayed with his wife's father, Ikaksuk (Ikaaqsaq). He stayed with us most of that night and told us all the news about the Eskimo families on the coast, and about my uncle and his estranged wife (see above), now staying at Tuluak Lake to do some fishing, and then towards morning he started walking back to his family on the Okokmilaga River. Then quite a few Nunamiut families went over [south of the Arctic Divide] to the John River, but they found no caribou there. My parents meanwhile had dried sheep meat, but they hid it on a creek, not at our camping place, because everybody was hungry, and people went looking for our meat cache but couldn't find it. It was a big starvation time, and while I don't remember the details, there were not many ptarmigan either. All fishing was poor, and there was a second big starvation among the Nunamiut.

And then we went over to Tuluak Lake, where my uncle was staying, and they, my uncle and others, had lost nearly all of their dogs [that had either run away or had been eaten by the starving Nunamiut]. Only two of them were left. Then we went down the Anaktuvuk River to a place where my uncle had left some whale oil, flour, sugar, molasses, rice, and mush [oatmeal or cornmeal], and we took two whole sled loads of marmot and white sheep-

person starving to death over in Chandler River, over in the fishing hole. And one old lady, my uncle's wife's mother and brother and my uncle's wife's father, stepson, them, are died from hunger. After two years seven people starving. And we moved around by the Anaktuvuk mouth with Arctic John's parents. No caribou up that way. And my father and Arctic John's stepfather walk quite a ways up, all the way up to the Rooftop Ridge. And no caribou. And they went back to us and we started moving by dog pack over northwest of Anaktuvuk mouth. And that is where they found a few calf.

And Arctic John's stepfather, he got five caribou that time, my father got nothing. And then we went up the river and I remember we saw only one caribou track. And all a bunch of people there together and surveying at the same time. And after they travel three or four days they had to take a rest. And especially the dogs they got to take a rest, work hard, and you have got to let them take a rest one day or two days. And the men, way up in the hills, with powerful telescope, I don't think they see any, and absolutely no caribou.

And finally when we come close to the mountains over Ulo Pass, Ulo Valley, people was disappear. I don't know where they went. And one family and us together and we went to Ulo Lake. And especially my mother and other woman and boy and I, we get nothing. No ptarmigan, maybe a few ptarmigan, but we was too young yet. And my father and the men and Utakuruk, uncle of Arctic John, they were up in the mountains somewhere looking for sheep. But they got nothing, no sheep too. So my parents started back to the other side of the mountain line. When we come to Galbraith Lake, we stay there one day and my father looking around for sheep but didn't find nothing. The next day we start up the streams of the Galbraith, outlet streams, the area of Natravak, that meaning lots of lakes. Then when we pass all the mountains, there, I guess all day long and found a bunch of family over in the south valley, and we went up river and down to Savoiyuk River, on south of Anaktuvuk, of course. Then people were doing some fishing and hooking and set a gill net and get a few fish, but not enough to go around. And then three or four families started down that way, follow the river and my parents went too and the Kayana family, Kakruk family and Puguruk and old Morry and mother and wife's father, old fellow Ikaksuk. Then one day we went on the side of the mountain and all the men went away to somewhere by snow shoeing. And all the men was

skins that my parents had got that summer. My father traded my uncle for some of his stuff, including a lot of black powder for his rifle, because my uncle had enough for himself, and for trading. We traveled on, and found May and her mother Panuluk, and a young guy who was taking care of his stepsister [May?]. They were catching fish down there and sometimes got enough to go around for supper. And farther on, near Rooftop Ridge, down where the fishing pools are, they, and we, looked for ptarmigan. They had a lot of ptarmigan snares [of sinew], and my father had a lot of shells for his old Winchester .44-caliber rifle. He had a reloading outfit, and we shot a lot of ptarmigan, enough to go around. And we had arrows from my uncle.

We also had a little sheep fat left over from what my parents had got to take us through the summer. Then my uncle was going down to the Colville River at the mouth of the Anaktuvuk to get his skin boat, *umiak*, that he had cached there. He had only two dogs for carrying his goods, and my parents finally helped him get down to the Colville. And when we went down with him my uncle got fifty pounds of flour, and two hundred and fifty pounds of brown sugar, which to me was like candy. And we were all right.

A big bunch of other Eskimos were camping at the same place on the Colville, and they told us that three more Nunamiut had starved to death on the Chandler River at the fishing hole [described above]. They were one old lady who was my uncle's wife's mother, and her brother, and my uncle's wife's father's stepson, so in two years seven people had starved to death. Then we moved back to the mouth of the Anaktuvuk with Arctic John's parents [Arctic John, a Nunamiut, was born in 1895; Grant Spearman, personal communication], but we found no caribou up that way. And my father and Arctic John's stepfather walked all the way up the Anaktuvuk River to Rooftop Ridge without finding caribou. And they came back to us and we started walking with our pack dogs northwestward from the mouth of the Anaktuvuk. And that is where we found a few caribou calves.

And Arctic John's stepfather got five caribou there, but my father got nothing. Then we went back up the Anaktuvuk River, and I remember that we saw only one caribou track, and we found a bunch of Nunamiut Eskimos surveying [hunting] at the same time. And after having traveled three or four days they and we, and especially the dogs, had to rest. The dogs had worked

FIGURE 34   Lunch in the uplands between Anaktuvuk Pass and the Savioyok River valley. Note the brisk small fire of dead spruce twigs under the coffee pot that is hung on a cantilevered pole. Photograph by Robert L. Rausch, 1968.

scouting around the country looking for caribou or sheep. And they went down and return home and it was empty, they were very tired. They went back up that way for several days without the sleeping bag, scouting the country, but it was no caribou in that time no place. And no fishing much, only May Kakinya's mother and my mother they catch only one or two or maybe three, not big size too, while my father and men, they look for animal up in the hills somewhere. But they find nothing and we start again down, down the Itkillik River.

When we come close to Anaktuvuk mouth they said there must be caribou and that night we hear a wolf howling. And they said, that it might be caribou around. And they was happy. Then they wake up early in the morning and they eat together over in skin tent or hut, *itchalik*. They eat together, a little. We are very low on flour and some other things and not very much meat either. When there is day light, still dark . . . They went out and they saw some caribou, but before they come close to it, two wolves, scare them away.

hard, and you have to let them rest for a day or two. The men went hunting way up in the hills, with a powerful telescope [a ship's spyglass; see Chapter 2, note 4], but I don't think they saw game, and they found absolutely no caribou.

We and another family went on north to Ulo (Ulu; Itkillik) Lake, where my mother and the other woman and her boy and I got nothing. There were no ptarmigan, or maybe a few, but we were too young yet to snare or shoot them. And my father and the men or man and Utakuruk (Utaqsiruaq), Arctic John's uncle, were up in the mountains somewhere, looking for sheep, but they got nothing.

Then we crossed the ridge that separates the Itkillik Valley from streams feeding Galbraith Lake, and when we came to Galbraith Lake we stayed there one day, and my father looked for sheep, but did not find any. The next day we started up the lake's outlet stream [actually its inlet stream], a locality named Natravak (Narvavak), which means "many lakes." We were traveling south now,

FIGURE 35   Simon at Tuluak Lake in Nunamiut winter clothing made of caribou skins. Each suit is tailored precisely to the wearer's measurements (see Campbell 1998: pls. 12, 13). Behind him is a rack of thirty-seven wolf skins, and in the background is a pair of snowshoes whose style was most probably borrowed centuries ago from neighboring Athapaskan Indians. Rasmuson Library, University of Alaska, Fairbanks. Photograph by Laurence Irving, 1952.

And they only got two caribou, and they only little bunch that they could find in this area. And then that is two caribou is lots to have, but it will never last long. But anyway, can't help it. And my parents they keep on going while they have a little meat for on the way. And we camped over to one of the lake between the Anaktuvuk mouth and Itkillik and there is a lot of willows in that lake. What they call it the dry lake. And my father went on to our skin boat which we left in the fall and they also have a cache, meat cache in the ground.

And left some meat and fish and maybe a little bit of flour and some other things, over in our skin boats, which is racked up in the willows. And then we almost run out of everything at that time. I was very tired to wait for my father, very hungry for something to eat. And he is not very far but my thought is that he did not come home early enough. And finally he came home in the night and after it get dark and he brought some fish, frozen fish and flour and some other things and the molasses I kind of like very much.

east of the Itkillik River valley. I guess that took us all day long, and then we crossed over into the south part of the Itkillik Valley where we found a bunch of Nunamiut families. From there we traveled up the Itkillik, crossing the Arctic Divide and on down to the Savioyak (Saviuyuk) River, which is south of Anaktuvuk Pass of course (Figure 34). The people were fishing there, both with hooks and a gill net, and they had caught a few fish, but not enough to go around. Then three or four families started down that way, following the Tinayguk (Tinaiyuk) River, and my family went too, together with the Kayano (Qaiyaana) and Kagruk (Qaġrug) families, and old Morry Maptigak and his [father and] mother, and his wife's father, the old fellow Ikaksuk. Then one day we camped on the side of a mountain, while all of the men went hunting somewhere on snowshoes. They were scouting the country, looking for caribou or sheep, and when they returned home they had nothing and were very tired. They went back up that way for several days, without sleeping bags [sleeping in their caribou skin clothing; Figure 35], scouting the country, but there were no caribou in that time or place, and very little fish either. Only May Kakinya's mother and my mother caught one or two, or maybe three, not very big fish while my father and the other men were looking for game somewhere up in the hills. But they found nothing, and we started back again down the Itkillik River.

And when we came close to the Anaktuvuk mouth we heard a wolf howling at night and the older people said that might mean there were caribou around, and we all were happy. We woke up early the next morning and ate together in a skin tent, an *itchalik*, but had little to eat because we were very low on flour, and some other things, and had not very much meat either. We were now on the hills right up from the Itkillik River, and the hunters started out before daylight, and found some caribou, but before they could get close to them they saw two wolves scare them away.

They got only two caribou from that little bunch, the only caribou they could find. And those two caribou were all that we had, and they would not last long, but anyway, we couldn't help it. Then we kept on going while we still had a little meat for along the way. We camped on one of the lakes between the Anaktuvuk mouth and the Itkillik, and there were a lot of willows on that lake, known to the Nunamiut as the Dry Lake. Then my father went on to our skin boat that we had left behind in the fall, and where we also had a meat cache in the ground.

We had left some meat and fish in the cache,[14] and a little bit of flour and some other things in our skin boat that was up on a willow pole rack in the willows. And while my father was gone to the boat and the meat cache we almost ran out of everything. While I waited for my father I was very hungry for something to eat. I knew that he was not very far away, but I thought he would not come home early enough. Then he came home in the night, after dark, and he brought some frozen fish, and flour, and some other things, and the molasses that I liked so very much.

THE LAST OF THE OLD DAYS

Because of the ravages of white man's diseases, the enticements of his modern northern settlements, and the money to be made in trapping the coastal-dwelling arctic fox, by 1920 the Nunamiut had abandoned their traditional territory, some of them moving as far inland as Fairbanks, but most of them settling in scattered camps along the Arctic Coast.[1] Then in 1938 and 1939, with the decline of the fur trade, and longing for home, these surviving members of the old Nunamiut tribe returned to their ancient camping grounds in the headwater valleys of the Chandler and Killik Rivers, getting there from the coast by tracking their *umiat* up the lower reaches of the Colville River (see Campbell 1998a: pl. 58), then walking and sledding southward up the Arctic Slope. There were thirteen families, whose members ranged in age from infants to men and women in their sixties, and for six years, until they were visited in 1945 by a U.S. Geological Survey party led by George Gryc (Metzger 1983), they remained isolated and nearly unknown to the outside world.

This return to the wilderness required putting into practice many of the old artifacts and techniques of survival, among the more prominent of which were year-round or winter dwellings of caribou hides or sphagnum moss, and winter clothing of hides and furs. Others, to name a few, included big game drives, snowshoes, traditional fishing tackle, sheep horn ladles, bow drills, and, in one memorable instance related here, skin boats.[2] Nevertheless, while in theory these families might have survived by abandoning all civilized accoutrements and adopting in its entirety their traditional inventory of tools and techniques, in reality this was practically impossible.

Mainly because of the fur trade, the Nunamiut had long since acquired modern rifles and ammunition together with steel knives and other cutting tools, steel sled runners, spyglasses, metal pots and pans, and other Western items that to one degree or another they could hardly do without (see Chapters 3 and 4). Additionally, they had acquired tea, coffee, sugar, and tobacco, luxuries, we might think, but luxuries (tobacco particularly) that in the minds of the Nunamiut had become indispensable. These and other white man's commodities could be got only from white traders, but for the reestablished Nunamiut camps on the Arctic Divide, the lines of supply were remarkably long and thin. The traders were sedentary, and their posts nearest to the high country of the central Brooks Range included one at Beechy Point, on the Arctic Coast; one on the middle Kobuk River; another at Allakaket, the confluence of the Alatna and Koyukuk rivers; and a fourth at Bettles, on the Koyukuk near the mouth of the John River. And summer or winter, as we shall see, a round trip from the Chandler Lake–upper Killik regions to any of the trading posts took days or weeks of hard travel.

There was another complication. Having little or nothing in the way of money, the Nunamiut did business by bartering, exchanging in this case furs and hides for the above-listed essentials. But as I have noted, and as Paneak explains further, the fur trade had fallen on hard times, the white traders were reluctant to extend credit, and besides that, Nunamiut territory had never contained the most desirable of the northern fur animals.[3] Still, for the thirteen Nunamiut families, mastheaded as it were on the summit of the Brooks Range, trading expeditions were among life's imperatives, and this chapter tells of those adventures.[4] Further though, and of value in their own right, are Paneak's explanations, feelings, and opinions relative to details of both his own history and traditional Nunamiut lore and belief.

Story about traveling back in 1940

In the fall of 1939 we was got by freeze-up before we gone up the river on Colville River. Accordingly, John W. Smith Crews was late coming back from Pt. Barrow who was take a trip to Barrow in every summer to meet his freight in Barrow. And his business is a behind because fur prices went down and he tight up. He cannot give away so much. He is too old to taking care of his own family. He has 3 kids and he was afraid if he lost his business, he cannot trap any more like he used to be when he was in middle age. And he was told us about finding better living in some where else. I know some mining peoples in Koyukuk river like Bettles – Allakaket and Wiseman. By that times I am bad luck only I catch one Lynx & one wolfs and I was afraid to go to John W. Smith to see him without Much furs I know he would not give me an Credit. So I had to stayed in the Mountain. And that time I have enough Ammunition for that summer but Absolataly Nothing I have no tobacco – no tea – no sugar – flour, just live on the Meat Alone. And no way without money or furs only have to work hard Hunt in every day Most looking for Animals and I have to take walk & walk for distance Many times found None and few times I found Some Animals.

In spring of 1940 in March we had trap lines down to Near Crevice Cr. and see an old cabin but nobody been for some years. And we are together in the long hours and have lunch together in Elijah Kakinya skin tent and talk over with each men about trip to Bettles and see what going on the Koyukuk river. And in earlier down at Bettles Village one trading post the importand for us we could find a Store at Bettles and then we do not have enough meat all we could have. No Caribou there but few Mooses in some where in some creek and we only have to driven down to the mouth of creek and in next morning Peter Morry & I we are going up to mountain ridge by no deep Soft Snow and then we saw 2 Moose in Valley from top of mountain ridge and we was above them and

Story About Traveling Back in 1940

In the fall of 1939, freeze up [of the sea] came before we started up the Colville River. Accordingly, John W. Smith's crew was late getting back [to his trading post on Beechey Point] from Point Barrow, which they reached each summer [by boat along the Arctic coast] to receive Smith's freight [following its arrival by ship from the south]. Smith was a white trader married to an Eskimo woman, and he was poor because of the drop in fur prices. He could not extend much credit, and he was too old to support his family by other means. He had three children, and he feared that if he lost his trading business he could not make a living at trapping, as he could have when he was middle-aged.

He told us about trying to find a better living elsewhere, and I told him that I knew of some mining people [including Nunamiut; see following] who lived in the Koyukuk River villages of Wiseman, Bettles, and Allakaket (Map 2). (Except where noted, all place names mentioned in this chapter are shown in Map 3; see also the hand-drawn maps reproduced herein). I had had bad luck, and having trapped only one lynx and one wolf I was afraid to try trading with Smith because I knew that he would not give me credit. So I had to remain with my family in the mountains, where at that time I had enough ammunition for the following summer, but absolutely nothing else. We had no tobacco, tea, sugar, or flour, and we lived on meat alone. Without money or furs we survived by living off the land. I hunted every day, walking long distances, many times seeing no game, and a few times finding [caribou or white sheep].

In March 1940, we had trap lines near Crevice Creek on the John River. And we spent long hours together talking and eating in Elijah Kakinya's hide tent. And we talked of traveling on down the John River to Bettles, on the Koyukuk River, where at least in earlier days there had been a trading post. [In 1899, a gold rush on the Koyukuk (see Marshall [1933] 1991:29–44) resulted in the village

then we run down and Scare them by holler and whistle in Loud Noise and 3 mens was sit & wait for Moose all day long. Then we can tell by the Moose tracks they are heading toward 3 mens to who was waiting on both side of valley and two Moose were killed and then next day we are going to bring the meat home and we are pile the meat aside and for our family meat.

Then Frank Rulland & I we have meat for 10 days Supplys and Start early morning and travel all day long and had a camp late in evening. We do not carry any tent had to sit by good open fire, had to rolls our skin Sleeping bags. And in next early morning had to thaw meat for our dog - two Sled teams and feed our dogs before we start. In John river still no track of man until we reach Timber Creek.

I know government cabin in mouth of Timber Creek and then soon we come near we saw track in front of cabin and soon we reach cabin. My! Two sled tracks is fairly fresh we was look for tobacco and other crub there is nothing to find in this cabin anyway good trail toward Bettles Village and we have troubles much on the trail too narrow for our heavy Sled and get in Old Bettles Village in late evening at Sometimes 10: P.M. And then we had to stop in front of Roadhouse and a man of Roadhouse first I met. And ask him about peoples who was in the village. And he was told me about Mr. David Tobuk family are here. And then I ask him where they are and he said, is right close. And then he ask, I take you to David Tobuk.

Our dogs is still in bank & Frank Rulland & a man & I take walk. And he knocking David door and opened by one of David daughter and she must be surprising. Perhaps she never did see me before and even David he did not recognized me eighter because we did not met since 1919. And then David jumb from his chair took gas lantern given us light when we tight up our dogs and Serving good dinner especially white mens food are test very good after we live on straight meat. And how we are enjoy together. And Frank Rulland & I we rolls a cigarettes with Prince Albert tobacco. Mr. David Tobuk just got home from Allakaket in few days. He had to go down to Allakaket to get his groceries two trading post in Allakaket. And no trading post in Bettles, only Roadhouse in Bettles. Only place we pay our groceries in Allakaket distance about approximetely 37 miles by Sled trail or government trail. Our dogs are pretty tired. Then Rulland & I we had to stayed in Bettles & take rest our dogs after we travel in two days from Hunt Fork lots of deep soft snow in that times.

of Old Bettles.] Finding a trading post was important because we did not have enough meat. We had no caribou, but we had found a few moose on a creek, and the next morning Peter Morry and I climbed a ridge to get above them, and hollering and whistling we drove them down to where, lying in wait, three of our party shot two of them. The next day we brought the meat to our camp and piled it aside for our families [who had remained behind, upriver].

Then Frank Rulland and I had meat enough for ten days, and starting early in the morning we traveled all day toward Bettles, and camped late in the evening [the two men were traveling by dogsled over the ice of the John River]. We had no tent, but rolled out our skin sleeping bags beside a good fire. The next morning, after thawing meat for our two sled teams, we started again, but found no track of man before we reached Timber Creek.

I knew of a government cabin at the mouth of Timber Creek, and when we arrived we found fairly fresh tracks of two dogsleds in front of the cabin. [During gold rush times the U.S. government had built cabins and trails in this region.] We looked for tobacco and other grub, and while we found nothing in this cabin, a good river trail led toward Bettles.

The trail gave us trouble because it was too narrow for our heavy sleds, but we reached Old Bettles Village in the late evening at about 10:00 P.M., where we stopped in front of a roadhouse. At the roadhouse, I asked a man if there were [Eskimo] people living in the village, and he said there were, David Tobuk and his family, and that he would take us to them. [Paneak's use of the term "man" signifies white man.]

Our dogs were still on the riverbank, and Frank Rulland and I and a white man walked to David's house, whose door was opened by one of David's daughters. They were most surprised to see us. I had not seen David since 1919, and at first he did not recognize me, but then he jumped from his chair, and taking a gas lantern helped us tie our dogs, and then invited us in for a dinner of white man's food that tasted very good after a diet of straight meat. How we enjoyed being together while Frank Rulland and I rolled cigarettes with [David's] Prince Albert tobacco.

A few days before, David Tobuk had arrived home from Allakaket where he had gone to get groceries. He told us that there were two trading posts in Allakaket, but only the roadhouse in Bettles, so to get our groceries Frank Rulland

Some few white man is resident of Bettles was told us better go down to Allakaket to get what we need. Sure enough we plan to go down to Allakaket and start in the morning again we are trouble on the trail of David Tobuk we did not make in that day had to camp we know is close we are but we do not like reach in the Night. And then we get there early morning. Gee! When we got there Stop on the river. Some man was saying Hello! Hello! And I say hello! And I say we are coming from Arctic side and some ones Say again, Arctic side, I say yes.

And one an old fellow coming down from front of house met us his name is Willie Williams. He was nice Smiling to us but he could not talk in engles but he pointed out by his hand and I understand that we could driven our dogs teams to front of Village houses. And then we get up soon Some of my parent friend I recognized an among old Indian peoples. Oh how they are nice peoples and invited and Come in – Come in have a tea break and talk. And among an old Indian cannot speak in english except all young peoples can speak very good in english. And they was talk about my grandfather Noisilaa and his brother Tulukana, everybody was so nice to us. And that evening one of Indian took us over to store. The owner of trading post his name is Sam Dubin he is an old timers in Koyukuk. And we pay little stuffs from him in reasonable price and he also told us he will move up to Bettles by river boat. And he will have lots of stuff and Nearest to us also that is nice to know and he was friendly too. I know him before in 1917 in Bettles before he bought all trading post – Northern Commercial Co. And he told us better coming in the fall after freeze up and he will give us better Supply. He also told us he know how to be poor, without Money. Lots of times go without grub just live on Rabbits Snaring. And next day Frank Rulland &. I we was start home and camp between Hand Saw Creek & Bettles. And accordingly our dogs are very tired and get to Bettles stayed with David Tobuk. And next day David Tobuk told us to stayed and let our dogs rest and he has dog food for one night. And we did and in second day we started off and leave Bettles and then our dogs is go along fine. Of course, our sled trail is fine and camp near Crevice Creek. And next day we make it where we leave our family.

And missed They are moving toward North and found some meat for us. And in next morning we go again and found our family at Hunt Fork. And in next day we started travel by Hunt Fork to northward and take bridge over to Okominilaga Valley found Old Morry & Homer

and I had to go on [down the Koyukuk] to Allakaket, about thirty-seven miles by sled trail on the river ice, or by government trail in the woods along the river. Our dogs were tired after having come down in the soft snow on the John River ice all the way from Hunt Fork in just two days, so we stayed over in Bettles to rest them.

There were a few white men in Bettles, and they advised us that we had better go to Allakaket to get what we needed. We started in the morning, but again had trouble with the snowy, river trail as we followed David Tobuk's sled tracks, and had to camp before reaching that village. We knew we were close, but did not want to arrive there in the dark (because of potentially unfriendly people; see below).[5] Accordingly, we arrived early the next morning, where we stopped on the ice in front of the village, and heard a man call "Hello! Hello!" And I called back, "Hello!" and I said we had come from the Arctic side [north of the Brooks Range] and someone said "Arctic Side!" and I said yes.

Then an old fellow [an Indian] whose name was Willie Williams came down from his house to meet us, and he was smiling, and very nice to us, although he could not speak English [or Eskimo, obviously], but with signs he made us understand that we could tie our dog teams in front of the village. Then we met the Indians, who were very nice, and invited us to come in and have a tea break and talk. Among the older of them I recognized some of my parent's friends. The old Indians could not speak English, but the young ones spoke it very well, and they interpreted stories of my grandfather Nuisillaa and his brother Tulukana.

Everyone was very nice to us, and that evening one of the Indians took us to a store whose owner was the white man Sam Dubin, an old timer on the Koyukuk. He sold us a little stuff at reasonable prices, and he was friendly, and told us that he was going to move up to Bettles by river boat, where he would have lots of stuff and be closer to where we were living on the Arctic Divide. I had known him in Bettles in 1917, before he bought the Northern Commercial Company store there, and he told us that we should come to Bettles this fall after freeze-up, when he would have more to sell. He said that he knew what it was like to be poor and without money, and that lots of times he had lived on snared rabbits. The next day Frank Rulland and I started home, and because our dogs were very tired we camped between Hand Saw Creek [Henshaw Creek] and Bettles.

Mekiana & my father, Tunngana. Stayed with Old Morry Maptigak at Okominilaga Valley, have winter camp without traveling – no wolfs but few wolverine and a few colored foxes no lynx in North Side of divide, of course, no Rabbits by that times Caribou are fewer than today. Here the sketch map of Okominilaga river and head water of Hunt Fork.

Then after we met Morry Maptigak and Nice times together in Several days and talk about going to see Jack W. Smith at Beechy Point. And some men decide to go to Upper Kobuk. Old resident Harry Brown who has been running his own trading post for many years in Upper Kobuk area.

We are travel together by Sled & dogs and then we reach Killik. And then in few days all the man are ready to go and pay what wanted for Summer Supply. Most of man has Not Many furs – no money available to every body is really an Eskimo old Eskimo life, just live on Meat.

On that times 3 man plan to trip down to Beechy Point and see J. W. Smith, the trader in Beechy Point and all along in Arctic Coast for 10 years Elijah Kakinya – Homer Mekina – Peter Morry. And other man are the name as follow Frank Rulland – John Morry – Billy Morry, went to Kobuk. That was early part of April and left rest of all family. I did not go myself Perhaps no wolf & furs to buy my Needy Supply very poor I was. And later part of April weather was gotten warmer for 2 week end and Finally Killik river break up and flooded in Killik. And we can tell all the man who was going to Kobuk & Beechy Point was gotten by break up the river. But still we expected 3 men returned from North Slope except we do not expected returned from Kobuk. And Near last part of April 3 man Show up by top hill. Snow is almost gone melted by extremely warm weather. And early in June Frank Rulland Billy Morry and Stanely Cris from Kobuk Come by Walking Alway from Shungnak Village, by dog bag bring little Supply – No Money that why.

A Raymond Paneak was born on 17 of June 1940. In that time I made my mind how I could get my income but I had take a walk & walk. I only have water tight Seal skin Knee Mukluk. No shoes in that times. If I carry Skin needles and thimbles and Sinews in my cartridges bag would be Save & last longer if I keep patching when worn bottom of my Knee boots & I had to carry patching outfit and I had to turn inside out to dry first and turn out side before too dry & after dry have to oiled every time no lazy.

That night we stayed with David Tobuk, at Bettles, who invited us to remain another day to rest our dogs because he had enough dogfood [fish or game] for one more night. So we did, and the next day, with our dogs in fine shape, we started off north, over the ice of the John River, and of course the trail was fine because we had been over it only a few days before, and we got as far as Crevice Creek, from where, the following day, we made it to where we had left our families.

But we missed them; they had moved north [after having got the moose meat we had left above Crevice Creek?]. However, the next morning we found them at Hunt Fork, and from there we traveled northward, and then over the ridge into the valley of the Okokmilaga River where we found Old Morry, and Homer Mekiana and my father, Tunngana, who with their people had wintered there. And we stayed with Old Morry Maptigak. Old Morry stayed in camp without traveling that winter. There were no wolves there but there were a few wolverines and a few colored foxes, there on the northern side of the Arctic Divide, but there were no lynx or rabbits, of course [because these are forest animals], and the caribou were fewer than today. Here is my sketch map (Figure 36).

After we had stayed several days and had nice times together we talked of going to see Jack W. Smith at Beechey Point, or going to the upper Kobuk River to trade with the old white trader Harry Brown, who had lived there for many years (see Burch 1998:336). So we traveled together by dogsled to the Killik River, and a few days afterwards several of us were ready to go trading for our summer supplies. Most of us had few furs, and just as in the old days we were living on meat. Three of our men started off toward the post at Beechey Point, where J. W. Smith had been trading all along the Arctic Coast for ten years.

It was early April, and leaving their families on the Killik, Elijah Kakinya, Homer Mekiana, and Peter Morry started by dogsled for Beechey Point, while Frank Rulland, John Morry, and Billy Morry started by dogsled for the Kobuk. I did not go because I was so poor that I did not have wolf or other furs with which to buy my needed supplies. For two weeks in the latter part of April the weather became very warm, causing the breakup of the river ice and flooding of the Killik River, and we knew that the men headed both toward Beechey Point and the Kobuk had been caught in the breakup.

Still, we expected the return of the three men who had gone down the North Slope to Beechey Point, although

In later part of June we started to moved by dog bags and packing some own also. Robert Paneak had to ride on top of my pack. We do not have mosquitoes repellent only do have Buhach. No help. Much. Here is the sketch map here in bellow drawing.

We cannot moving in every day take times about a Month to reach the head water of Kivigiak River where we could stayed long. And Saw Several grizzly bear & Many Mountain Sheeps & Caribou just enough for what we could used we take. And in July I have shots 4 or 5 wolfs. I think one wolf bounty are $30.00. And in August we started hunt marmots. I know how to set rock dead fall for marmot and learned from my dad who is experience for inland animal how to catch. And we catch quite a few.

When we started Frank Rulland Elijah Kakinya & I we had to leave our family and Stayed Away in Several days we did not expect to see the three who had gone to the Kobuk. In the last part of April those who had started for Beechey Point, but who had turned back at breakup, showed up on the top of a hill near camp. Then, to our surprise, in early June, when the snow was nearly gone because of the extremely warm weather, Frank Rulland, Billy Morry, and Stanley Cris (a Kobuk [Kovagmiut] Eskimo) came walking in, all the way from Shungnak Village, with their dogs now carrying packs rather than pulling sleds. For lack of money, they brought little in the way of supplies.

Our son Raymond was born on 17 June, and I made up my mind how I was going to get money, but I would have to walk and walk for it. At that time I had no white man's shoes, but instead wore waterproof sealskin knee boots that I patched with skin needles, thimbles, and sinews

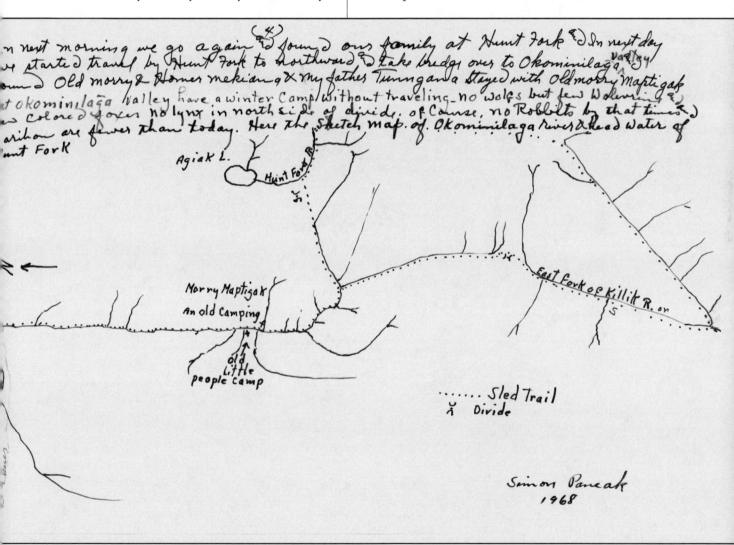

FIGURE 36 Paneak's illustration of his travels.

and after we stayed out in mountain we carry 8 × 10 tent carried by dog. And one other times we was going our own way check our stone deadfall and had to skinned what we catch. We shoot Some marmots. I had 22 Horned Winchester model 70 and Frank Rulland has 2520 Winchester and Elijah Kakinya has 2520 Remington. All those little caliber is right size for marmots. And one day started home we go by our own way. And I had 6 shots only and I spotted big Grizzly head of me he was sleeping on top of Caribou Carcas. And I just take walk if he see me I does not care if he was Scared. And I have load of marmot skin kind of heavy on my pack. Pretty soon I come close about approximately 100 yds. away and took my pack off and I had all my shells on 22 horned and ready

carried in my cartridge bag, and that I dried carefully. In the latter part of June we began traveling, moving our gear both by dog pack and on our backs. Robert Paneak had to ride on top of my backpack. We had no mosquito repellent, only Buhach (a commercial powdery repellent burned in a tent or tent door) that was no help, and we moved very slowly, taking about a month to reach the head of the Kivigiak (Qiviġiaq) River or Easter Creek, where we settled our families for a stay of several months. Here is a sketch map (Figure 37).

On our way from the Killik to the head of the Kivigiak we saw several grizzlies, and many caribou and sheep, and we killed only as many as we needed. In July I shot four or five wolves, the [federal] wolf bounty being $30.00, and in

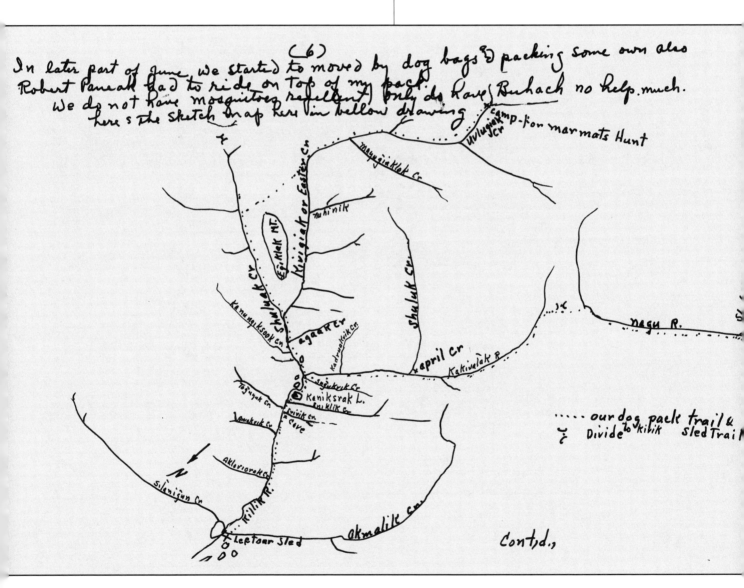

FIGURE 37   Paneak's illustration of his travels.

to shoot the bear. And I hala! Wake him and lift up head up and tighten my tricker and the big bear are moving his head and pull my tricker. My little 46 grain bulled hit right in bear ear make him nervice, roll-roll haul. And I had to wait stopping rolling but the big bear was running toward me and I shoot him in Second Shot and downfall a bit and got up and running other way and I took shot & aimed in Shoulder plate and he was fall to death and I only have 3 More Shells I was save.

And we almost cleaned all marmots but few yet there. Elijah & I we was talk about going to Bettles. I have caught about at least 150 marmots and Elijah caught 70 marmots and Frank Rulland caught 50 marmots and we caught few wolfs same times. And myself caught 7 wolfs. And we started to move over to Agiak Valley in upper Hunt Fork. My father was move to Agiak 2 week head of us and he was killing around 20 Caribou and few marmots.

In middle of September we make 4 bull Caribou and 2 ram skin added 4 Caribou skin we clipped off the hair of skin and sewing together to make waterproof and make 2 bundles easy on one dog pack. The sketch map about Elijah Kakinya & Simon Paneak take a trip to Bettles thru Hunt Fork &., John River. Elijah Kakinya &.. I we ready every things we could used. And we desired to take good 10 dogs & with pack, and loaded our dogs packs in the evening. And wake early morning and breakfast nice boiled fat meat and soon after we finished eating. And then we start that morning its snow on the mountain that was middles part of September. And we saw one wolfs on our way but could not catch it. And then we reaching the mouth of Kivik Cr. to where we could built. Late in evening it was fairly chilly and soon our 10 dogs tied up and we pitch our 8 × 10 wall tent. 8 oz duck no stove we carry and built a good open fire nice and warm we have plenty dead good wood. And then we cook some meat and ate for supper and drink meat broth like a Hundred years ago peoples who are living that way and roll our skin Sleeping bag and have nice Sleep we has. And then we wake from our nice Sleep built our fire outside of tent. And we carry only one little boy axe good enough cutting Small common spruce hauled together into one place. And we was looking willow root to tie together connection of Umiak frame. Perhaps we do not have any nails – no hammer we have. And we use Some green willows for rib for Umiak and then we almost finished before noon

August Frank Rulland, Elijah Kakinya, and I began hunting marmots, and we caught quite a few. I had learned how to set rock deadfalls for marmots from my father, who was experienced in trapping inland animals.

On these marmot hunting trips we had to be away from our families for several days at a time. We took an 8' × 10' commercial canvas tent carried by dog pack, and sometimes each of us went his own way to skin marmots caught in his deadfalls. We shot some of them; I had a .22 Hornet Winchester Model 70, Rulland had a .25-20 Winchester, and Kakinya a .25-20 Remington. These small calibers were the right size for marmots.

One day, when we started home, each of us going his own way, I spotted a big grizzly ahead of me, sleeping on top of a caribou carcass. I had only six cartridges left and decided that if he saw me I would just walk away. I was carrying a heavy load of marmot skins on my back, and when I was about 100 yards from the bear I took off my pack, and with my .22 Hornet loaded with all six cartridges, got ready to shoot him. I shouted "Hala!" to wake him, and as he lifted and was moving his head, I pulled the trigger. The little 46-grain bullet hit him in the ear. He rolled over and over, and I waited until he stopped rolling, but then the big bear got up and ran toward me, so I shot him again, and down he fell. Then, however, he got up and ran the other way, and aiming at his shoulder I fired again, and killed him. That left me with three shells.[6]

We had by now caught most of the marmots in that locality, and Elijah and I talked about going to Bettles to trade. I had caught at least 150 marmots; Elijah, 70; and Frank Rulland, 50, and we had killed a few wolves—I had seven. So we moved to the Agiak (Agiaq) Valley on the upper Hunt Fork, where my father had gone two weeks earlier and had killed about 20 caribou and a few marmots.

In the middle of September, beginning with the skins of four bull caribou and two white sheep rams, and then adding four more of caribou, after clipping the hair from the hides we sewed together waterproof dog packs which fit easily on each dog. [In general design, Nunamiut dog packs were much like saddlebags; see Campbell 1998a:23, 25.] Elijah Kakinya and I were ready to head for Bettles, and choosing ten good pack dogs, and gathering our furs and our gear, we loaded the dog packs the evening before we traveled. Then early the next morning, with fresh snow on the mountain, and a breakfast of nice, boiled fat meat,[7] we started off (Figure 38).

except we have to do some Sewing the raw skin to make water tight and put the Skin over the frame and stretch and tie by willow roots. Here drawing in below the frame how look like.

About length 20 ft. and 8ft width &. bow & stern is about the same Wideness. All connection are tight with all Willow roots is strong to hold. And after all finished done we put Skin over and Stretch all we could do it pretty tight. And soon we have lunch we hauled down to Kivik water Seem to be no leak but still we never know until we loaded with 10 fat dogs and our gears.

And we have got to makes 2 long poles and one paddles and one oar and then we load and how high we ought to have above water lines and about couple foot above water lines. We say pretty good. Then we off the Kivik and

We saw one wolf that day, but were unable to shoot it, and reached the mouth of Kivik (Kivviq) [Kevuk] Creek late in the evening. We tied our dogs and pitched our 8' × 10' wall tent of eight-ounce duck. It was fairly chilly, and we had no stove, but there was plenty of good deadwood, and we built a good fire in the open, and cooked some meat and drank the broth, just the way people did one hundred years ago. We rolled out our sleeping bags, had a nice sleep, and in the morning built another nice fire outside our tent.

We carried only one "little boy" axe, but it was good enough for cutting small spruces, which we piled together. Then, having neither hammer nor nails, we looked for willows with which to tie together the frame of an *umiak*. We used green willows for ribs, and before noon were nearly finished, having only to sew a waterproof cover of

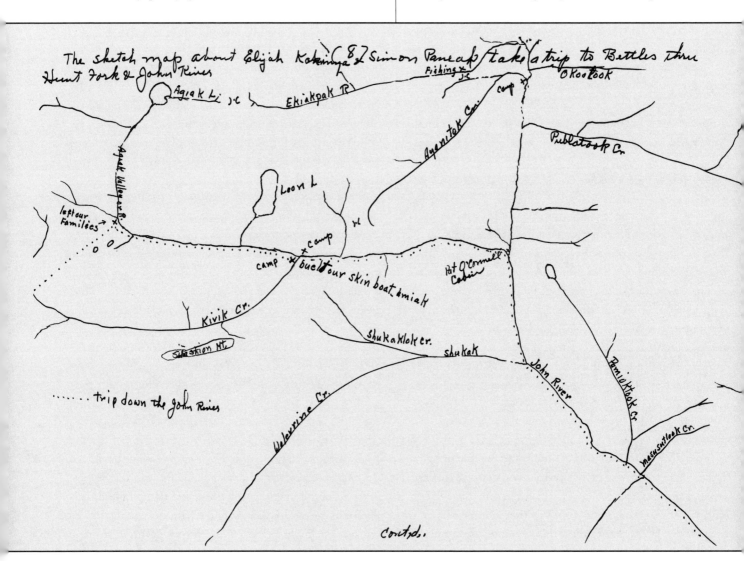

FIGURE 38   Paneak's illustration of the travels described in this chapter.

floating along nicely before we come to Several big boulder rocks & Some drift wood which was hanging round the big boulder and water was rough like boiled. Current was so Swift and again & again and then we almost tip over in Several times before reach the mouth of Hunt Fork in John river.

After we past Hunt Fork we alright but is darkness late in evening. And we camp we do not want travel by night. And then early morning we off & floating along fine. Shortly after we starting big bull Moose is standing front of and we shot him and we skinned fat Moose and we took most of meat because I know some Native like meat. Still hight enough our boat from water lines. Weather was so nice partly cloudy see More Moose in along John river water was Smooth and stop at England cabin the old times

skins and stretch and tie it to the frame with willow roots. This drawing shows how the frame looked (Figure 39).

It was about twenty feet long, had a bow-to-stern width of eight feet, and all connections were tied with strong-holding willow roots. We put on the skin cover, stretching it as tight as we could, and after lunch launched the boat in Kevuk Creek where it seemed not to leak, although we would never know until we loaded it with ten fat dogs, our gear, and the two of us. We then made two long poles, and a paddle and an oar, and after loading the boat, and finding that we had two feet of freeboard, we said that it looked pretty good. We started off down the Kevuk, and floated along nicely until we came to big boulders, hung with driftwood, around which the water was rough and boiling. The current was so swift that we nearly tipped

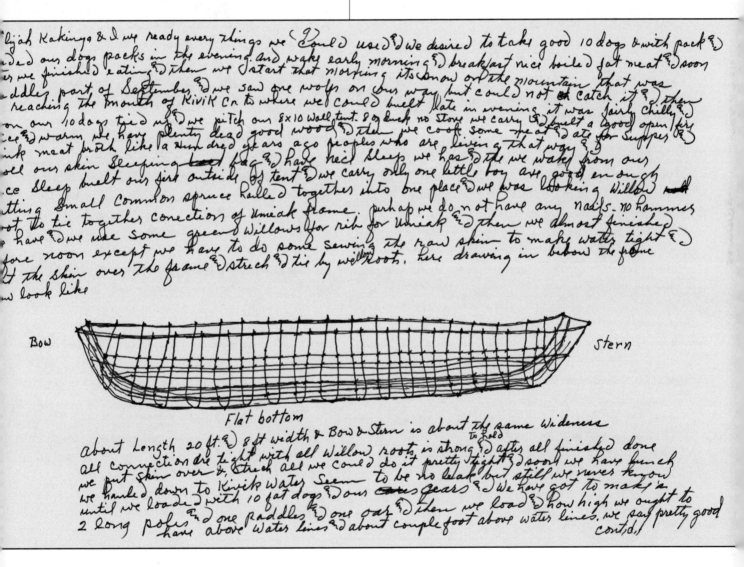

FIGURE 39   Paneak's illustration of boat travel.

resident of Koyukuk river. And we leave some dried meat and Some Moose Meat for our return Supplies in meat cache. And we off the ground again. So far is no man and no tracks of man and we Saw Some mountain Sheep on mountain side by that times no sport hunters.

And we keep going on – Elijah oaring and myself paddling & Steering the Slow boat. Pretty soon we hear Some one was chopping or cut Spruce by the axe and come near we spot a man standing on the bank and waiting for us and we could not tell what kind of man he is. And I say Hi! in loud – he say Hi! And I recognize Sound like a Big Charley Suckik. And I still not quite sure.

I say in english we are coming from Arctic Side and we are Arctic Man. And ea, he said and coming down to beach of the river and pretty soon we come close. I recognize he is Big Charley Suckik he ask me where is your father he is still alive? I said yes except my mother are past away in long ago and he say Natook! That mean Absulately Nothings he has no tobacco to smoke – no tea – no coffee and no nothing he has. He said I only have cooked moose meat. We say thank you – Koyanak. We have nice Jak-Jak and ate nice fat moose meat cooked by fire side.

And he also Smoked his 3 big Moose Meat hanged by good spruce and he had long fire to keep the Meat from rotten and keep from blue flies too. And he was going to make good size raft, big enough for 3 Moose Meat. He say that have enough Meat Supply for the coming winter & family he asking us carry moose meat to his family in Bettles but we have plenty meat we carried in our Umiak we could give some meat when we get to Bettles. And he was told us he be reaching Bettles after two days. And he also told us Mr. Sam Dubin is there with plenty of everythings in his new Trading Post Store and he also told us Mr. Frank Bishop got a grub at Crevice Cr. if we really need it he is very nice man but any way we do not wanted to bothered, of course, we do not know him before.

And Elijah &. I we off again and then we past Crevice Cr. And we saw big grey wolf on river bars head of us. And the wolf see us but it Standing by probably could not tell what things floating along in the river and we shot him and caught him and after we skinned the wolf we keep on going.

And pretty soon darkness being on in late evening and camping or camp at near 3 Men Mountain in Eskimo name are Omatikyuk meaning shape like heart looking over several times before we reached the mouth of Hunt Fork. We got past the mouth and into the John River all right, but it was then late in the evening, and dark, so we camped because we did not want to travel by night. The next morning we were off and floating along fine when we shot a big bull moose that we found standing in front of us, and we skinned the fat moose and took most of the meat with us because I knew that some Natives [Indians, at Bettles] liked meat.

Our boat still floated well, the weather was partly cloudy and nice, and we saw more moose along the smooth-flowing John River before we reached the deserted cabin of England, an old-time white resident of the Koyukuk River. Here, we left in his cache some moose meat for our return trip and were off again, so far having seen no sign of man, although we did see, in those years before sport hunting, sheep on the mountainsides. We kept on, Elijah using the oar, and I paddling and steering the slow boat, and soon we heard someone chopping wood, and then saw a man standing on the bank waiting for us, but we could not tell what kind of man he was. So I called, "Hi! in a loud voice, and he called back, "Hi! and I thought I recognized the voice of Big Charlie Suckik (Sukkiq). But I was not quite sure, so I said in English that we are coming from the Arctic side, and that we are Arctic men, and he said "Ea (Iiyaa), and coming down to the beach I saw that he was indeed Big Charlie Suckik. [For a fascinating biographical sketch of this famous Nunamiut Eskimo and his loved ones, see Marshall [1933] 1991:88–95.] He asked about my father, who I said was still alive, but that my mother had passed away long ago, and then Big Charlie said, "Natook! meaning that he had nothing, no tobacco, tea, or coffee. He said that he did have moose meat, and we said, "Koyanak (Quyanaq), thank you, and sat and had a nice Jak-Jak (yak-yak) [chat], and ate fat moose meat by the fireside.

He also had hanging the meat of three big moose that he was smoking over a long-burning fire which kept it from rotting, and from blue [blow] flies too. He said that the three moose would provide enough meat for his family during the coming winter, and that he was going to build a big raft with which to take the meat downriver [to Bettles]. He asked us to take some of this meat to his family, in Bettles, but we told him we had plenty of meat in our boat, and that we would give them some when we arrived. He said he would follow us in two days, and that Mr. Sam Dubin [the white trader] was in Bettles.

from distance. And we start off again next early morning but the river are twisted too much current is not so Swift and we are floating along Slowly. Here sketch map beginning from Bettles and up the river.

All day long and toward evening weather was gotten sour – raining and we are soaken wet on our skin parka. And before we reach Old Bettles – darkness being on and Finally we reach Fork and saw bright light from Sam Dubin New Store – gas light, no electric there yet in that times.

And when we come near River boat is tight up on the front of Road House or Cafe' the last freight boat to Sam Dubin. And I know where David house and stopped at front of David house. And then our 10 dogs was so Noisy after long ride in all day long and heard by David Tobuk

Big Charlie said that Mr. Dubin had plenty of everything in his new trading post there, and he told us that a Mr. Frank Bishop [a white man] was camped at Crevice Creek, and that he was a nice man and could give us food when we got there. Elijah and I did not know this man, however, so we passed the mouth of Crevice Creek without stopping, and then found a big gray wolf on a river bar ahead of us. He was standing still, watching us, and wondering what might be floating toward him, and we shot him and skinned him, and kept on going.

In the evening we camped near Three Men Mountain [known commonly as Three Time Mountain], whose Eskimo Name is Omatikyuk (Uummatiyyuk), meaning that it looks heart-shaped from a distance, and the next

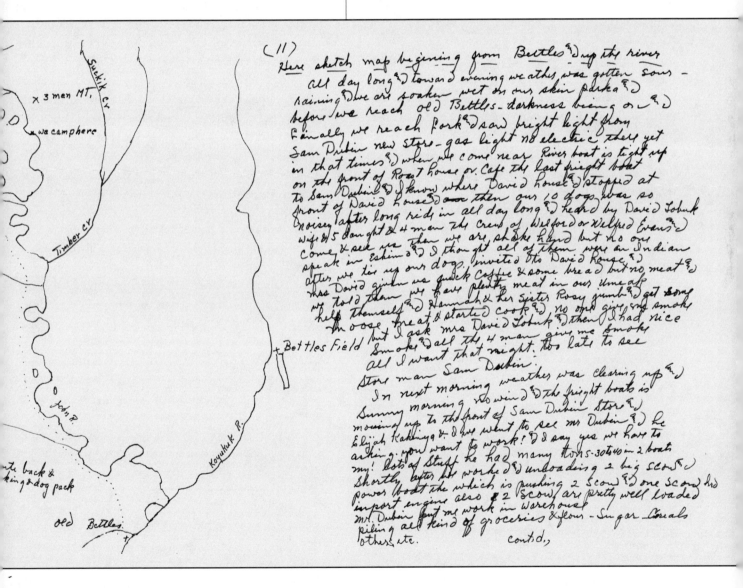

FIGURE 40   Paneak's illustration of travels described in this chapter.

wife & 5 daughter &.. 4 men the crew of Wilford or Wilfred Evans and come and see us.

Then wc are shake hand but no one speak in Eskimo and I thought all of them were an Indian. After we tie up our dogs, invited to David house and Mrs. David given us quick Coffee & some bread but no meat and we told them we have Plenty Meat in our umiak help Themself and Hannah & her Sister Rosy jumb and get Some Moose Meat & started cook. And no one give me smoke but I ask Mrs. David Tobuk and Then I had Nice Smoke and all the 4 man give me Smoke all I want that night. Too late to see store man Sam Dubin.

In next morning weather was Clearing up and Sunny morning no wind and the frieght boats is moving up to front of Sam Dubin Store. And Elijah Kakinya & I we went to see Mr. Dubin and he asking, you want to work? And I say yes we have to. My! lots of Stuff he had, Many tons – 30 to 40 in 2 boats. Shortly after we worked and unloading 2 big Scow and power boat the which is pushing 2 Scow and one Scow in port engine also 2 Scow are pretty well loaded. Mr. Dubin put me work in warehouse piling all kind of groceries & flour – Sugar – Cereals others, etc. We are empted up 2 big scow almost all day long. And Elijah & I we earn some money for our help unloading.

About $2.00 an hourly, but he told he could give me $3.50 an hourly. He is selling reasonable price on his stuff Coffee 1 # @ $.50, tea $1.25 per lbs. And everythings is fairly cheap. He give me tobacco in free charge while I am working. And he give other job by next day. And third day Elijah Kakinya &. I we sell our marmot skins and wolf bounty we credit forth. I have 7 wolf and over 100 marmot skin and I am very well fix except my 5 dogs cannot carry much so I leave Some of Extra Money for in the fall after freeze up by dogsled.

On fourth day Elijah Kakinya & I we had to leave Bettles by walking and our dogs had pretty good load – dog pack full and ourself had to pack some too. And in two first day we did not go very far in case our dogs pack worn & torn in thick forest in the wood and we stop & Sewed good things we carry Needles & Sinew and Thimbles & then we run out Sinew and Mrs. Mary Smith given me one spool hand cotton thread she is an Indian from Nulato in Yukon. She is help us on the thread.

And on our way back we saw Several Moose & grizzlies bears except no Black bear they are in den in later part of September. And Saw quite bit Beaver. And we

morning we started early, but the river became so twisted (Figure 40) and had such little current that we floated along slowly. [Campbell knows very well this slow, frustrating stretch.] The weather had gotten sour and rainy. In our skin parkas we were soaking wet, and it became dark before we reached Old Bettles. Then, finally, from the fork [the confluence of the John and Koyukuk rivers] we saw the bright gas light in Sam Dubin's new store. In those days there were no electric generators in Bettles.

When we had floated down the Koyukuk the short distance to Bettles, we found this year's last freight boats to Sam Dubin tied up in front of the roadhouse or cafe. [This typical small Alaska "roadhouse" was a combination restaurant, bar and hotel; see Figure 16.] Because I knew the location of David Tobuk's house, we stopped there, and our dogs were so noisy after the long day's boat ride that they soon attracted the attention of David's wife and five daughters, plus four men of Wilford (or Wilfred) Evans's crew. [Wilfred Evans had a white father and a Koyukon Indian mother.] We shook hands, but none of the four men spoke in Eskimo, so I knew they were Indians.

After we had tied our dogs, we were invited into David's house, where Mrs. David gave us coffee and bread but said she had no meat. We said we had plenty in our *umiak*, and to help themselves, and Hannah and her sister Rosy jumped up, got some of the moose meat, and started cooking. No one offered me a smoke, but when I asked, Mrs. Tobuk and all four of the men gave me all the tobacco and cigarette papers I wanted that night. It was too late to see the trader Sam Dubin. The next morning the weather was clear, and the freight boats were moving up in front of Sam Dubin's store. When Elijah and I went to see Mr. Dubin he asked us if we wanted to work, and I said yes, we had to. My! he had lots of stuff. He had thirty to forty tons in two boats. We started to work, unloading two big scows and the powerboat that was pushing them. One of the scows had an inboard engine too. And we unloaded all kinds of groceries: flour, sugar, cereals, etc. By the end of the day we had nearly emptied the two scows, and Elijah and I had earned some money for our help.

He told us that he usually paid $2.00 per hour, but that he would give us $3.50. His stuff was reasonably priced—a number one can of coffee for $.50, and a pound of tea for $1.25, and he gave me free tobacco while I was working (Elijah did not smoke).[8] He gave us other jobs the next day, and on the third day Elijah and I traded our marmot and wolf skins for credit. I had seven wolves and nearly

stop at one of the lake – I know the lake in 1919 Some Northern Pike and built afire there and make good tea we only have one hook and caught 3 Pike and forth one pull right off burst the fish lines and we boiled Pike because we run out of meat. And then toward evening we saw bunch of Beaver Elijah Kakinya Say Beaver is pretty good meat. And pitch tent before we come Near to Beaver den and tight our dogs also let them rest good after work hard and we go Come Near to Beaver den. And Many Muskrats in that lake. And then we shoot, take 6 Beaver that we got enough and quit.

And Elijah Kakinya know how skinning and handles the meat first cut gaster out of the Beaver and I learned how too. We skinned all good fat Beaver and boiled and Ate. But after we eat my stomach is not good. Perhaps first times I ate during all my life times and next day I won't Never eat again and travel all day long and reach our Meat which we lefted in Cache. And I had Nice Supper and then we pull out again by early morning and we found 2 sheep on riverside and got it and still pretty good meat for us and we continue keep on moving in every day and in 9 ½ days we reach our family from Bettles to Agiak Valley.

And Then we all fix – have Nice Coffee and Nice tea all we could drink, hot cake in the morning and in two days we Cached our dried Meat. Of course, we have to walk back Kiiik for long away to our Sled in Akmalik in Killik river it is snow on the ground already but is not too thick and we are travel in 5 days and reach our Sled and winter cloth and others etc.

one hundred marmots, and was very well fixed except that my five dogs could not carry much on their backs, so I left some credit to use after freeze-up when I returned by dogsled. On the fourth day Elijah and I left Bettles on foot, with full dog packs, and carrying some of the load on our own backs.

We did not get very far the first two days because our dog packs were torn in our travel through the thick forest. We stopped and mended them with our needles, thimbles, and sinew, and when we ran out of sinew we used a spool of cotton thread given to me in Bettles by Mrs. Mary Smith, who was an Indian from Nulato, on the Yukon (Map 2).

On this trip we saw several moose and grizzly bears, and quite a few beavers, but no black bears because they are in their dens by late September. And we stopped at a northern pike lake, that I had known in 1919, where we built a fire and made tea, and then with the only hook we had we caught three pike and lost a fourth one that broke the line. We boiled the pike because we had run out of meat, and that evening we came upon a bunch of beavers.

Elijah said that beaver meat was pretty good, so we pitched our tent before we got close to the beaver den, and tied our dogs to let them rest [and to keep them from scaring the game]. Then we moved up near the beaver den. There were many muskrats in the same lake, and we shot six beavers—all we needed. Elijah knew how to skin and handle the meat after first cutting out the castor [gland]. I learned how by watching Elijah, and we skinned all of the good, fat beavers, and boiled and ate the meat. But afterwards my stomach was not good. This was perhaps the first time in my life that I had eaten beaver, and the next day I thought I would never eat [beaver?] again.

We traveled all that day, reaching meat that we had left in a cache, and having a nice supper. We pulled out again early the next morning, finding and shooting, beside the river, two sheep that provided us with good meat. And we continued along, day after day until nine and a half days out of Bettles we reached our families in the Agiak Valley.

Then we were all fixed. We had all the nice coffee and tea we could drink, and hot cakes in the morning, and after two days we cached our dried meat. Of course we had to walk a long ways back for our sleds at our Akmalik (Agmaalik) camp in the Killik River valley, but there was snow on the ground already, although not too deep for good walking, and in five days of travel we reached our sleds and winter clothes, etc.[9]

Epilogue

In the epilogue of my recent book of Paneak's drawings, I summarize what has happened to the Nunamiut, and to Anaktuvuk Pass, since the canvas tent and sod house days of the middle 1950s. Among my observations therein are that the present population of the town of Anaktuvuk is on the order of 275 Nunamiut and 25 whites, that its citizens live in split-level houses, that the school system serves grades K through 12, and that the town is accommodated five days a week by four scheduled airlines. These sample statistics, while incomplete, are enough to give the reader an idea of the transformation of Nunamiut society (see Figures 41 and 42). A metamorphosis of grand proportions, it has resulted from the development of the Prudhoe Bay oil fields, and the awarding of government lands to north Alaska Eskimos, in each case prompted and accelerated by the recent political activism of native Alaskans, and of Native Americans in general. And not unnaturally, the Nunamiut have welcomed the change. During the California Gold Rush, this writer's great grandfather, John C. Campbell, rode a saddle horse from Gettysburg to Sutter's Mill, but if there had been a train he would have taken it, and a century later it was the same sort of thing with the Nunamiut. Fur-clad Eskimos breaking trail for sled dogs (Figure 43) make for a charming picture, but the Nunamiut would rather have ridden snowmobiles.

One summer in the 1960s, Elijah Kakinya sought me out to show me his "big pup." It was the first snowmachine in Anaktuvuk Pass, and it was followed by an avalanche of modern technology that has certainly modified the accoutrements of traditional culture. Gone are the sled dogs, but the sleds are towed behind snowmachines. The walrus ivory fish lures still show up on occasion in a man's tackle box along with his mepps and daredevils. Skin mittens and boots are commonplace, but pants and parkas are not. Snowshoes are still made and used, but not often. Sheep horn ladles and stone malls are rare, but *ulus* and cooking fires of willow twigs are as important today as they were in the past, thus mingling with modern technology and outlasting other artifacts and techniques that had prevailed among north Alaska Eskimos for generations. What is known now of the traditional Nunamiut is preserved, therefore, only in artifacts housed in scattered museums, and in a small body of literature.[1]

Still, the Nunamiut are hunters. Each year, ranging far and wide on their gasoline-powered snowmachines and "all-terrain vehicles," they kill four or five hundred caribou, choosing only the fat and the healthy, and eating all of them. As State of Alaska biologist Sverre Pedersen tells me, "wild caribou are better food than plastic wrapped meat, and hunting them is far more satisfying than going to a grocery store." And they are trappers too. Killing wolves and wolf pups for their bounties is a thing of the past, but nowadays a good winter wolf skin is worth four hundred dollars or more, followed in value by those of wolverines and red foxes. Today, few if any of the skins of these fur bearers reach the white man's market. Instead, because of their continuing popularity for parka ruffs or other trim (Figure 44), they are sold or traded among the Nunamiut themselves, or to neighboring north Alaska tribes.

FIGURE 41 The Nunamiut camp at the summit of Anaktuvuk Pass in the summer of 1957. At this time of year the families have moved out of their sod winter houses and are living in canvas-wall tents. Photograph by JMC.

FIGURE 42 The town of Anaktuvuk Pass in 1996 in a picture taken from nearly the same place as shown in Figure 41. Photograph by Mary Mekiana.

FIGURE 43 Tough sledding in the country near the Savioyok River valley. In snow of this depth it was necessary for men and women to break trail ahead of the dogs. Photograph by Robert L. Rausch, 1963.

FIGURE 44 Mabel Paneak, daughter of Simon and Suzie, in the typical mid-twentieth century, short dress parka. Made here, in Anaktuvuk Pass, its cuffs and inner ruff are of high-quality wolverine fur, and its outer ruff is cut from an exceptionally good wolf skin. Photograph by Stephen C. Porter, 1960.

So with all this mechanized hunting and trapping, what has become of the natural world of the Nunamiut, the wilderness that I experienced first in the summer of 1956? Well, very little, as it turns out. My field notes, most of which relate here to the valleys of Chandler Lake and the Kalutagiak (Qalutaġiaq) River (Figure 45) have the following to say about the central Brooks Range as it was in 1956. By the time our four-man expedition (see Campbell 1998a) arrived on the ice of Chandler Lake in the last days of May, our landing field, a mile wide, five miles long, and five feet thick, had become bordered by a shore lead of open water that widened as, melting inward, the field's edges fell into the lake. Weather, as it evolved from those early days of spring, was by midsummer to provide enough warmth to turn the tundra green, but wind was its most abiding characteristic. Entrenched between tall mountains, the narrow valley was swept by gales and half-gales that ploughed furrows in the lead, blew down our tents (Figure 46), and as the days passed drove thou-

sands of tons of ice ashore on Chandler's north and south beaches. For a few days, we got from solid ground to lake ice over a snowdrift in front of camp, one of many around the lake that provided bridges, thereby allowing us to walk the length and breadth of Chandler, and to cross dry-shod to its other shores. But as the lead widened the bridges fell into open water, thus ruining for the summer the best walking to be had in the valley.

In our first week, a wolverine, following its nose to camp, came lumbering across the lake ice right up to the edge of the lead, twenty yards from our tents. A few days afterward a gray wolf came by, and one morning we were brought tumbling out of our cook-tent by the crashing roar of a great piece of bedrock, big as a house, as it fell down the mountain across the lake. We had been told by our support people—The Naval Arctic Research Laboratory, at Pt. Barrow—that they would see us later in the summer, when open water would allow float plane landings on Chandler Lake. Meanwhile, without a radio,

FIGURE 45 A view westward up the Kalutagiak River following an eighteen-hour late June storm. Such summer snows are not uncommon on the Brooks Range Divide, and this one destroyed countless numbers of the eggs and young of ground-nesting birds. Photograph by JMC, 1956.

with neither track nor trace of other humans and with the nearest road one hundred and seventy air miles away, we were isolated quite conclusively from the rest of the world. One will appreciate, therefore, our astonishment the morning we found four men approaching over the ice from the direction of the south beach.

They were Nunamiut hunters, and they were dragging behind them more than one hundred pounds of lake trout caught, as one of them, Jonas, explained—in the same English as that used by Paneak—on walrus ivory lures jigged from the edge of the ice. Walking overland from the Nunamiut encampment in Anaktuvuk Pass, the hunters, the night before, had pitched their tent a discreet quarter mile above us on what we had named Camp Creek. The fish were for their dogs, left tied near their tent, and Jonah said that on their walk from Anaktuvuk they had shot three caribou: food for men, but not for dogs, when fish could be caught.

In early June, I set off in the direction of Anaktuvuk Pass, as the raven flies a distance of only about thirty miles across

the mountain tops, but what with "heading" creeks to get above dangerous water, and going around mountains, it was a good fifty. I walked up Camp Creek to a narrow pass leading into the valley of the Kalutagiak (Figure 45), and two days later, in a dense fog, found my way to the Nunamiut camp by following the fragrance of its willow fires. They would say later that I was the first *tanik* (white man) to travel overland between Chandler Lake and Anuktuvuk, and when I arrived their first question was, "Where is your airplane?" White men came in airplanes, so I must have lost mine in the mountains.

But whether or not I was the first *tanik* to walk in from Chandler Lake, that traverse, and two others that summer, set the course of my future Brooks Range work. I met Simon Paneak at Tuluak Lake. At the summit of Anaktuvuk Pass I was given a flint spearhead by the elegant ten-year-old Anna Hugo, a gift that was to result in the discovery of the Kayuk Site (Campbell 1959), and on the banks of the Kalutagiak I found an abandoned Nunamiut camp of moss houses, the last of its kind.

FIGURE 46   Our 1956 camp on the east shore of Chandler Lake. Because of the total absence of all but the smallest willow twigs, our stove fuel that summer was a ton of gasoline. Photograph by JMC.

As for wilderness, one of the more fascinating aspects of the country lying between the lake and Anaktuvuk is that Camp Creek and the Kalutagiak share a common source even though they flow in opposite directions. At the summit between the two streams, a torrent pouring out of a side canyon split, part of it running, eventually, north to the Arctic Ocean; and the other part, the Kalutagiak, running south and then west to the Pacific. Then, down the long valley of the Kalutagiak, I found a herd of seventy-five caribou bulls; sheep on the hills; two snowshoe (varying) hares; a marmot on a snowdrift; a gyrfalcon's nest on a canyon wall; and a swan on a tundra pool.

And they are there now, together with wolf dens and grizzly bears. Given, most particularly, today's mechanized Nunamiut forays, and, more generally, such modern intrusions as the Prudhoe Bay oil fields, and their public access, by highway, from Fairbanks, it is remarkable that all but miniscule parts of Arctic Alaska remain as wild and woolly as any nature-lover could ask. Still, there are the nibbling encroachments, few of which have much to do with how the Natives are treating their environment.

Americans love roads, helicopters, airplanes (the last time I looked there were two ugly plane wrecks on the south shore of Chandler Lake), and now, at least, it is unthinkable that we do without oil. We love wilderness too, but mind you not too much of it, so it is hard to say what these mountains and barrens will be like a century or two down the line.

APPENDIX 1

Paneak's Plants and Animals

———

Robert L. Rausch

Paneak	English	Latin	Iñupiaq
PLANTS			
caribou lichen	caribou moss	*Cladonia* spp., etc.	niqaat (pl.)
spruce	white spruce	*Picea glauca*	napaaqtuq
willow (of large size)	willows	*Salix alaxensis;*	uqpik
		S. arbusculoides;	
		S. lanata	
cloudberry, akpic	cloudberry	*Rubus chamaemorus*	aqpik
mashoo, maso	licorice root	*Hedysarum alpinum*	masu
legrice root	Indian potato	*Hedysarum alpinum*	masu
cranberry	lingon berry	*Vaccinium vitis-idea*	kimmigñaq
blueberry	blueberry	*Vaccinium uliginosum*	asiaq
smoking tobacco	tobacco, smoking	*Nicotiana* sp.	taugaaqiq
chewing tobacco	tobacco, chewing	*Nicotiana* sp.	uiḷaaksraq
sand tobacco	tobacco	*Nicotiana* sp.	
navy tobacco	tobacco	*Nicotiana* sp.	
greenleaf tobacco	tobacco	*Nicotiana* sp.	
INVERTEBRATES			
lice, louses	head louse	*Pediculus humanus capitis*	kumak
mosquito	mosquito	(several genera and species)	kiktuġiaq
blue flies	blow flies	(several genera and species)	nuviuvak
FISHES			
whitefish	least cisco	*Coregonus sardinella*	iqalusaaq
whitefish	round whitefish	*Prosopium cylindraceum*	saviġuunnaq
grayling	arctic grayling	*Thymallus arcticus*	sulukpaugaq

Paneak	English	Latin	Iñupiaq
herring	common herring	*Clupea harengus*	marine—not present
lake trout	lake trout	*Salvelinus namaycush*	iqaluaqpak
arctic char	arctic char	*Salvelinus alpinus*	iqalukpik
salmon	chum salmon	*Oncorhynchus keta*	iqalugruaq
salmon eggs			suvaich (pl.)
northern pike, pike	northern pike	*Esox lucius*	siilik
sucker	longnose sucker	*Catastomus catastomus*	qaviqsuaq
ling cod	burbot	*Lota lota*	tittaaliq

Birds

yellow bill loon	yellow-billed loon	*Gavia adamsi*	tuuklik
black bill loon	common loon	*Gavia immer*	taasiŋiq
pacific loon	arctic loon	*Gavia arctica*	malġi
swan	tundra swan	*Cygnus columbianus*	qugruk
goose	various	various species	niġliq
duck	various	various species	qaugak
scaup ducks	greater scaup	*Aythya marila*	qaqłukpalik
	lesser scaup	*Aythya affinis*	qaqłuktuuk
rough legged hawk	rough-legged hawk	*Buteo lagopus*	qilġiq
marsh hawk	northern harrier	*Circus cyaneus*	papiktuuq
grayfalcon	gyrfalcon	*Falco rusticolus*	aatqarruaq
duck hawk	peregrine falcon	*Falco peregrinus*	
pigeon hawk	merlin	*Falco columbarius*	tiŋmiaġruum kirgavia
ptarmigan	willow ptarmigan	*Lagopus lagopus*	aqargiq
	rock ptarmigan	*Lagopus mutus*	niksaaktuŋik
arctic white owl	snowy owl	*Nyctea scandiaca*	ukpik
short eared owl	short-eared owl	*Asio flammeus*	nipaiḷuktaq
raven	common raven	*Corvus corax*	tulugaq
crow	common crow, and others	*Corvus* sp.	not present
arctic shrike	northern shrike	*Lanius excubitor*	iraiyayuuq

Mammals

big shrew (myth)	giant shrew	——	ugruŋnaqpak
wolf	wolf	*Canis lupus*	amaġuq
gray wolf	wolf	*Canis lupus*	amaġuq
dog	dog	*Canis lupus* forma familiaris[1]	qimmiq
fox	red fox	*Vulpes vulpes*	kayuqtuq
colored fox	colored fox	*Vulpes vulpes*	
cross fox	cross fox	*Vulpes vulpes*	qianġaq
silver fox	silver fox	*Vulpes vulpes*	qiġñiqtaq
silver gray fox	silver fox	*Vulpes vulpes*	qiġñiqtaq

Paneak	English	Latin	Iñupiaq
white arctic fox	arctic fox	*Alopex lagopus*	tiġiganniaq
white fox	arctic fox	*Alopex lagopus*	tiġiganniaq
grizzly	brown bear	*Ursus arctos*	akłaq
grizzly bear	brown bear	*Ursus arctos*	akłaq
brown bear	brown bear	*Ursus arctos*	akłaq
black bear	black bear	*Ursus americanus*	iggaġriq
polar bear	polar bear	*Ursus maritimus*	nanuq
weasel	mouse weasel	*Mustela nivalis*	naulayuq
ermine	ermine	*Mustela erminea*	itiġiaq
wolverine	wolverine	*Gulo gulo*	qavvik
lynx	lynx	*Lynx canadensis*	niutuiyiq
walrus	pacific walrus	*Odobenus rosmarus*	aiviq
seal	seal	generic	natchiq
bearded seal	bearded seal	*Erignathus barbatus*	ugruk
oogruk	bearded seal	*Erignathus barbatus*	ugruk
white whale	white whale	*Delphinapterus leucas*	sisuaq or
beluga	belukha (Russian)[2]	*Delphinapterus leucas*	qiḷalugaq
whale	bowhead whale	*Balaena mysticetus*	aġviq
caribou	wild reindeer	*Rangifer tarandus*	tuttu
reindeer	domestic reindeer	*Rangifer tarandus*	qunŋiq
moose	moose	*Alces alces*	tuttuvak
musk ox	musk ox	*Ovibos moschatus*	umiŋmak
mountain sheep	Dall sheep	*Ovis dalli*	imnaiq
marmot	arctic marmot	*Marmota broweri*	siksrikpak
ground squirrel	arctic ground squirrel	*Spermophilus parryi*	siksrik
beaver	beaver	*Castor canadensis*	pałuqtaq
mouse	voles, and brown lemming	(three genera)	aviŋŋaq
muskrat	muskrat	*Ondatra zibethicus*	kivgaluk
rabbit	varying hare	*Lepus americanus*	ukalliq

[1] See Herre and Röhrs (1973) for a discussion of the use of "forma" to designate domesticated animals derived from wild ancestors.

[2] "Belukha" is the correct Russian name for the white whale. "Beluga," which is the Russian name for the white sturgeon (*Huso huso*), is commonly misapplied to the whale.

Sources: American Ornithologists' Union 1998; Hultén 1968; MacLean 1980; McPhail and Lindsey 1970; Rausch 1951, 1953, and unpublished field notes; Wilson and Reeder 1993.

An Anaktuvuk Genealogy: 1959

Stephen C. Porter

SIMON PANEAK

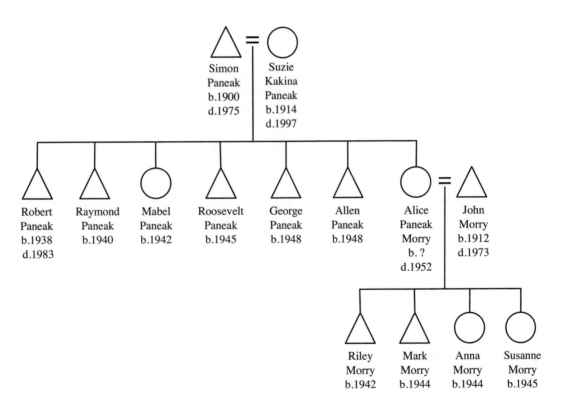

Known dates of death provided by Grant Spearman in 1999.

Elijah Kakinya

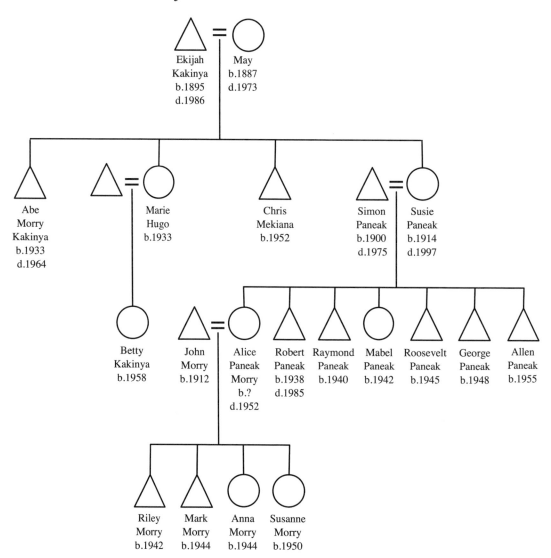

Inualurak (Old Hugo) part i

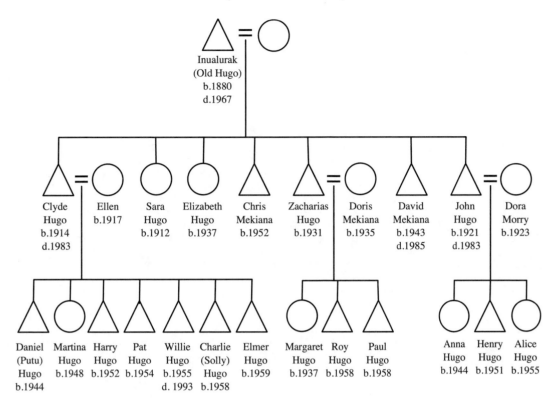

Inualurak
(Old Hugo)
b.1880
d.1967

Clyde Hugo b.1914 d.1983	Ellen b.1917	Sara Hugo b.1912	Elizabeth Hugo b.1937	Chris Mekiana b.1952	Zacharias Hugo b.1931	Doris Mekiana b.1935	David Mekiana b.1943 d.1985	John Hugo b.1921 d.1983	Dora Morry b.1923

Daniel (Putu) Hugo b.1944 • Martina Hugo b.1948 • Harry Hugo b.1952 • Pat Hugo b.1954 • Willie Hugo b.1955 d. 1993 • Charlie (Solly) Hugo b.1958 • Elmer Hugo b.1959

Margaret Hugo b.1937 • Roy Hugo b.1958 • Paul Hugo b.1958

Anna Hugo b.1944 • Henry Hugo b.1951 • Alice Hugo b.1955

Inualurak (Old Hugo) part ii

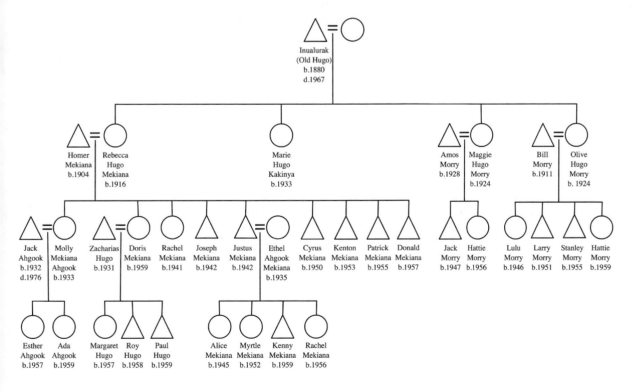

Inualurak
(Old Hugo)
b.1880
d.1967

Homer Mekiana b.1904 • Rebecca Hugo Mekiana b.1916

Marie Hugo Kakinya b.1933

Amos Morry b.1928 • Maggie Hugo Morry b.1924

Bill Morry b.1911 • Olive Hugo Morry b. 1924

Jack Ahgook b.1932 d.1976 • Molly Mekiana Ahgook b.1933 • Zacharias Hugo b.1931 • Doris Mekiana b.1959 • Rachel Mekiana b.1941 • Joseph Mekiana b.1942 • Justus Mekiana b.1942 • Ethel Ahgook Mekiana b.1935 • Cyrus Mekiana b.1950 • Kenton Mekiana b.1953 • Patrick Mekiana b.1955 • Donald Mekiana b.1957

Jack Morry b.1947 • Hattie Morry b.1956

Lulu Morry b.1946 • Larry Morry b.1951 • Stanley Morry b.1955 • Hattie Morry b.1959

Esther Ahgook b.1957 • Ada Ahgook b.1959

Margaret Hugo b.1957 • Roy Hugo b.1958 • Paul Hugo b.1959

Alice Mekiana b.1945 • Myrtle Mekiana b.1952 • Kenny Mekiana b.1959 • Rachel Mekiana b.1956

JESSE AHGOOK

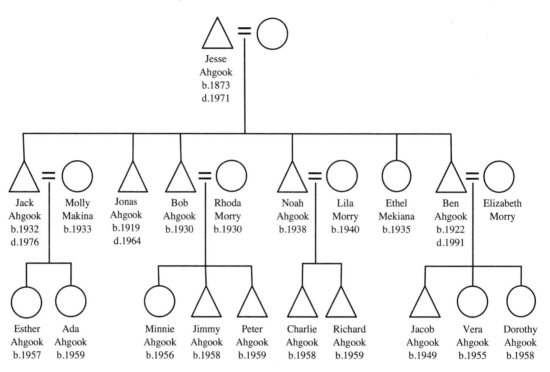

Jesse
Ahgook
b.1873
d.1971

Jack
Ahgook
b.1932
d.1976

Molly
Makina
b.1933

Jonas
Ahgook
b.1919
d.1964

Bob
Ahgook
b.1930

Rhoda
Morry
b.1930

Noah
Ahgook
b.1938

Lila
Morry
b.1940

Ethel
Mekiana
b.1935

Ben
Ahgook
b.1922
d.1991

Elizabeth
Morry

Esther
Ahgook
b.1957

Ada
Ahgook
b.1959

Minnie
Ahgook
b.1956

Jimmy
Ahgook
b.1958

Peter
Ahgook
b.1959

Charlie
Ahgook
b.1958

Richard
Ahgook
b.1959

Jacob
Ahgook
b.1949

Vera
Ahgook
b.1955

Dorothy
Ahgook
b.1958

FRANK RULLAND

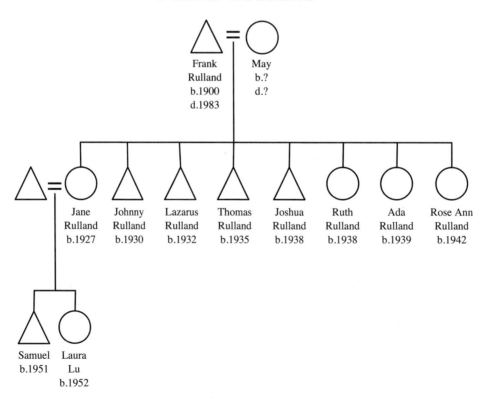

Frank
Rulland
b.1900
d.1983

May
b.?
d.?

Jane
Rulland
b.1927

Johnny
Rulland
b.1930

Lazarus
Rulland
b.1932

Thomas
Rulland
b.1935

Joshua
Rulland
b.1938

Ruth
Rulland
b.1938

Ada
Rulland
b.1939

Rose Ann
Rulland
b.1942

Samuel
b.1951

Laura
Lu
b.1952

MORRY MAPTIGAK

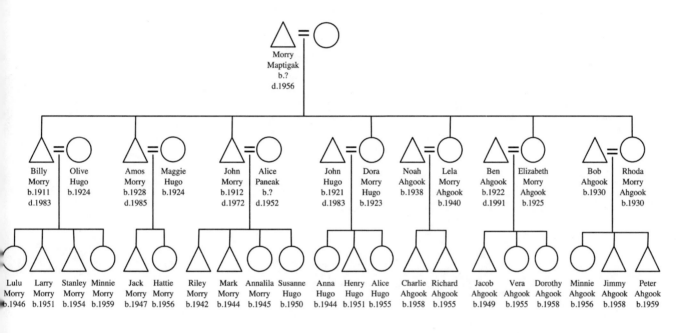

Notes

FOREWORD

1. Modern Iñupiaq spellings (provided by James Mumiġana Nageak) are noted in parentheses following the first occurrence of each word, including place names and proper names. Thereafter the (various) historical spellings, as documented in Paneak's sketchbook and in contemporary literature, are retained.

INTRODUCTION

1. For essays on the archaeology of north Alaska, from earliest known sites to historically occupied Native localities, see Solecki (1950), W. Irving (1953), Campbell (1959, 1962, 1972), Giddings (1964), Humphrey (1966), Alexander (1969, 1987), Hall (1970, 1976), Levin (1972), Stanford (1976), Reanier (1995), Clark (1996), and Morlan (2000).

2. As Paneak's original sketchbooks and recorded audio tapes attest, the terms "Eskimo" and "Indian" were an accepted part of the Alaskan Native vocabulary during the mid-twentieth century. For this reason, and for the purposes of consistency, these terms are used throughout.

3. For Eskimo and north Alaska Indian ethnography see Murdoch (1892), Weyer (1932), Osgood (1936a, 1958), Rausch (1951), Ingstad (1954a, 1954b), Spencer (1959), Hadleigh-West (1963), Gubser (1965), McKennan (1965), Chance (1966), Oswalt (1979), Nelson (1973), VanStone (1974), Ray (1975, 1984), Amsden (1977), Dumond (1987), and Burch (1998). For place names, see the topographic maps produced by the U.S. Department of the Interior (1956) and Orth's 1967 detailed compendium.

4. By the end of 1968, exceptional essays on the flora and fauna of this uttermost end of North America included those by Rausch (1951, 1953), Walters (1955), Bee and Hall (1956), Irving (1960), Wiggins and Thomas (1962), Hultén (1968), and Skoog (1968).

5. See, for Arctic Alaska and western Arctic Canada, Bandi (1995), Blackman (1989), Bodfish (1991), Burch and Mishler (1995), Fienup-Riordan (1994), Metayer (1972), Sheehan (1995), and Raboff (2001).

CHAPTER I

1. Each place name is given a map reference on its first mention only.

2. Life history data relative to those Nunamiut who were resident in the central Brooks Range in 1959 are presented in Appendix 2.

3. Apparently, however, none of these early white missionaries actually preached in Nunamiut territory. Rather, the Nunamiut learned about Christianity on visits to the Arctic Coast, or from contacts with the Kovagmiut and Noatagmiut who had been converted by the Kotzebue Sound Moravians (see Stefansson 1913:81).

4. For their occurrences among the Copper Eskimos of northwestern Arctic Canada, see Stefansson (1913); for their elaborations among north Alaska Indians, see Osgood (1936a, 1958) and McKennan (1965); and for a more eclectic perspective of their roles in native societies, see Lessa and Vogt (1958).

5. In this chapter, stories of the three brothers, flying whale, mosquitoes, and mouse are from previously unpublished parts of Paneak's 1969 sketchbook, and their titles are his. I have given names to the remainder, which are from his untitled, taped narratives (see Introduction).

   Fragments of the flying whale (Koptogak) tale, and Parent of All Mosquitoes, appear in Campbell (1998a) and (1998b), respectively, and see Ingstad (1954a, 1987) and Gubser (1965) for fragments or different presentations of the following Raven, Muskoxen, and Arlvaloirvak stories.

6. For this and other animals and plants mentioned by Paneak here and in subsequent chapters, see Appendix 1.

7. Labrets, or lip plugs, of stone, bone, ivory, or wood were worn by men in incisions cut through the corners of the lower lip, and were held in place by their enlarged ends. Among north Alaska Eskimos, labrets survived as adornments—associated commonly with social or religious belief—through most of the nineteenth century (see Murdoch 1892:143–48; Nelson 1899: 44–50).

8. Apparently, native Alaska musk ox became extinct in the 1890s (they have since been reintroduced), the last of them having been killed by Indians and whites in the Kutchin Athapaskan region of the Chandalar River (Map 2; McKennan 1965:18). Their more northern Alaska tundra populations, however, seem to have been exterminated forty years earlier when Eskimos are reported to have killed the last known Arctic Slope herd in 1858 (Bee and Hall 1956:255, and see Rausch 1951:192–93).

    Left unanswered is the question of whether the last of the tundra herds were killed with native weapons or with rifles (see Campbell 1978:200–202), and the question of the sizes of prehistoric and protohistoric Alaska tundra musk ox populations. Curiously, in view of the several hundred Brooks Range and Arctic Slope archaeological localities that have been excavated over the past five decades, the remains of only one musk ox, from one locality, have been recovered to date (Gerlach 1989:332).

CHAPTER 2

1. For the relative roles of fishes, birds, and mammals in protohistoric Nunamiut economy see Campbell 1968, 1998a.
2. See Campbell 1998a for Paneak's drawings of traditional Nunamiut trapping techniques.
3. In the 1950s, the older Nunamiut talked of how in former times there were few if any game animals to be found on the eastern parts of the Arctic Slope.
4. Few modern artifacts were more dear to Nunamiut hunters than telescopes, ships' spyglasses got from Yankee whalers or from Arctic Coast trading posts (see Campbell 1998a:23).
5. A partnership was a more or less formalized reciprocal alliance between two individuals belonging to two different bands or, sometimes, tribes (see Gubser 1965:160–61).
6. In a typically coffin-less Arctic desert, the forested Kobuk River valley provided wood.
7. Most probably, Paneak refers here to the large-caliber, single-shot cartridge rifles manufactured in the U.S. from about 1875 to 1885. Made for commercial bison hunting on the Great Plains, and known as "buffalo guns," they came on the market just as the last of the big bison herds were exterminated, thus becoming obsolete nearly as soon as they were introduced (see Barnes 1965:110–18). Naturally, the surpluses would find their way to the Arctic.

CHAPTER 3

1. Stories in this chapter relating to early trade, trading to the Arctic Coast, and riveted iron pots are from Paneak's taped narratives, and I have provided their names. The remainder are from his 1969 sketchbook (see Introduction) and retain his own titles.
2. By the beginning of the eighteenth century, tobacco, a New World plant, was cultivated by various East Asian people from whom it reentered North America via Bering Strait trade (Winter 2000). Spotted, light-colored reindeer skins were procured by the Siberian Eskimos from the domestic herds of their neighbors, the non-Eskimo Reindeer Chukchee (see Bogoras 1904–1909). This is the same deer (*Rangifer tarandus*) as the wild North American caribou and the wild Greenlandic reindeer, but in parts of northern Eurasia its centuries-old domestication has resulted in phenotypical modifications, including light-colored, spotted skins.
3. That 7,000 Eskimos lived between Itkillik Lake and Howard Pass is a demographic impossibility. In fact, excluding the Arctic Coast, for the whole of north Alaska north of the Brooks Range Divide, a figure of 2,000 men, women, and children is much closer to the mark (see Campbell 1968).
4. Because of their size, numbers, their return downriver after spawning, and the geography involved, these fish could not have been silver salmon (*Oncorhynchus nerka*), nor any other salmon for that matter. Instead, they were one or another species of whitefish, or cisco, of the genus *Coregonis* (see Appendix 1; McPhail and Lindsey 1970, and Morrow 1980).
5. The black navy, derived at least indirectly from the British Royal Navy, probably came in twists; the sand tobacco, apparently a better grade, may have been cut and packed like modern loose tobacco for pipes or hand-rolled cigarettes (Joseph Winter, personal communication 1999; and see Winter 2000 and Spence 1959:24, 25).
6. Fort McPherson, in Kutchin Indian territory (Osgood 1936a, 1936b; McKennan 1965), was established by the Hudson's Bay Company in 1840 (Usher 1971:86), and we agree with Simon when he says that this gun "probably" came from that isolated fort. We assume further, because Fort McPherson lay so far (more than one hundred air miles) south of Eskimo territory, that the flintlock was traded first to an Indian who then traded it to an Eskimo somewhere far down the MacKenzie.

CHAPTER 4

1. In this chapter, the story of mock combat is from Paneak's 1969 sketchbook and contains his own title. The others are from his tapes, and I have provided their names.
2. This is Arctic tundra land lying north of the boreal forest. The Indians are Koyukon or possibly Kutchin Athapaskans (Osgood 1936a; McKennan 1965; Clark 1996). The Noatak and Kobuk rivers run through the traditional territories of the Noatagmiut and Kovagmiut Eskimos, respectively (Kroeber 1939; Oswalt 1979).
3. As they are known to anthropologists, the northernmost Athapaskans were forest people (Osgood 1936a; McKennan 1965; Nelson 1973; VanStone 1974; Clark 1996) who in the

old days built houses and other wood structures without benefit of metal axes and saws, the kinds of tools to which Paneak seems to refer. Probably their houses were of stone (covered with hides) simply because the Indians summered north of the northernmost trees (and see Figs. 19, 20).

. In moving to the tundra regions of Howard Pass, the refugee Indians settled again, rather oddly, among Eskimos whose numbers included, or consisted entirely of, Nunamiut.

. This is one of Simon's more interesting observations. Contrary to the wishful thinking of modern romanticists and revisionists, there is very little evidence that in early times north Alaska Indians and Eskimos practiced conservation of food resources (for an example of evidence to the contrary, see Stoney 1900: 838). Further, Simon, the Eskimo, endows here his ancestral enemies, the Indians, with a wisdom he says is lacking in his own people.

. Gubser (1965:46–47) describes these same events, but adds that the twenty dead men were buried subsequently by the Indian women and children in the top of a little isolated hill that stands about a mile north of Tuluak Lake (Fig. 33). Given that the soils of this hill remain frozen the year around (see below), that the common grave had to be large enough to accommodate twenty men, and that the surviving women and children were abandoned by the Nunamiut to fend for themselves (Gubser 1965:47), the story assumes a certain mythical quality.

However, as late as the 1950s the story of this bloody battle was so widely known and repeated by the Nunamiut that in the summer of 1961 my field assistants and I examined the supposed burial site, and at a depth of a few inches below ground surface found several hand-hewn spruce timbers, laid side by side as if to cover whatever lay beneath. This discovery was of interest because the nearest, most easily available spruce trees grow on the John River, forty air miles south-southwest of the hill.

Beneath the timbers we found a matrix of cobbles, gravels, and soils frozen so imperviously that we gave up the project. Then, William N. Irving (personal communication), while surveying in the eastern Kutchin area (Map 1), met an elderly Dihai Indian woman who had been told of this battle between her own people, the Kutchin, and the Nunamiut, and while her testimony to Irving supports the Nunamiut account, it leaves unresolved the mystery of who, or what, lies buried in the hill.

. This reference to an early nineteenth (or eighteenth) century sod house contradicts this writer (Campbell 1998a: pl. 17), who believed that among the Nunamiut it was a mid-twentieth century innovation; and see Gubser 1965:71.

. The chief reason for this prolonged famine was the temporary, radical crash of north Alaska caribou populations, a recurring phenomenon discussed by Skoog (1968), and whose consequences during these years is interpreted further by Campbell (1978).

. Depending upon their sex, adult Brooks Range caribou in good condition weigh from about 200 to 350 pounds (Rausch 1951: 189), and at mid-twentieth century a Nunamiut family of six

individuals and their dogs are said to have required normally seventy caribou per year (Ivar Skarland as cited by Solecki 1951). This explains why, after the meat from their successful spring caribou hunt ran out, Simon's family was soon living on white sheep and fish, both of which, to the Nunamiut way of thinking, were inferior to caribou.

10. In late July 1969 I witnessed a middle-aged Nunamiut man gill-netting ciscos (a type of whitefish) at this same fishing hole (see Morrow 1980:29–31; Campbell 1998a: pl. 30 and app. 2).

11. When used as unharnessed pack animals, the Nunamiut dogs liked nothing better than deserting their owners to chase after game animals (adventures from which the not-so-faithful dogs sometimes did not return). Accordingly, hunting parties left their dogs tethered in camp until the shooting was over.

12. When successful, the hunters immediately eviscerated, skinned, and quartered each animal, then covered its quarters with its hide, hair side up, to protect them from rain or snow. In caribou hide shoulder bags the men took home marrow bones and a little meat, and afterwards the pack dogs carried the quarters to camp (see Campbell 1998a:25).

13. North Alaska wolves are known to have occasionally mistaken sled dogs and their drivers for game animals, as was experienced by William N. Irving (personal communication) when he was working in the upper Noatak River–Howard Pass region in March 1962 (Campbell 1963), and four wolves, one of which he shot, threatened to attack his dog team. But this does not mean that in either of these two instances the wolves would have pressed home their attack, regardless of whether or not one of their pack was shot. North Alaska wolves had learned long since to keep out of the way of humankind.

14. This was a subterranean cache, dug into the permafrost (see Campbell 1998a:9, pls. 41–42).

CHAPTER 5

1. For a perspective of Nunamiut economy during the first half of the twentieth century see Brower ([1942] 1994:243, 246–7); Solecki (1950); Rausch (1951:154, 158–9); Spencer (1959:18–28, 130), and Gubser (1965:23–25).

2. For illustrations or textual descriptions of these Nunamiut artifacts see Rausch (1951:160, 162, 191); Ingstad (1954a:60, 61, 89, 96, 97; 1954b:33, 160); Irving (1960: pls. 7, 8, 11); Metzger (1983:61), and Campbell (1998a: pls. 12–18, 24, 26, 29, 34–36, 41, 54–56).

3. The beaver, fur seal, land otter, marten, mink, muskrat, and sea otter either did not range in traditional Nunamiut territory, or occurred there rarely (see Hall and Kelson 1959).

4. This chapter reproduces in its entirety a handwritten account contained in Paneak's 1969 sketchbook. Some of the descriptions appeared first in Paneak 1960:12–13, 53.

5. North Alaska Eskimo-Indian warfare (see Chapter 4) had long since gone out of style. Indeed, in the 1950s we met an old Eskimo-Indian couple at Bettles who had been married for

fifty years. Still, here and elsewhere in this story Paneak is cautious when approaching strangers, and when they turn out to be Indians he makes sure to tell us how nice they were.

6. Any modern, knowledgeable big game guide will tell you it is suicidal to shoot at a grizzly with this tiny bullet for the reason that it will make the great bear even more ferocious than usual. Modestly, but proudly, Simon is telling us here of how, with his straight shooting, he got away with it.

7. Note here, and following, Paneak's references to "fat" meat—not just any meat—a universal Eskimo need and craving that, while it flies in the face of modern dietary theory, has yet to be demonstrated as having deleterious effects among traditional Eskimos. As we observed in our field work of the 1950s, the Nunamiut ate all the "fat" meat they could lay their hands on. When the autumn caribou hunting was good, they let cows and calves go by, shooting instead the fat bulls (Campbell 1970, 1998a:8). Vilhjalmur Stefansson, who died of old age in his middle eighties, was so convinced of the beneficial properties of the Eskimos' fat meat diet that ten years following his (1946) thought-provoking, and controversial, *Not By Bread Alone,* he entitled its revised edition (1956) *The Fat of the Land.* (Sue Campbell and I recall dining with the Stefanssons when, in addition to requesting a steak without vegetables or salad, he astonished the waiters by ordering a half pound of butter.)

8. According to my Nunamiut friends of the 1950s, Elijah (rascal that he could be) did not smoke—until, that is, everyone in camp was running low on tobacco. Then, borrowing Prince Albert and cigarette papers, he smoked "to lighten up the load," as he would say.

9. Over the time span described in this story, Simon traveled some 3,000 miles as measured by foot, dogsled, and skin boat. Wilderness dog-sledding, incidentally, involves far more walking than riding.

EPILOGUE

1. Working with older Nunamiut men and women (nearly all of whom are now dead), Grant Spearman, during his twenty-five years of residence in Anaktuvuk Pass, has compiled a far-ranging, detailed account of traditional Nunamiut material culture and survival skills, including drawings and detailed textual descriptions of implements and technologies, from fishing tackle to dogsleds. Used as a text in local schools, it will perforce be a final ethnographic portrait of old-time Nunamiut material culture.

References Cited

lexander, Herbert L., Jr.

969   *Prehistory of the Central Brooks Range—An Archaeological Analysis.* Unpublished Ph.D. dissertation, University of Oregon, Eugene.

987   *Putu: A Fluted Point Site in Alaska.* Department of Archaeology Publication no. 17. Burnaby, British Columbia: Simon Fraser University.

merican Ornithologists' Union

998   *Check-List of North American Birds: The Species of Birds of North America from the Arctic through Panama, Including the West Indies and Hawaiian Islands,* seventh ed. Lawrence, Kansas: Allen Press.

msden, Charles Wynn

977   *A Quantitative Analysis of Nunamiut Eskimo Settlement Dynamics: 1898 to 1969.* Unpublished Ph.D. dissertation, University of New Mexico, Albuquerque.

andi, Hans-Georg

995   Siberian Eskimos as Whalers and Warriors. In *Hunting the Largest Animals: Native Whaling in the Western Arctic and Subarctic.* Allen P. McCartney, ed. Pp. 165–84. Edmonton: Canadian Circumpolar Institute, University of Alberta.

arnes, Frank C.

965   *Cartridges of the World.* Chicago: Follett.

ee, James W., and E. Raymond Hall

956   *Mammals of Northern Alaska.* Miscellaneous Publication no. 8. Lawrence: University of Kansas, Museum of Natural History.

lackman, Margaret

989   *Sadie Brower Neakok: Iñupiak Woman.* Seattle: University of Washington Press.

Bodfish, Waldo, Sr.

1991   *Kusiq: An Eskimo Life History from the Arctic Coast of Alaska.* Fairbanks: University of Alaska Press.

Bogoras, Waldemar

1904–1909   *The Chukchee.* American Museum of Natural History Memoirs vol. 11. New York.

Brower, Charles D.

[1942] 1994   *Fifty Years Below Zero: A Lifetime of Adventure in the Far North.* Fairbanks: University of Alaska Press.

Burch, Ernest S., Jr.

1974   Eskimo Warfare in Northwest Alaska. *Anthropological Papers of the University of Alaska* 16(2):123–45.

1998   *The Iñupiaq Eskimo Nations of Northwest Alaska.* Fairbanks: University of Alaska Press.

Burch, Ernest S., Jr. and Craig W. Mishler

1995   The De'haii Gwich'in: Mystery People of North Alaska. *Arctic Anthropology* 32: 147–72.

Campbell, John M.

1959   The Kayuk Complex of Arctic Alaska. *American Antiquity* 25:94–105.

1962   Cultural Succession at Anaktuvuk Pass, Arctic Alaska. In *Prehistoric Cultural Relations Between the Arctic and Temperate Zones of North America.* J. M. Campbell, ed. Pp. 39–54. Technical Paper no. 11. Ottawa: Arctic Institute of North America.

1963   Arctic. *American Antiquity* 29:576–81.

1968   Territoriality Among Ancient Hunters: Interpretations from Ethnography and Nature. In *Anthropological Archaeology in the Americas.* Betty J. Meggers, ed. Pp. 1–21. Washington, D.C.: Anthropological Society of Washington.

1970   The Hungry Summer. In *Culture Shock: A Reader in Modern Cultural Anthropology*. Philip K Bock, ed. Pp. 165–70. New York: Alfred A. Knopf.

1972   *Anaktuvuk Prehistory: A Study in Environmental Adaptation*. Unpublished Ph.D. dissertation, Yale University, New Haven.

1976   The Nature of Nunamiut Archeology. In *Contributions to Anthropology: The Interior Peoples of Northern Alaska*. E. S. Hall, Jr., ed. Pp. 2–51. Archaeological Survey of Canada. Mercury Series no. 49. Hull, Quebec: Canadian Museum of Civilization.

1978   Aboriginal Human Overkill of Game Populations: Examples from Interior North Alaska. In *Archaeological Essays in Honor of Irving B. Rouse*. R. C. Dunnell and E. S. Hall, Jr., eds. Pp. 179–208. The Hague, Netherlands: Mouton.

1998a   *North Alaska Chronicle: Notes from the End of Time*. Santa Fe: Museum of New Mexico Press.

1998b   Notes from the End of Time. *Alaska: The Magazine of the Last Frontier* 64(7):27–29.

Chance, Norman A.
1966   *The Eskimos of North Alaska*. New York: Holt, Rinehart and Winston.

Clark, Annette McFadyen
1996   *Who Lived in This House? A Study of Koyukuk River Semisubterranean Houses*. Archaeological Survey of Canada. Mercury Series no. 153. Hull, Quebec: Canadian Museum of Civilization.

Dumond, Don E.
1987   *The Eskimos and Aleuts*, revised ed. London: Thames and Hudson.

Driver, Harold E., and William C. Massey
1957   Comparative Studies of North American Indians. *Transactions of the American Philosophical Society* n.s. 47(2):165–456. Philadelphia.

Fienup-Riordan, Ann
1994   Eskimo War and Peace. In *Anthropology of the North Pacific Rim*. William W. Fitzhugh and Valérie Chaussonnet, eds. Pp. 321–35. Washington, D.C.: Smithsonian Institution Press.

Gerlach, S. Craig
1989   *Models of Caribou Exploitation, Butchery, and Processing at the Croxton Site, Tukuto Lake, Alaska*. Unpublished Ph.D. dissertation, Department of Anthropology, Brown University, Providence.

Giddings, James L.
1964   *The Archeology of Cape Denbigh*. Providence: Brown University Press.

Gubser, Nicholas J.
1965   *The Nunamiut Eskimos: Hunters of Caribou*. New Haven: Yale University Press.

Hadleigh-West, Frederick
1963   *The Netsi Kutchin: An Essay in Human Ecology*. Unpublished Ph.D. dissertation, Louisiana State University, Baton Rouge.

Hall, Edwin S., Jr.
1970   Kangiguksuk: A Cultural Reconstruction of a 16t Century Eskimo Site in Northern Alaska. *Arctic Anthropology* 8(1):1–101.

1975   *The Eskimo Storyteller: Folktales from Noatak, Alaska*. Knoxville: University of Tennessee Press.

Hall, Edwin S., Jr., ed.
1976   *Contributions to Anthropology: The Interior Peoples of Northern Alaska*. Archaeological Survey of Canada. Mercury Series no. 49. Hull, Quebec: Canadian Museum of Civilization.

Hall, E. Raymond, and Keith R. Kelson
1959   *The Mammals of North America*, Vol. II. New York: Ronald Press.

Hanson, Charles E., Jr.
1955   *The Northwest Gun*. Publications in Anthropology no. 2. Lincoln: Nebraska State Historical Society.

Herre, Wolf and Manfred Röhrs
1973   *Haustiere-Zoologisch Gesehen*. Stuttgart: Gustav Fischer Verlag.

Hultén, Eric
1968   *Flora of Alaska and Neighboring Territories: A Manual of the Vascular Plants*. Palo Alto: Stanford University Press.

Humphrey, Robert L.
1966   The Prehistory of the Utukok River Region, Arctic Alaska: Early Fluted Point Tradition with Old World Relationships. *Current Anthropology* 7:586–88.

Ingstad, Helge
1954a   *Nunamiut: Among Alaska's Inland Eskimos*. New York: W.W. Norton.

1954b   *Nunamiut: Blandt Alaskas Indlands Eskimoer*. Copenhagen: Forlaget Fremad.

1987   *Nunamiut Stories Told by Elijah Kakinya and Simon Paneak*. Edited and translated by Knut Bergsland, illustrated by Ronald W. Senungetuk. Fairbanks: North Slope Borough Commission on Iñupiat History, Language and Culture.

Irving, Laurence
1953   The Naming of Birds by Nunamiut Eskimo. *Arctic* 6(1): 35–43.

960   *Birds of Anaktuvuk Pass, Kobuk, and Old Crow: A Study in Arctic Adaptation.* United States National Museum Bulletin 217. Washington, D.C.: Smithsonian Institution.

rving, William N.
953   Evidence of Early Tundra Cultures in Northern Alaska. *Anthropological Papers of the University of Alaska* 1(2): 55–85.

rauss, Michael E.
982   Native Peoples and Languages of Alaska. Map. Fairbanks: Alaska Native Language Center, University of Alaska.

roeber, A. L.
939   *Cultural and Natural Areas of Native North America.* Publications in American Archeology and Ethnology 38. Berkeley: University of California Press.

arsen, Helge, and Froelich Rainey
948   *Ipiutak and the Arctic Whale Hunting Culture.* Anthropological Papers 42. New York: American Museum of Natural History.

essa, William A., and Evon Z. Vogt
958   *Reader in Comparative Religion.* Evanston, Illinois and Elmsford, New York: Row, Peterson and Company.

evin, M. G.
972   *Ethnic Origins of the Peoples of Northeastern Asia.* Arctic Institute of North America: Translations from Russian Sources No. 3. Toronto: University of Toronto Press.

ogan, Herschell C.
959   *Cartridges: A Pictorial Digest of Small Arms Ammunition.* New York: Bonanza Books.

IacLean, Edna Ahgeak
980   *Iñupiallu Taŋŋiḷḷu Uqaluŋisa Iḷaŋich (Abridged Iñupiaq and English Dictionary).* Fairbanks and Barrow: University of Alaska and the North Slope Borough.

Iarshall, Robert
.933] 1991   *Arctic Village.* Fairbanks: University of Alaska Press.

IcKennan, Robert A.
965   *The Chandalar Kutchin.* Technical Paper 17. Montreal: Arctic Institute of North America.

IcPhail, J. D., and C. C. Lindsey
970   *Freshwater Fishes of Northwestern Canada and Alaska.* Fisheries Research Board of Canada Bulletin 173. Ottawa: Queen's Printer for Canada.

Ietayer, Maurice, ed. and trans.
972   *I, Nuligak.* New York: Pocket Books.

Ietzger, Charles R.
983   *The Silent River: A Pastoral Elegy in the Form of a Recollection of Arctic Adventure.* Los Angeles: Omega Books.

Morlan, Richard E.
2000   The Siruk Site, Alatna River, Alaska; A Koyukon Winter House. *Arctic Anthropology* 37(1):43–59.

Morrow, James E.
1980   *The Freshwater Fishes of Alaska.* Anchorage: Alaska Northwest.

Murdoch, John
1892   *Ethnological Results of the Point Barrow Expedition.* Bureau of Ethnology, Ninth Annual Report. Pp. 3–441. Washington, D.C.: Smithsonian Institution.

Nelson, Edward W.
1899   *The Eskimo about Bering Strait.* Bureau of Ethnology, Eighteenth Annual Report. Pp. 3–518. Washington, D.C.: Smithsonian Institution.

Nelson, Richard K.
1973   *Hunters of the Northern Forest.* Chicago: University of Chicago Press.

Orth, Donald J.
1967   *Dictionary of Alaska Place Names.* Geological Survey Professional Paper 567. Washington, D.C.: U.S. Government Printing Office.

Osgood, Cornelius
1936a   *Contributions to the Ethnography of the Kutchin.* Publications in Anthropology 14. New Haven: Yale University Press.

1936b   *The Distributions of Northern Athapaskan Indians.* Publications in Anthropology 7. New Haven: Yale University Press.

1958   *Ingalik Social Structure.* Publications in Anthropology 53. New Haven: Yale University Press.

Oswalt, Wendell H.
1979   *Alaskan Eskimos.* San Francisco: Chandler.

Paneak, Simon
1960   "We Hunt To Live." *Alaska Sportsman* 26(3):12–13, 55. Juneau: Alaska Northwest.

Pospisil, Leopold
1964   Law and Societal Structure among the Nunamiut Eskimo. In *Explorations in Cultural Anthropology: Essays in Honor of George Peter Murdock.* Ward H. Goodenough, ed. Pp. 395–431. New York: McGraw-Hill.

Raboff, Adeline Peter
2001   *Iñuksuk: Northern Koyukon, Gwich'in & Lower Tanana, 1800–1901.* Fairbanks: Alaska Native Knowledge Network.

Rausch, Robert
1951   Notes on the Nunamiut Eskimo and Mammals of the Anaktuvuk Pass Region, Brooks Range, Alaska. *Arctic* 4(3):147–95.

1953   On the Status of Some Arctic Mammals. *Arctic* 6(2):
        91–148. Ottawa: Arctic Institute of North America.

Ray, Dorothy Jean
1975   *The Eskimos of Bering Strait.* Seattle: University of
        Washington Press.

1984   Bering Strait Eskimo. In *Arctic. Handbook of North
        American Indians,* vol. 5. David Damas, ed. Pp. 285–302.
        Washington, D.C.: Smithsonian Institution.

Reanier, Richard E.
1995   The Antiquity of Paleoindian Materials in Northern
        Alaska. *Arctic Anthropology* 32(1):31–50.

Schrader, Frank Charles
1904   *A Reconnaissance in Northern Alaska across the Rocky
        Mountains, along Koyukuk, John, Anaktuvuk, and Colville
        Rivers, and the Arctic Coast to Cape Lisburne, in 1901.*
        Washington, D.C.: United States Geological Survey
        Professional Paper no. 20.

Sheehan, Glenn W.
1995   Whaling Surplus, Trade, War and the Integration
        of Prehistoric Northern and Northwestern Alaskan
        Economics, A.D. 1200–1826. In *Hunting the Largest
        Animals: Native Whaling in the Western Arctic and Subarctic.*
        Allen P. McCartney, ed. Pp. 185–206. Edmonton:
        Canadian Circumpolar Institute, University of Alberta.

Skoog, Ronald Oliver
1968   *Ecology of the Caribou* (Rangifer tarandus granti) *in Alaska,*
        Parts 1 and 2. Unpublished Ph.D. dissertation, University
        of California, Berkeley.

Solecki, Ralph S.
1950   New Data on the Inland Eskimo of Northern Alaska.
        Journal of the Washington Academy of Sciences 40:137–57.

1951   Archeology and Ecology on the Arctic Slope of Alaska. In
        Smithsonian Institution Annual Report 1950. Pp. 469–95.
        Washington, D.C.: Smithsonian Institution.

Spencer, Robert F.
1959   *The North Alaskan Eskimos: A Study in Ecology and
        Society.* Bureau of American Ethnology Bulletin 171.
        Washington, D.C.: Smithsonian Institution.

Stanford, Dennis J.
1976   *The Walakpa Site, Alaska: Its Place in the Birnirk and
        Thule Cultures.* Contributions to Anthropology no. 20.
        Washington, D.C.: Smithsonian Institution.

Stefansson, Vihjalmur
1913   *My Life with the Eskimo.* London and New York:
        Macmillan.

1946   *Not By Bread Alone.* New York: Macmillan.

1956   *The Fat of the Land.* New York: Macmillan.

Stoney, George M.
1900   *Naval Explorations in Alaska, with Official Maps of t.
        Country Explored by Lt. George M. Stoney.* Annapoli
        U.S. Naval Institute.

Stuck, Hudson
1920   *The Alaska Missions of the Episcopal Church: A Brief Sketc
        Historical and Descriptive.* New York: Domestic ar
        Foreign Missionary Society.

United States Geological Survey
1956   Bettles, Chandler Lake, Wiseman Quadrangle Map
        Alaska Topographic Series. Washington, D.C.: U.
        Government Printing Office.

Usher, Peter J.
1971   *Fur Trade Posts of Northwest Territories, 1870–197*
        Northern Science Research Group 71-4. Ottaw
        Department of Indian Development.

VanStone, James W.
1974   *Athapaskan Adaptations: Hunters and Fishermen of t
        Subarctic Forests.* Los Angeles: University of California.

1984   Exploration and Contact History of Western Alaska. *
        Arctic. Handbook of North American Indians,* vol. 5. Dav
        Damas, ed. Pp. 149–60. Washington, D.C.: Smithsoni
        Institution.

Walters, Vladimir
1955   *Fishes of Western Arctic America and Eastern Arctic Siber
        Taxonomy and Zoogeography.* Bulletin 106:255–368. Ne
        York: American Museum of Natural History.

Weyer, Edward Moffat, Jr.
1932   *The Eskimos: Their Environment and Folkways.* Ne
        Haven: Yale University Press.

Wiggins, Ira L., and John Hunter Thomas
1962   *A Flora of the Alaskan Arctic Slope.* Arctic Institute
        North Alaska Special Publication no. 4. Toront
        University of Toronto Press.

Wilson, Don E., and Dee Ann Reeder, eds.
1993   *Mammal Species of the World: A Taxonomic and Geograph
        Reference,* second ed. Washington, D.C.: Smithsoni
        Institution Press.

Winter, Joseph
2000   *Tobacco Use by Native North Americans: Sacred Smoke ar
        Silent Killer.* Norman: University of Oklahoma Press.

Index

———